IMAGES
of America

STERLING

On the Cover: Transportation by rail has heavily influenced Sterling's development since the early years of the community. By the early years of the 20th century, an average of 19 trains passed through Sterling daily. Pictured is one of the silk trains that carried silk to the West C7oast. (Courtesy Overland Trail Museum.)

IMAGES
of America

STERLING

Forrest Hershberger
with Jenni Grubbs

ARCADIA
PUBLISHING

ISBN 978-0-7385-8152-1

Published by Arcadia Publishing
Charleston, South Carolina

Printed in the United States of America

Library of Congress Control Number: 2010928647

For all general information, please contact Arcadia Publishing:
Telephone 843-853-2070
Fax 843-853-0044
E-mail sales@arcadiapublishing.com
For customer service and orders:
Toll-Free 1-888-313-2665

Visit us on the Internet at www.arcadiapublishing.com

This book is dedicated to the many area families who can trace their heritage to the time before northeast Colorado was organized into counties, when the city of Sterling was still in its youth as a town. It is also dedicated to the people who have a continuing interest in the history of their community.

Contents

Acknowledgments		6
Introduction		7
1.	Transportation: From Trains to Planes	9
2.	City Business: From Agrarian to Industrial	21
3.	City Buildings: Great and Small	35
4.	Homes and Churches: As Diverse as the Community	47
5.	Pioneers and Other Notable Folks: From Fields to Offices	57
6.	Daily Life and Special Events: Something to Celebrate	71
7.	Clubs and Organizations: Strength in Numbers	83
8.	Small Town: Big Education Opportunities	93
9.	Overland Trail Museum: Preserving History	109
10.	Nowadays in Sterling: Different but the Same	113

ACKNOWLEDGMENTS

Compiling the photographs and information in this book was a rewarding work of intrigue, as we learned more about Sterling than expected. This endeavor could not have been completed without the assistance of the Overland Trail Museum staff, Jack Annan and Northeastern Junior College, Russell Johnson and the use of his photograph postcard collection, and the *Sterling Journal-Advocate* newspaper's archived photographs. As a community, Sterling has a fascinating history, and we are delighted to be able to shine a light on some of the people, places, businesses, and events that have made that history so rich. While this book contains only a shadow of everything that has made Sterling special, we hope that readers are able to get a sense of the community we have long considered to be home.

INTRODUCTION

Transportation was key to Sterling long before the city was incorporated. The Sterling area has many trails (some still visible) dating back to when Native American hunters roamed the Midwest region, including those from the Arapahoe, Cheyenne, Crow, Blackfoot, Sioux, Kiowa, and Pawnee tribes. The first recorded visit to the area by Europeans, primarily French fur trappers, was in 1820. Organized exploration of the area began with Maj. Stephen Harriman Long's visit in 1820. At the time, Major Long referred to the area between the Missouri River and the Rocky Mountains as "The Great American Desert." As recently as when the first permanent settlers arrived, the Sterling area was described by newcomers as fit for rattlesnakes and little more.

The present location of Sterling is a crossroads of many paths and transportation routes. Today it is the intersection of Interstate 76, U.S. Highway 6, Colorado Highways 61, 14, and 138, and a railroad that is busy most hours of every day. The South Platte River also bisects the east edge of the city. Additionally, Sterling's airport dates to the 1940s, when it hosted a flight school, and is scheduled for expansion in coming years.

The area is also known for being the location of one of the last battles of the Indian Wars. The Battle of Summit Springs was decided southwest of Sterling near what is now Colorado Highway 63. The battle started near present-day Atwood and was between the U.S. Army, led by Col. Eugene A. Carr, and the Cheyenne dog soldiers, led by Chief Tall Bull. The final battle took place on July 11, 1869.

Many of the early settlers and explorers of the Sterling area arrived by the Overland Trail, a southwesterly branch of the famed Oregon Trail. The trappers were drawn to the fertile beaver ponds of the Rocky Mountains. In addition to game and furs, Rocky Mountain gold was always a lure to travel through the Sterling area. Nationally it was an era of opportunity, and Sterling was on the route to many of those opportunities. In some cases, Sterling was the doorway to new adventures.

Northeast Colorado's earliest European visitors were mostly French fur trappers on their way to Colorado's Rocky Mountains. As with most cross-country routes, not everyone made it to their destination. Of the trappers who brought families, many found new homes before arriving at the beaver-rich mountains. Some trappers discovered beavers along the South Platte River and set up homes on the plains, rather than continuing to the mountains. The first organized expeditions into the area were conducted in the 1820s, beginning with the expedition led by Maj. Stephen Harriman.

The curiosity of the Sterling area grew with each traveler using the Overland Trail—one of the most heavily traveled routes in the area. It also crossed northeast Colorado near present-day Sterling. History records have noted that thousands traveled the Overland Trail between 1862 and 1868. William Hadfield and John Iliff set their marks on areas near Sterling. Hadfield arrived in 1871, establishing his home on an island near the South Platte River south of Sterling. Iliff set up a massive cattle operation almost the same distance from Sterling to the north.

Early settlers of the original Sterling community located about 4 miles north of present-day Sterling first moved to Union Colony. The Union Colony settlement later became Greeley. When these settlers moved to Union Colony, they found that the best farmland was already taken. Many of them then decided to move back east along the South Platte River, eventually settling at the first Sterling community site. Excitement for the Sterling area grew in the late 1880s due the Union Pacific railroad's 1881 decision to expand west from Julesburg to LaSalle. The community eyed this expansion as an economic opportunity that must be addressed.

Leaders of the Sterling community recognized opportunity about to present itself, but one problem had to be overcome: location. Citizens of the old Sterling knew that if the railroad came, a town would have to be established. It would only make sense. The Overland Trail, South Platte River, and, theoretically at the time, the Union Pacific railroad were converging. By the late 1880s, the new Sterling location was busy with numerous trains passing through town daily.

Local community leader Minos King traveled to Omaha, Nebraska, to offer railroad officials 80 acres of land for a right-of-way if shops and a roundhouse were located at Sterling. Sterling's current site was first owned by John E. Boyd, who sold it to King for $400. The new site was platted and surveyed by railroad surveyor David Leavitt of Sterling, Illinois.

Leavitt resided in Sterling and served as justice of the peace, lawyer, and civil engineer. His wife was a physician and also served as the first postmaster of the new community.

The new Sterling was platted with 19 blocks. The east side was bordered by what is now Front Street, the south border at present-day Cedar Street; and the west side of Sterling was at what is now Fourth Street and Division Avenue. King also donated lots for a church, schools, public buildings, and a cemetery. That cemetery, then located north of Sterling, has since been abandoned.

In 2009, Sterling celebrated its 125th anniversary. In that time, the community has gone through numerous growth stages and economic cycles, but it has continued to stay connected to its agricultural history. Much of the economy in the Sterling area remains tied to the success of the farmers and ranchers in the area. More than 100 years ago, the community began celebrating the success of the season for sugar beet growers. The city still has a festival called Sugar Beet Days, a fall event that is as much a celebration of the sugar beet crop as it is a community gathering.

Sterling still recognizes the railroad as one of its biggest assets and largest employers, shipping freight through the community numerous times each day. Early in Sterling's history, it was estimated that at least 19 trains passed through town on a daily basis. Moving the community to accommodate the railroad has proven to be a forward-looking decision.

One

Transportation
From Trains to Planes

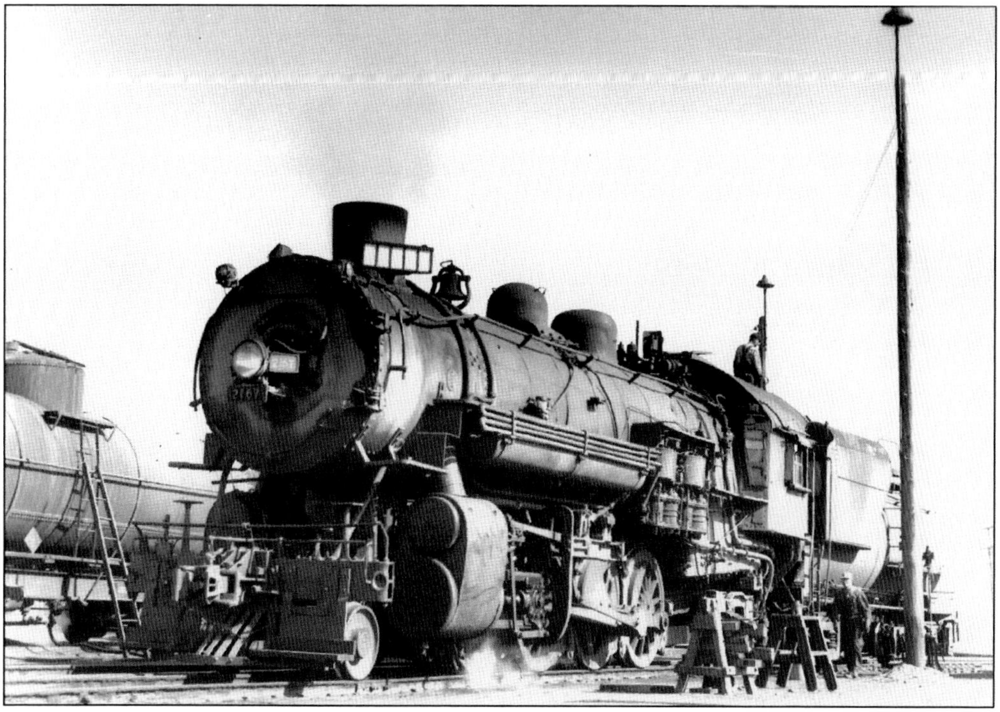

This photograph of Union Pacific engine No. 2167 was taken May 28, 1955. Steam engines still moved freight on most of the rail lines in the 1950s. (Courtesy Overland Trail Museum.)

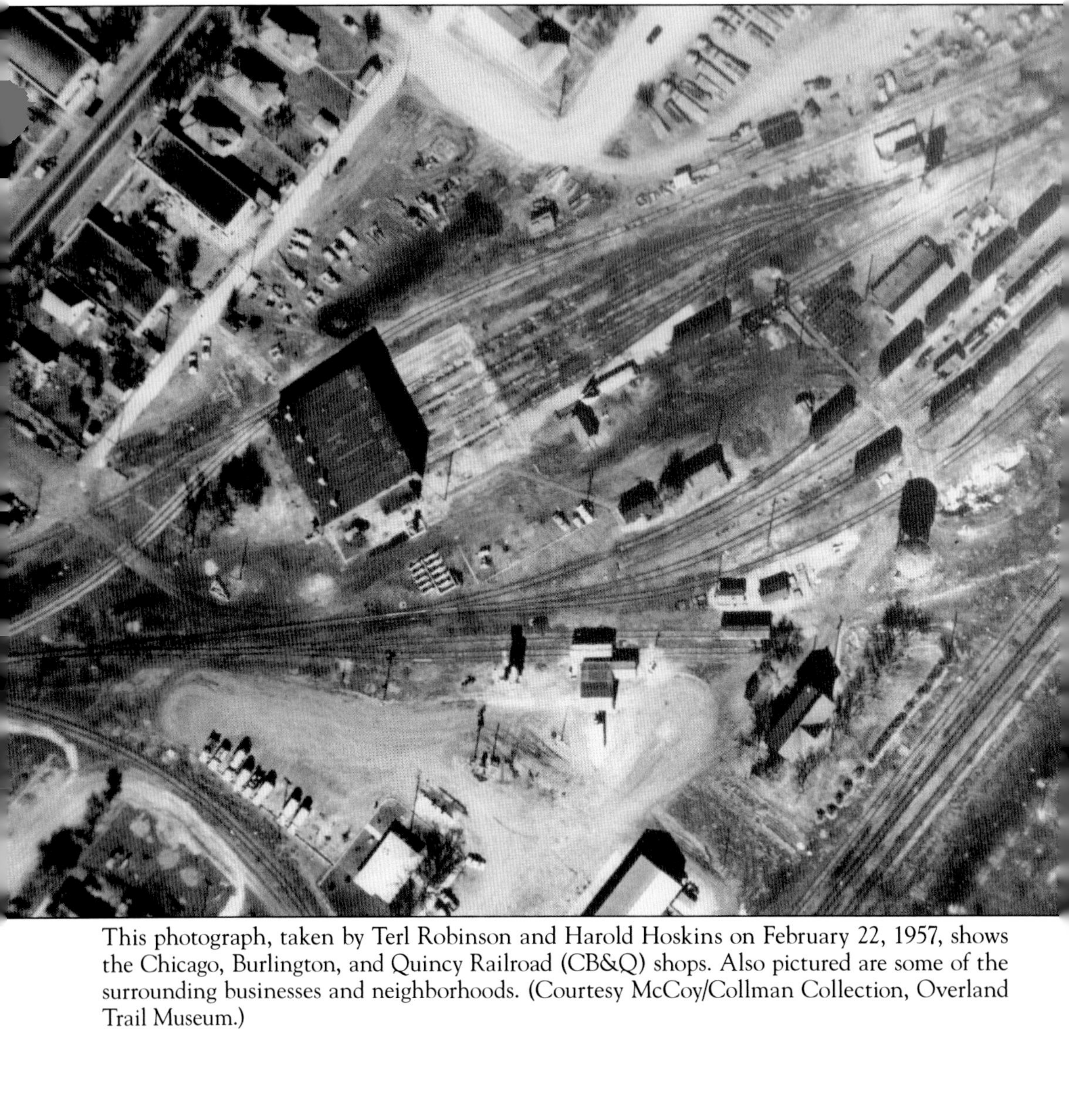

This photograph, taken by Terl Robinson and Harold Hoskins on February 22, 1957, shows the Chicago, Burlington, and Quincy Railroad (CB&Q) shops. Also pictured are some of the surrounding businesses and neighborhoods. (Courtesy McCoy/Collman Collection, Overland Trail Museum.)

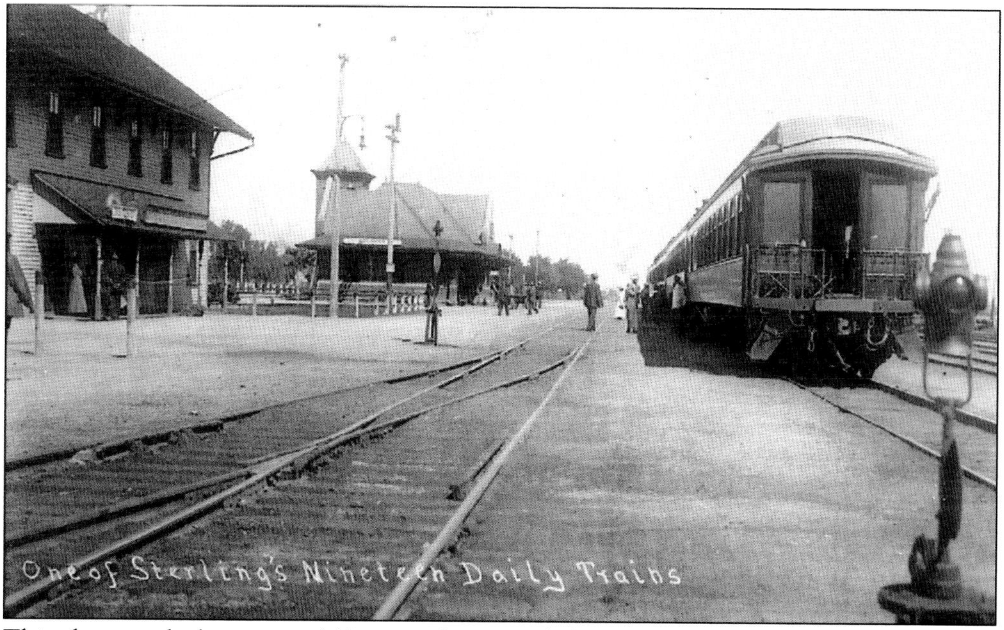

This photograph shows one of 19 trains that passed through Sterling in 1915 on a daily basis. Part of an old hotel and the Union Pacific depot can also be seen in this photograph. (Courtesy Russell Johnson postcard collection, Overland Trail Museum.)

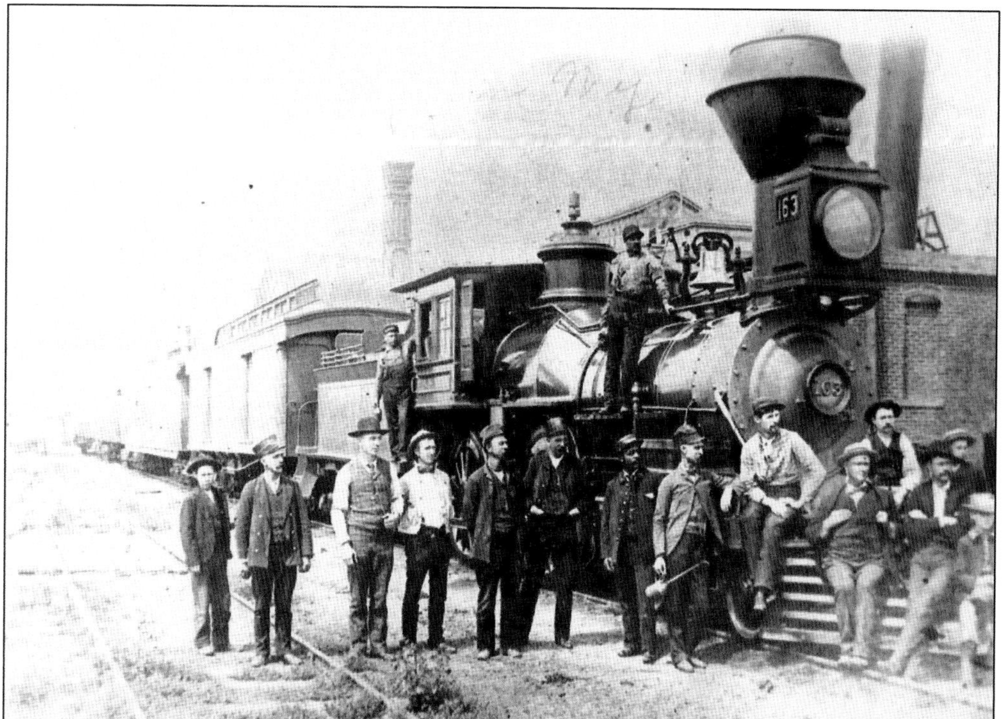

Pictured are the engine and crew of an early train on the Sterling-Cheyenne line of the Burlington railroad in 1889. This line was one of the silk trains, which carried silk eastward from the West Coast, with porters and other symbols of grandeur. (Courtesy Overland Trail Museum.)

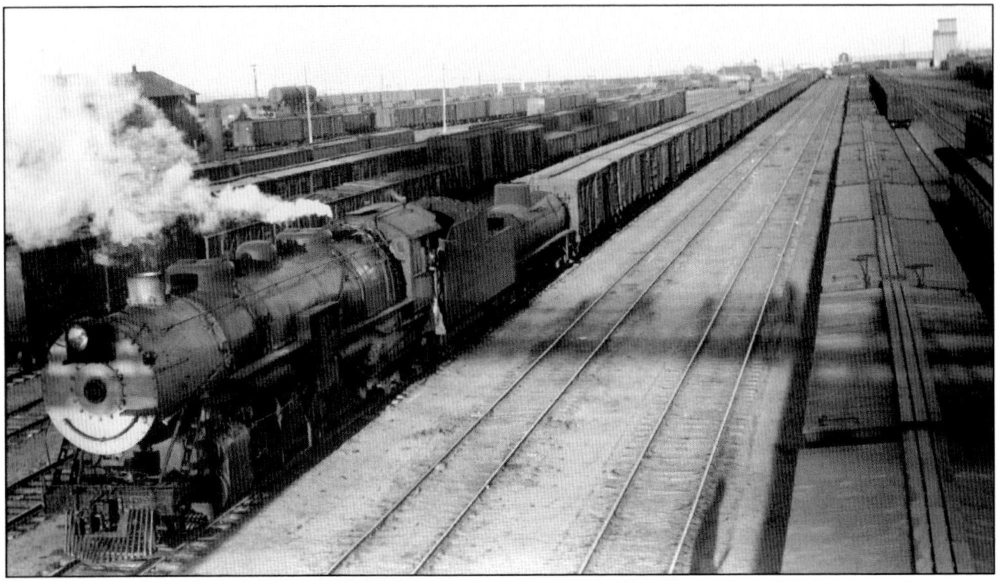

This is the Chicago, Burlington, and Quincy engine No. 6151 in a rail yard. Note how long this train is. It may very well have passed through Sterling, as the area remains busy with freight trains. Many of the trains passing through Sterling are delivering coal from or returning to the coal fields in Wyoming. (Courtesy Overland Trail Museum.)

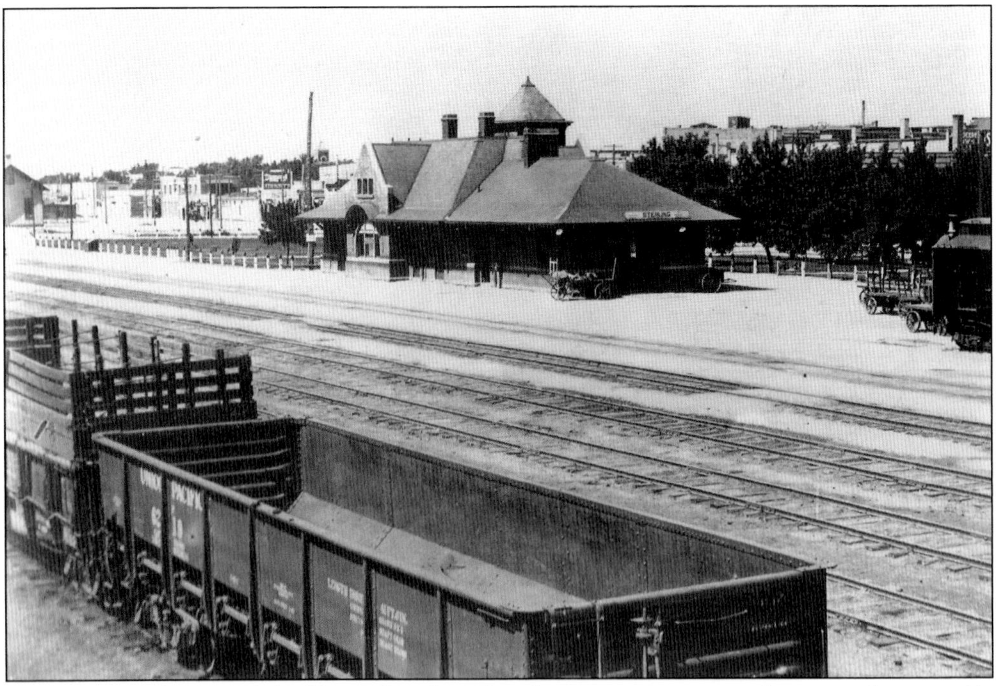

This is the back view of the Union Pacific railroad station in its original spot on the east side of Front Street in 1922. This view shows several sets of railroad tracks and some open-style cars. Many of the buildings around the Front Street area can also be seen. (Courtesy Overland Trail Museum.)

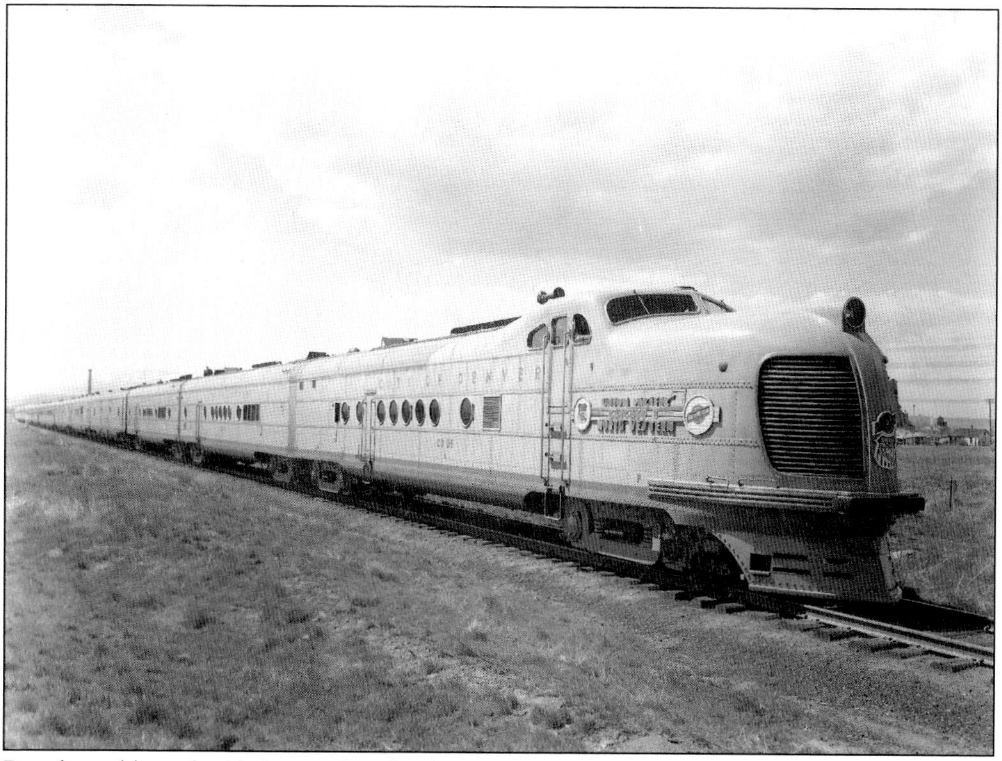

Dated possibly in the 1940s to 1950s, this front engine of the streamliner railroad car was a Union Pacific engine that went from Denver through Sterling to Chicago. The engine is on the tracks near the Sterling depot. (Courtesy Overland Trail Museum.)

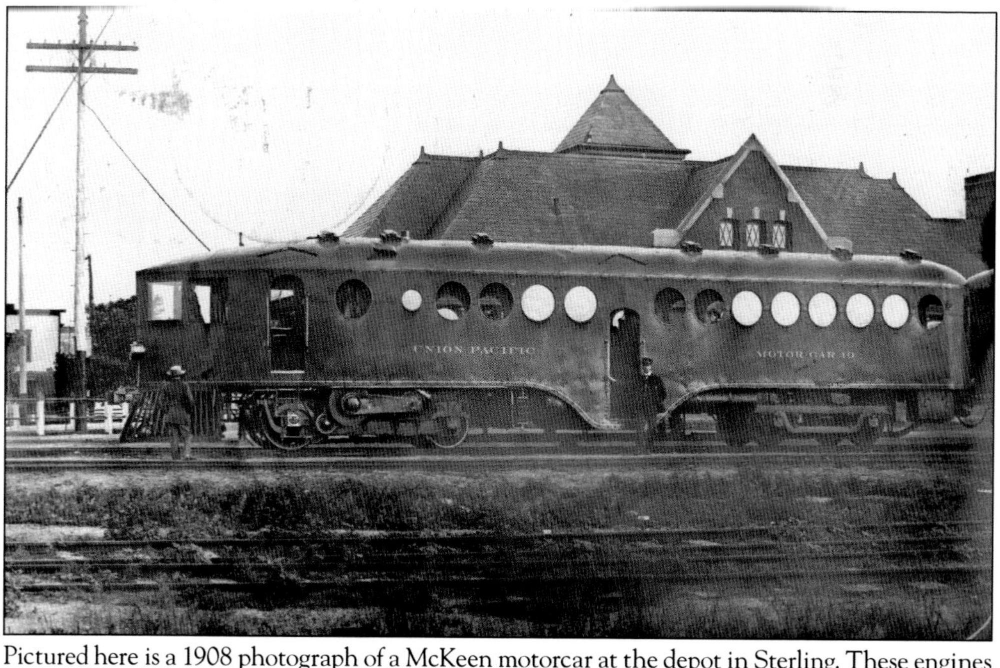

Pictured here is a 1908 photograph of a McKeen motorcar at the depot in Sterling. These engines were built in Omaha, Nebraska, for the Union Pacific Railroad. (Courtesy Russell Johnson.)

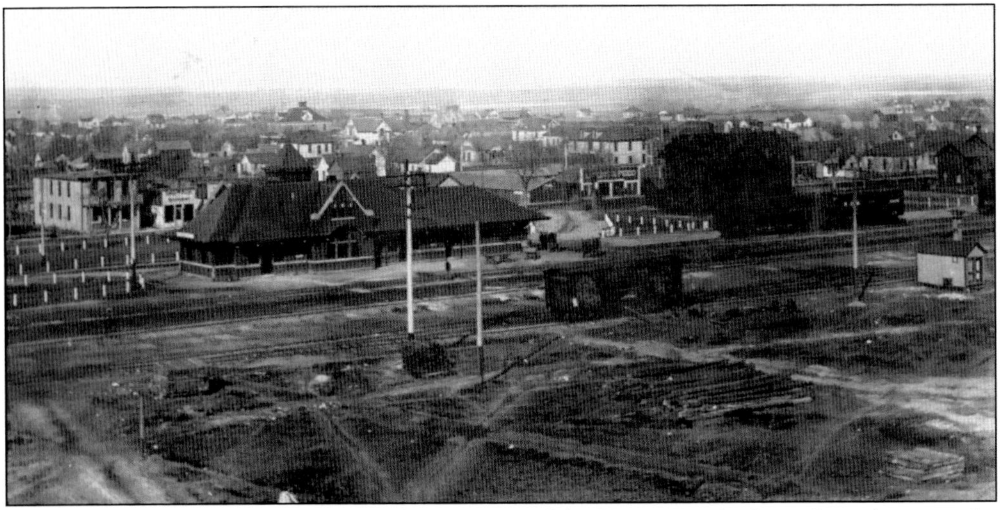

This photograph, taken around 1907, shows a view of the Union Pacific depot from the east side. Built in 1903, the depot originally was adjacent to the tracks but was moved west in 1984 to its current site across Front Street from the tracks. It now houses the Logan County Chamber of Commerce. (Courtesy Russell Johnson.)

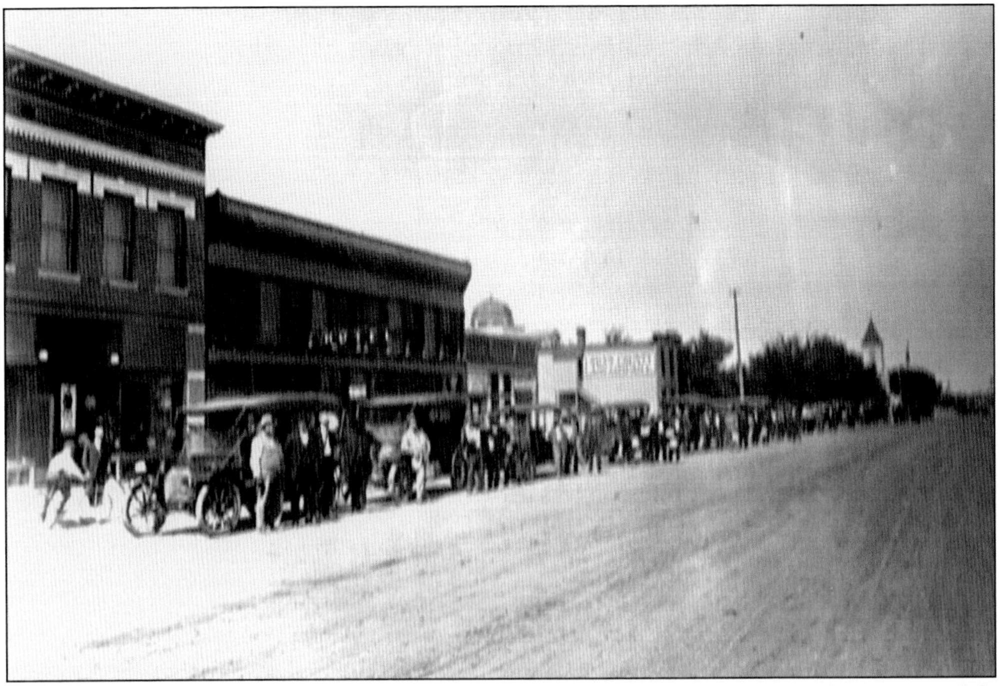

Countryside tours were an event in the early days of Sterling. In this 1913 photograph, an automobile tour is about to begin from downtown. The hotel in the picture is the current location of Larry Fetzer's accounting offices. The building to the right and the open space would become the building where Woolworth's was located. The Logan County Land Company was the forerunner of the Gillett Brothers Bank. They built a new structure at the west end of the block—the Foote Building, which was destroyed by a fire in 2002—and this building was razed and replaced by the I and M building, where Herb and Chris Vandemoer have their real estate business. (Courtesy Overland Trail Museum.)

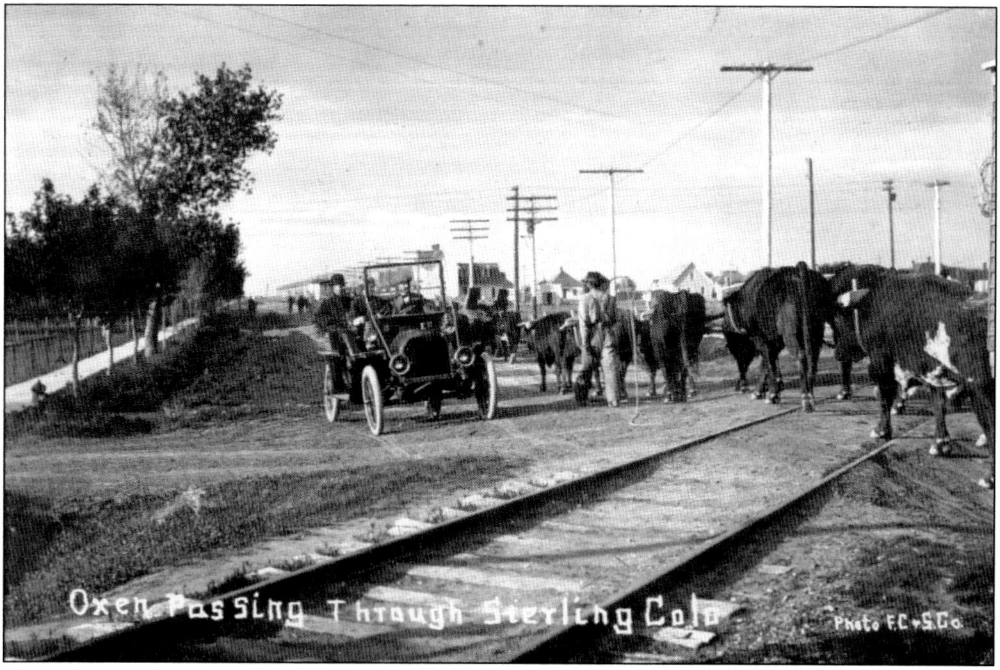

Three forms of transportation converge in this picture from 1909 as an automobile waits to cross while oxen pass over the railroad tracks near Sterling. (Courtesy Russell Johnson.)

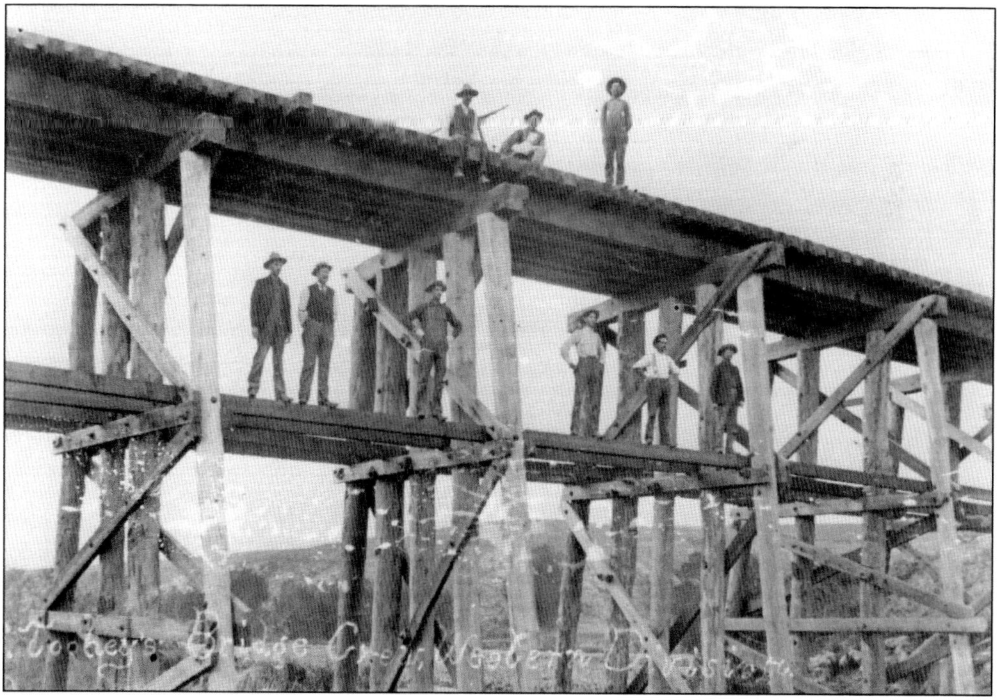
This photograph, taken between 1900 and 1904, shows a bridge crew working on a trestle for the Burlington and Missouri Railroad. These men worked under James S. Toohey, who was made roadmaster of the Sterling division in 1906. Toohey worked for the Burlington railroad for 50 years.

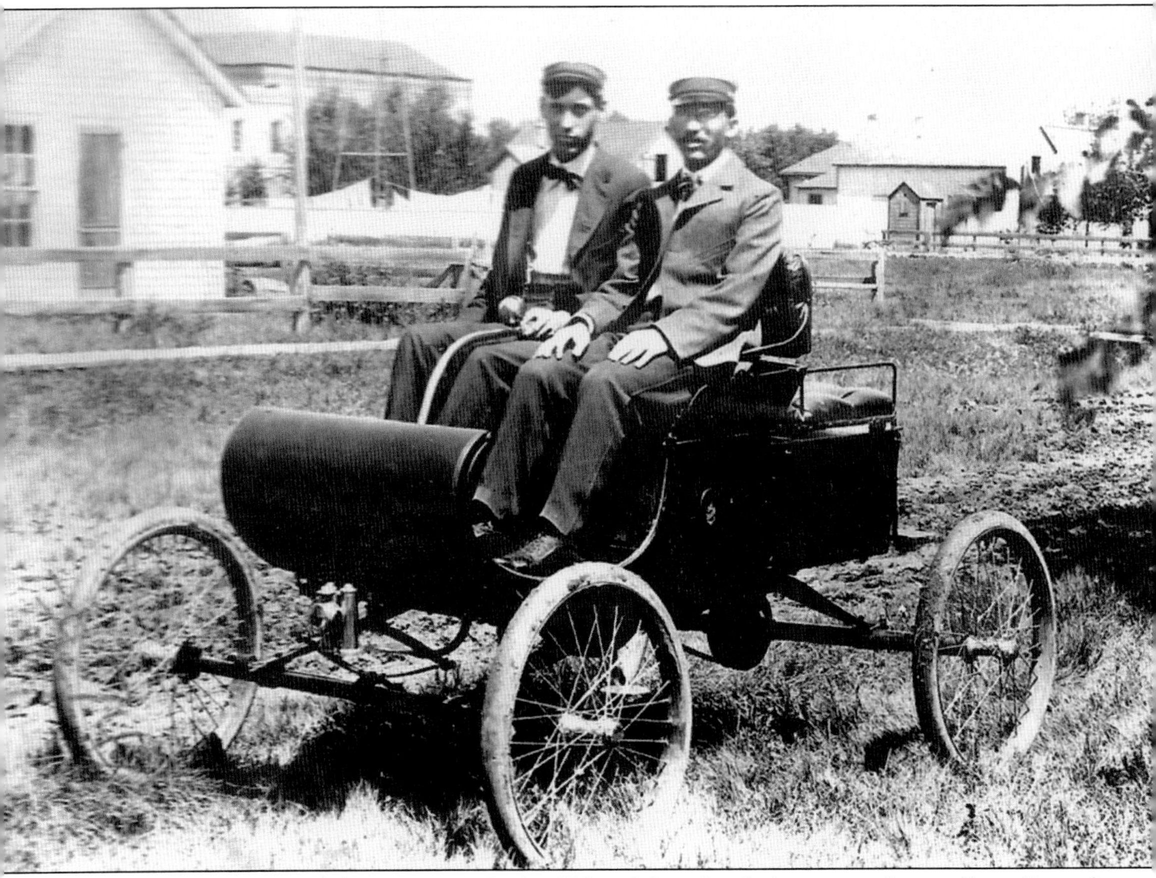

Sterling's first automobile was a one-cylinder Oldsmobile with a fuel capacity of two gallons. Owned by Sam Ard, it arrived after two days and two nights of travel from Denver in 1903. Occupants here are Claude Ard (left) and K. C. Sapero, itinerant medico. Ard was known for charging passengers 25¢ for a ride around a square block. (Courtesy Overland Trail Museum.)

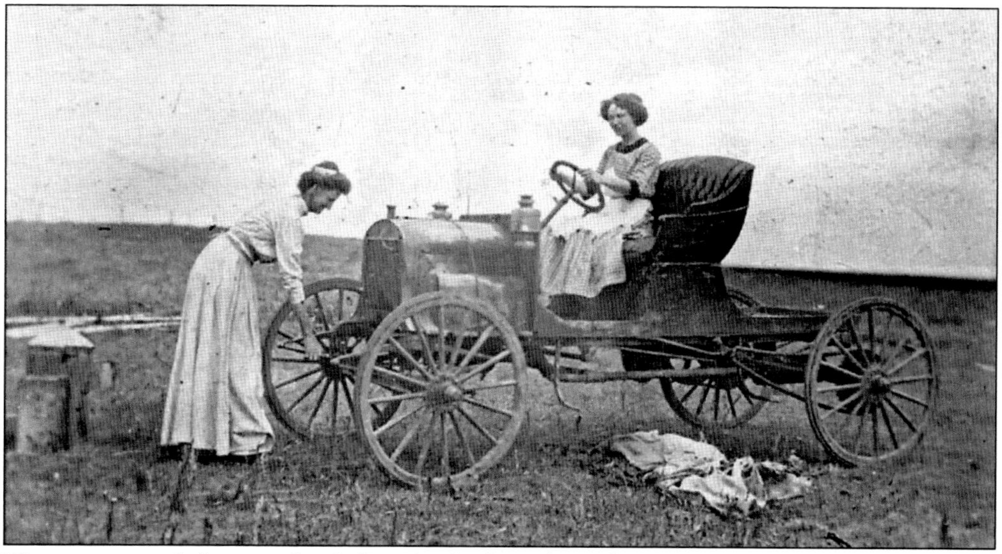

This is a postcard photograph—believed to be from the early 1900s—of two unidentified women with an early car. One is in the driver's seat, and the other is cranking the engine. A handwritten caption on the car says "One of Ard's first cars." This refers to Sam Ard, owner of the Central Hotel. (Courtesy Overland Trail Museum.)

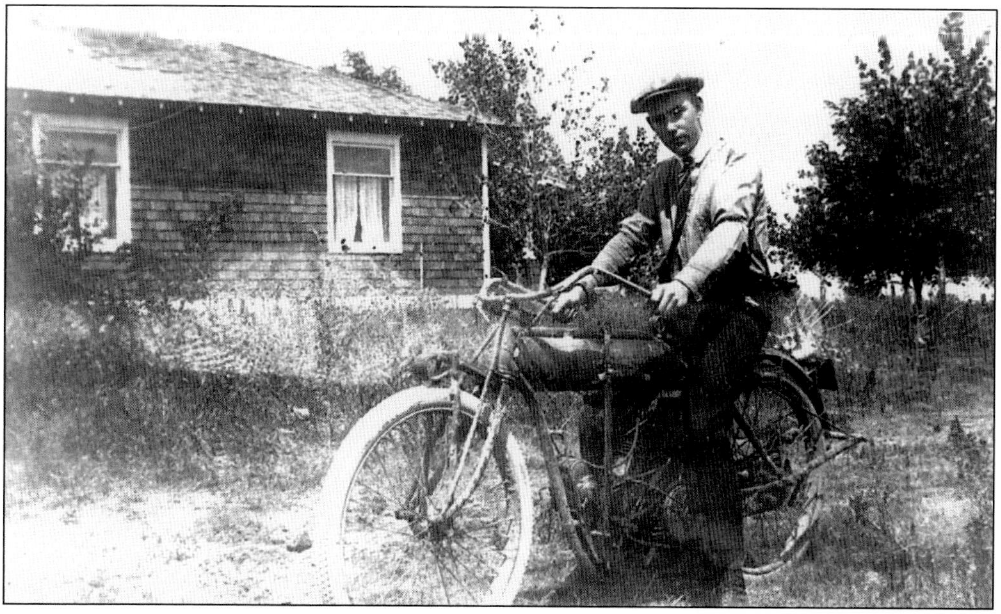

Sam K. Ard, grandson of Sam Ard, is pictured on an early motorcycle on North Third Street around the 700 block. He is pictured on the property where he would eventually open a garage and work on automobiles—and possibly motorcycles, which he raced. This photograph was probably taken in the 1920s. (Courtesy Overland Trail Museum.)

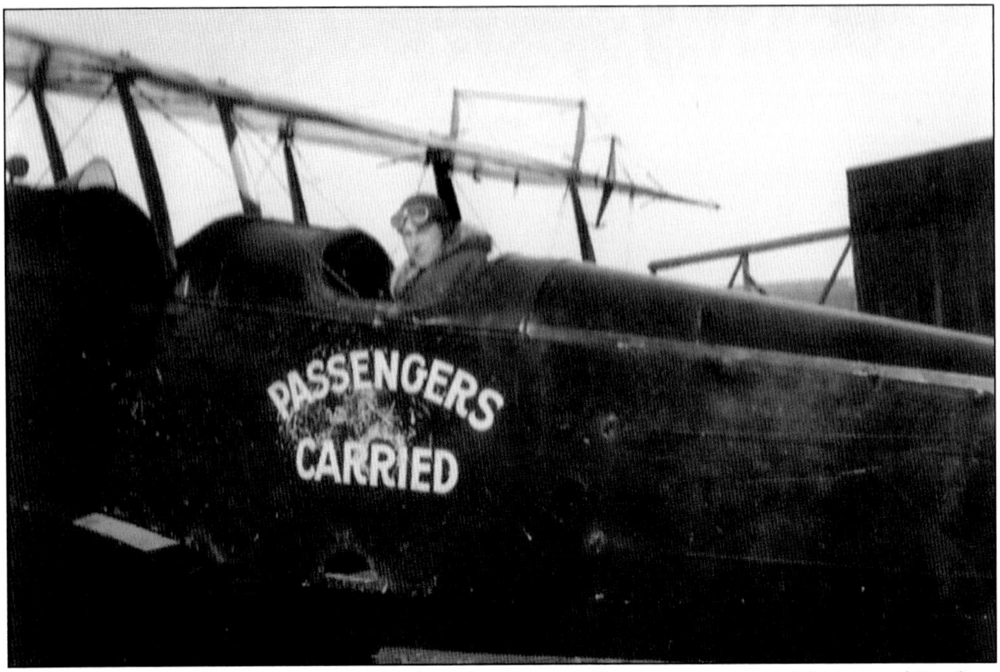

Pictured is local pilot Joe Crosson of Sterling Air Service. Crosson grew up in Merino and Sterling with his sister and fellow pilot, Marvel Crosson, before going to California and learning to fly. He also was a bush pilot in Alaska. Crosson was friends with Wiley Post and Will Rogers. He brought Rogers's body back to the state after the performer's plane crashed at Point Barrow, Alaska, in 1935. (Courtesy Overland Trail Museum.)

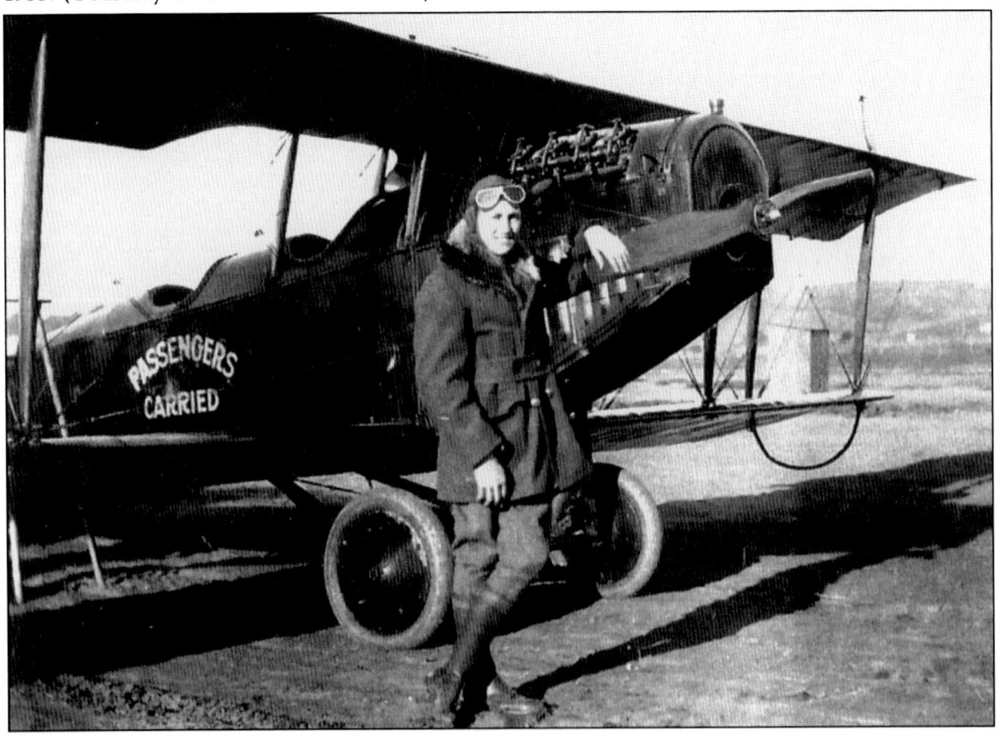

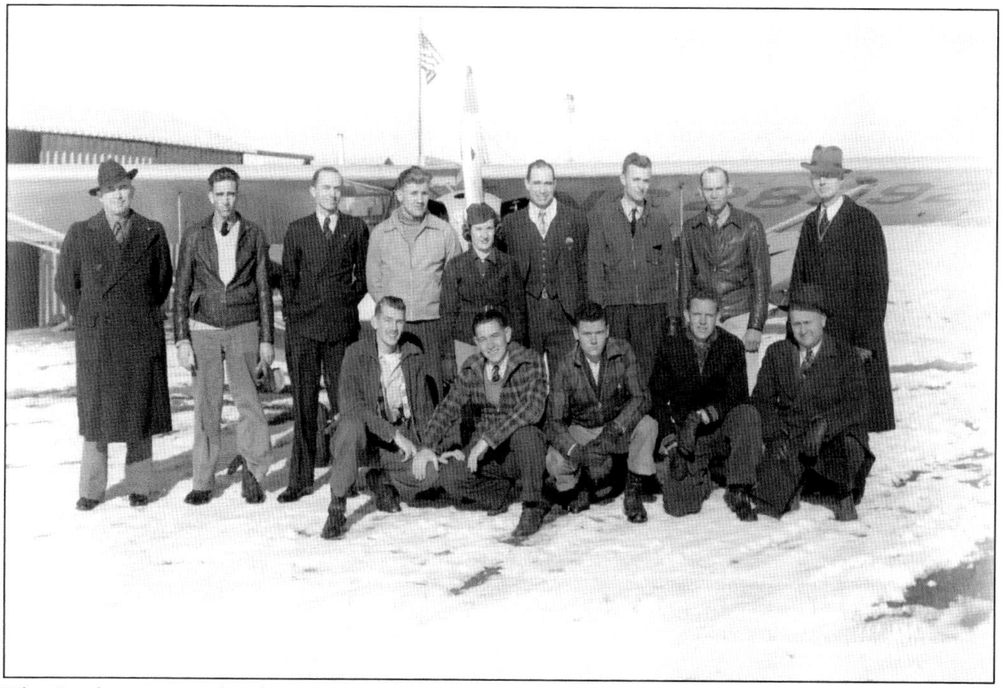

The Sterling airport has been an important part of the community from the time of the first runway. In 1941, the flight school of Sterling's training class consisted of, from left to right, (first row) Roger Parsons, Glenn Pence, Keith Baird, Dean Baird, Dick Smith; (second row) Herb Welsh, George Hair, Chesley Harris, Solomon Luft, Wilma Davis, David Detamore, Jack Stenback, Raymond Chadwick, and Roy E. Smith. (Courtesy Overland Trail Museum.)

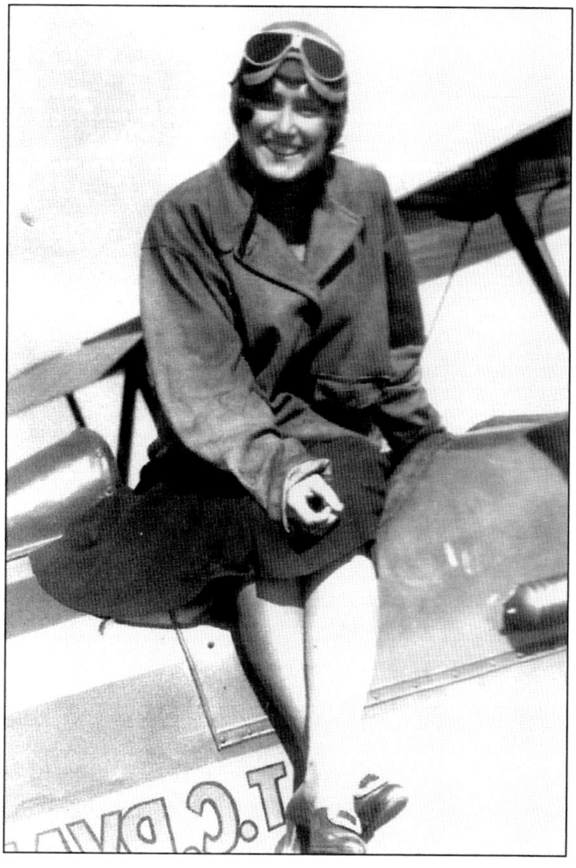

Marvel Crosson, along with her brother, Joe Crosson, grew up in Merino and Sterling before going to California, where they both learned to fly. Marvel competed in air races and set several altitude records before her untimely death during a race. (Courtesy Overland Trail Museum.)

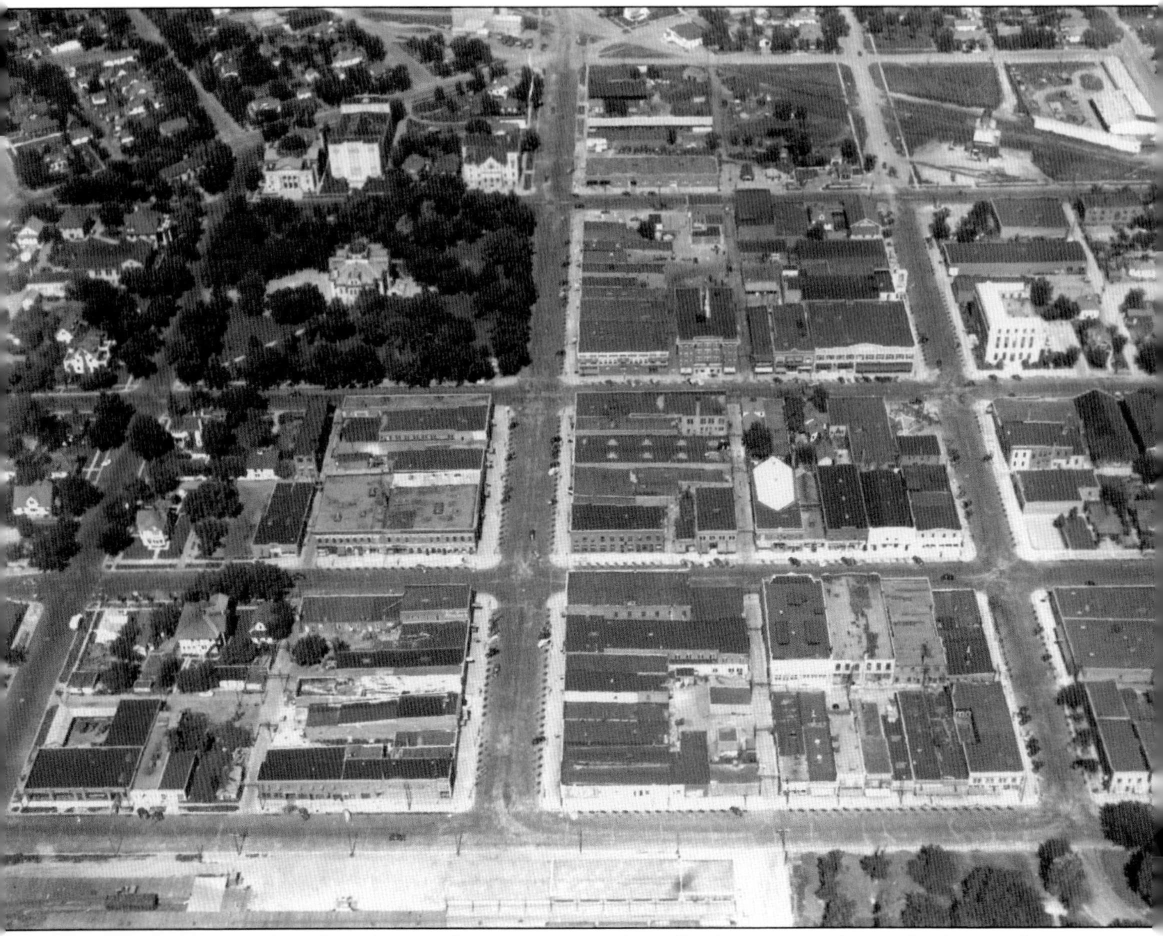

This photograph, taken during the early years of the 20th century, shows the Logan County Courthouse near the top left. Visible above the courthouse are the First Presbyterian Church, the Sterling Municipal Auditorium (which burned down in the early 1980s), and a church at the southwest corner of Fourth and Main Streets. (Courtesy Overland Trail Museum.)

Two

City Business
From Agrarian to Industrial

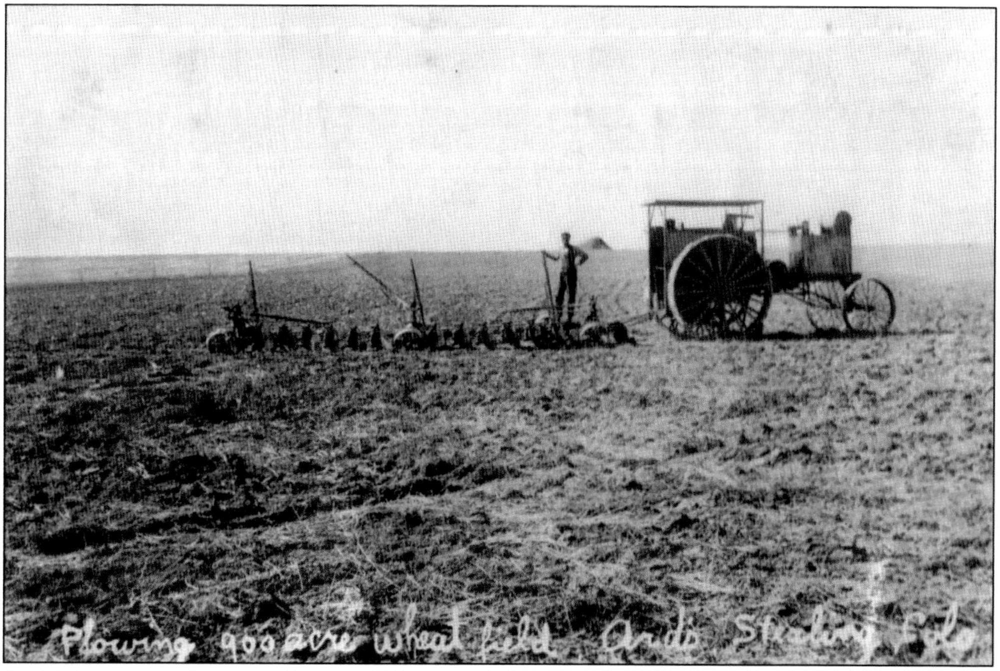

In this image, workers are plowing 900 acres of wheat on the Claude and Sam Ard farm, 7 miles west of the Sterling cemetery. (Courtesy Overland Trail Museum.)

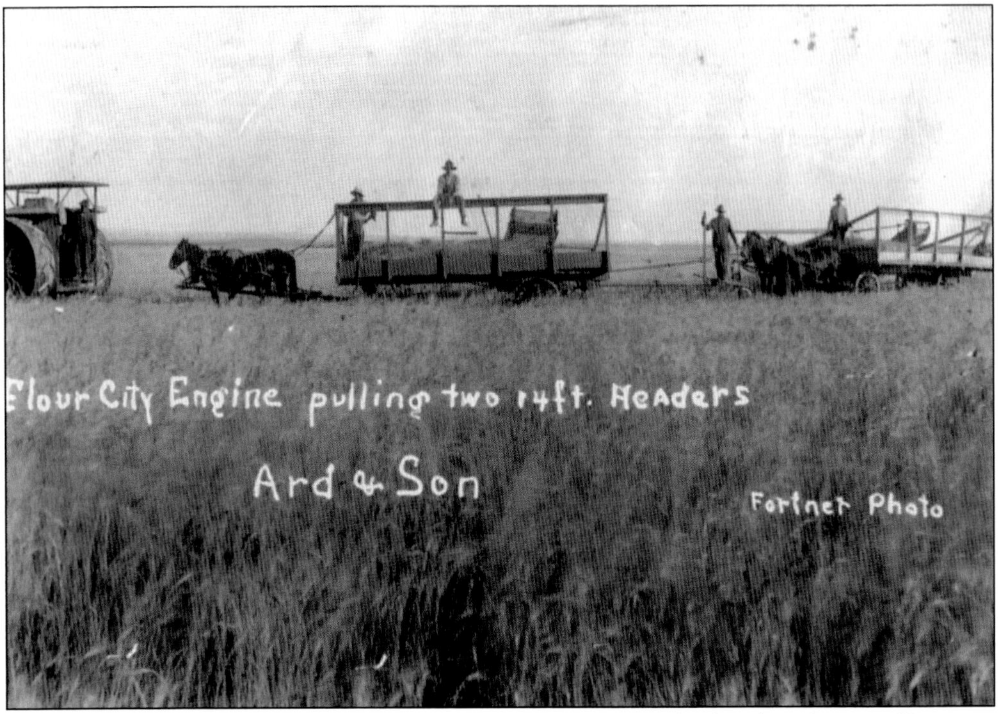

Workers on the Ard farm move two 14-foot headers in preparation for the wheat harvest. (Courtesy Overland Trail Museum.)

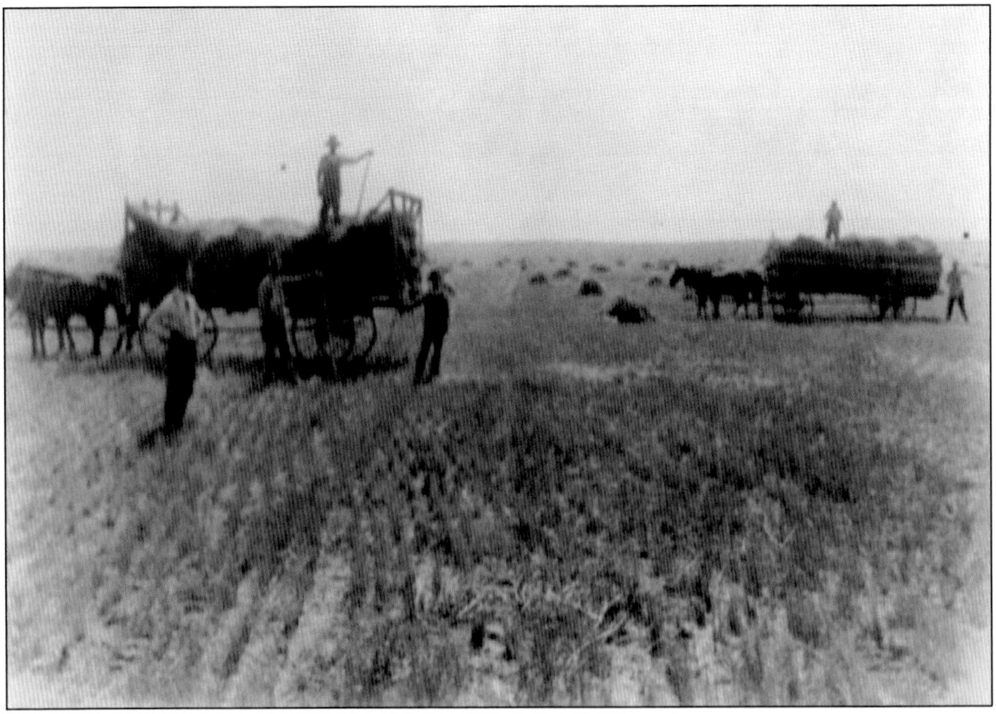

This is a picture of workers in the W. C. Harris hay field near Iliff. This photograph was taken before mechanized farming was introduced to the Harris Farm. (Courtesy Overland Trail Museum.)

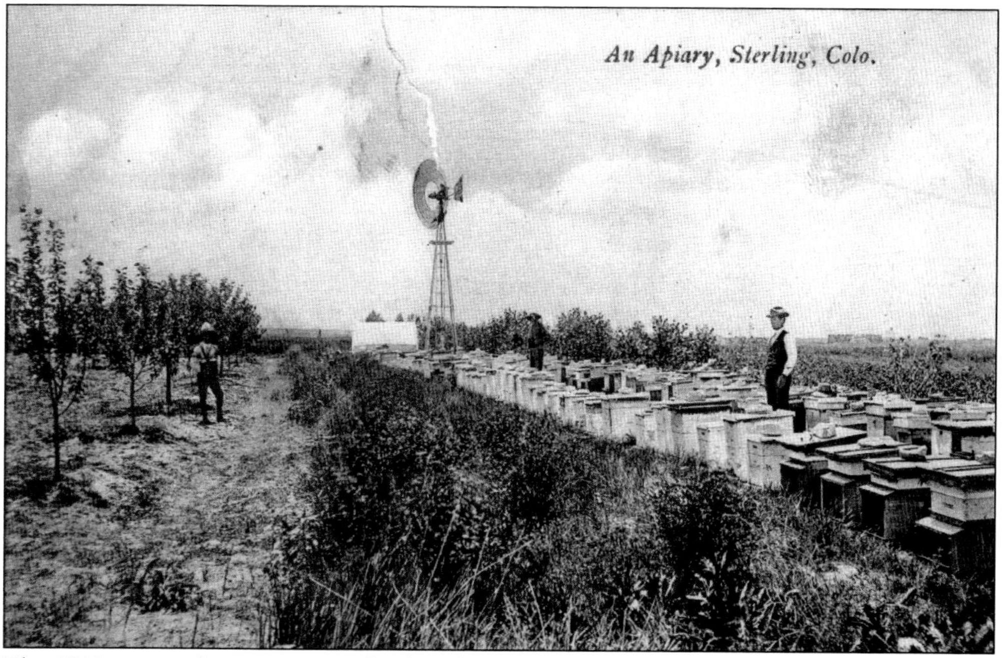

This 1910 picture shows an apiary (beehives) on a farm near Sterling. Honey is still produced by some farmers in the area, and bees are an essential part of many agriculture operations. (Courtesy Russell Johnson.)

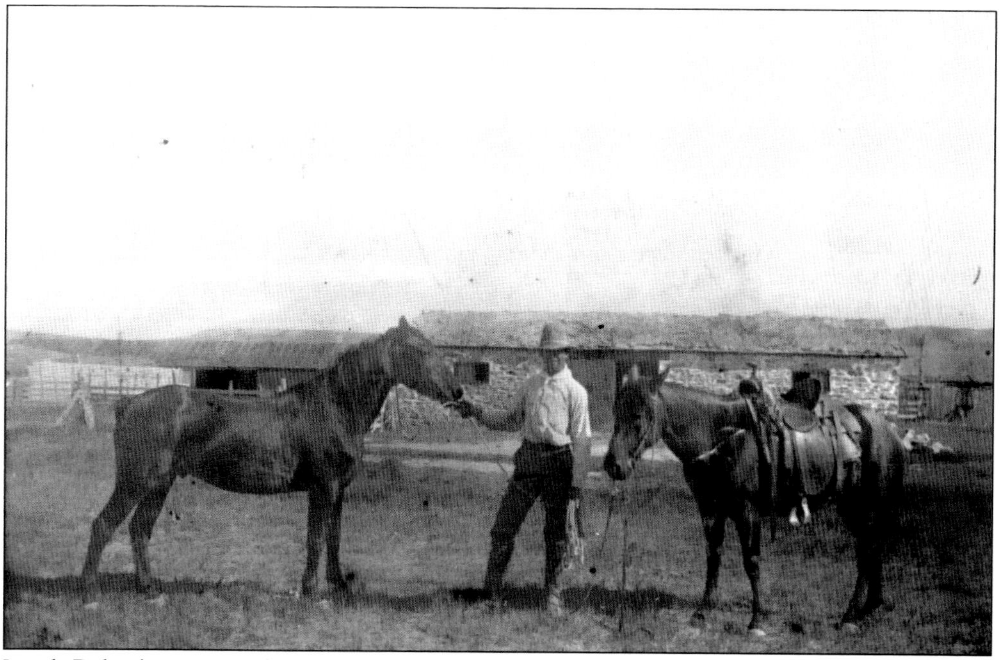

Leach Robuck is pictured with his saddle horses on the Uncle Billy Hadfield Ranch southeast of Peetz. Robuck worked as a cowboy on the ranch. The North Sterling ditch now runs through the place. (Courtesy Overland Trail Museum.)

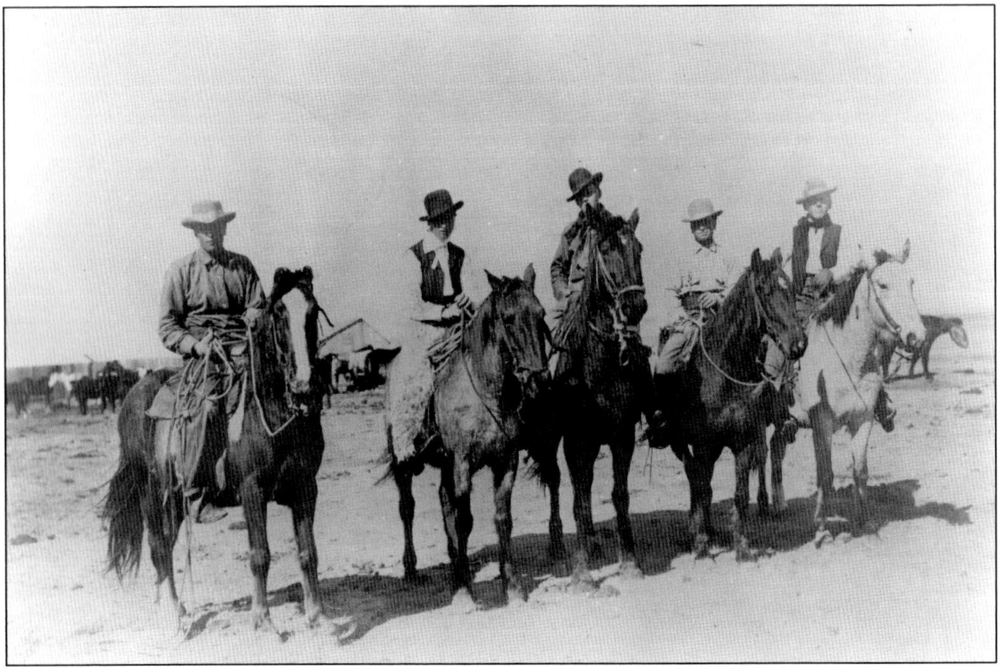

The scene made by these five cowboys was a typical sight in the early days of Sterling. Pictured from left to right are Robert Simpson, Sam Mathews, Rudy Brownell, Sam Cheairs, and John Mathews (no relation to Sam). (Courtesy Overland Trail Museum.)

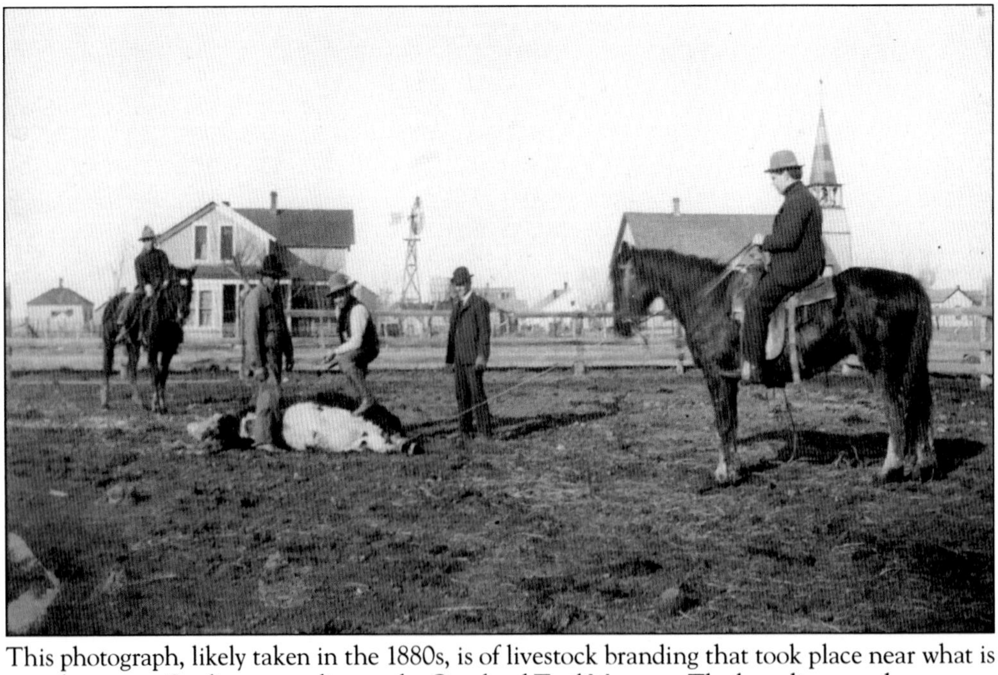

This photograph, likely taken in the 1880s, is of livestock branding that took place near what is now downtown Sterling, according to the Overland Trail Museum. The branding was done across from the present location of the Fox 5 Theatre, on the north side of Poplar Street between Third and Fourth Streets. A Baptist church is seen in the background at right. (Courtesy Overland Trail Museum.)

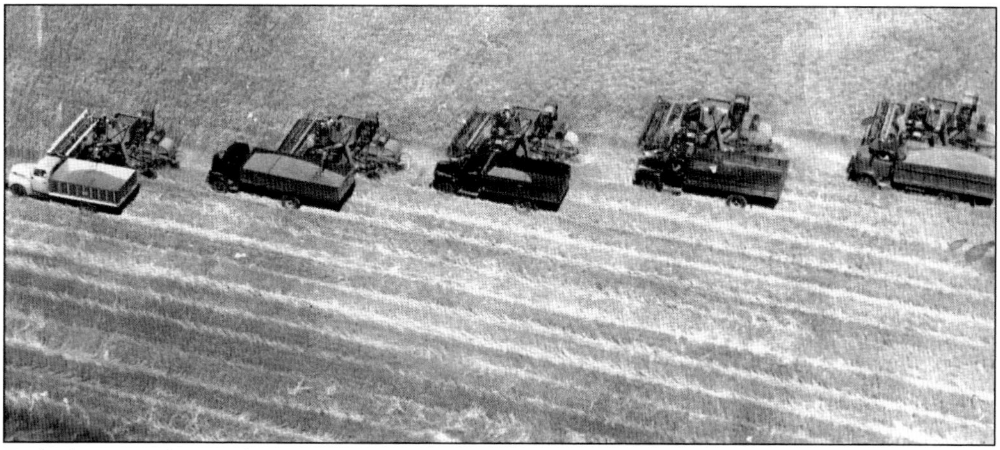

Early farm machinery harvests wheat on a Logan County farm around the 1940s. (Courtesy Overland Trail Museum.)

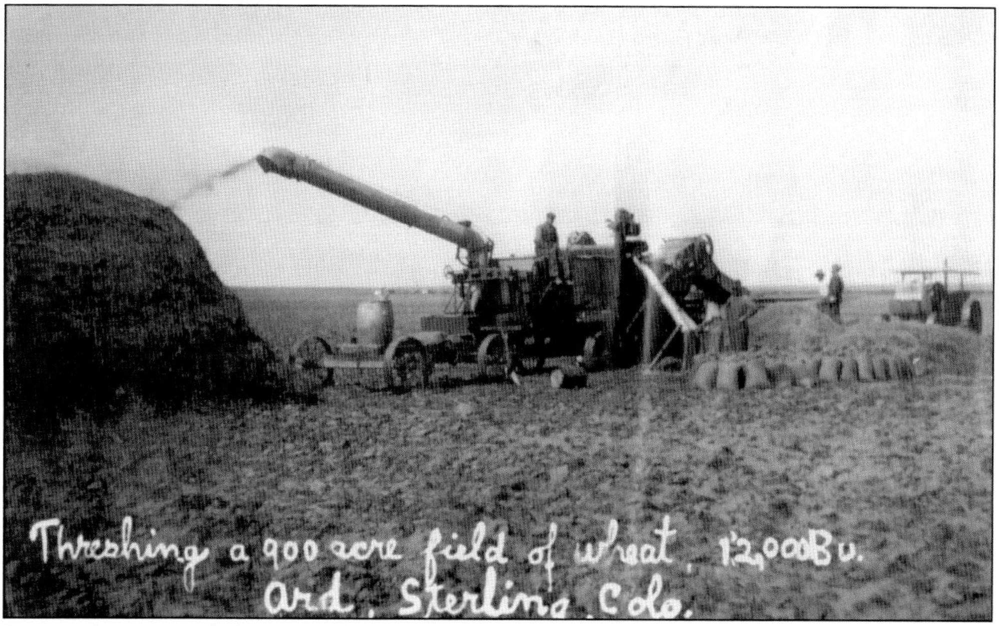

Farmworkers use early heavy machinery to thresh a 900-acre field of wheat on the Ard farm near Sterling. The yield was around 12,000 bushels. (Courtesy Overland Trail Museum.)

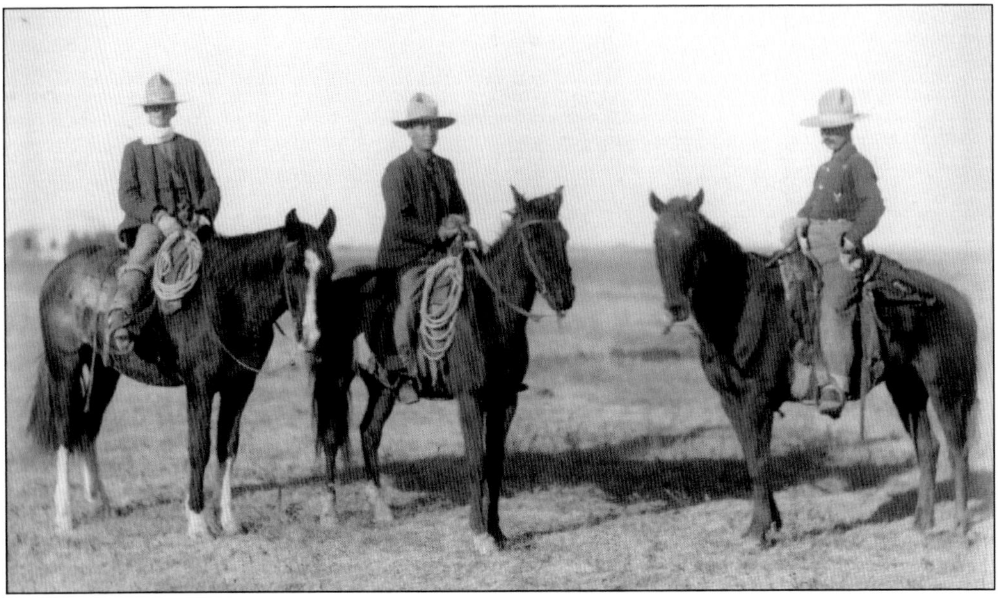

While the actual date of this photograph is unknown, these Sterling-area cowboys are dressed in what appears to be early-20th-century clothing. Pictured from left to right are Clarence Day, Prentiss McEndaffer, and Al Schindler. (Courtesy Overland Trail Museum.)

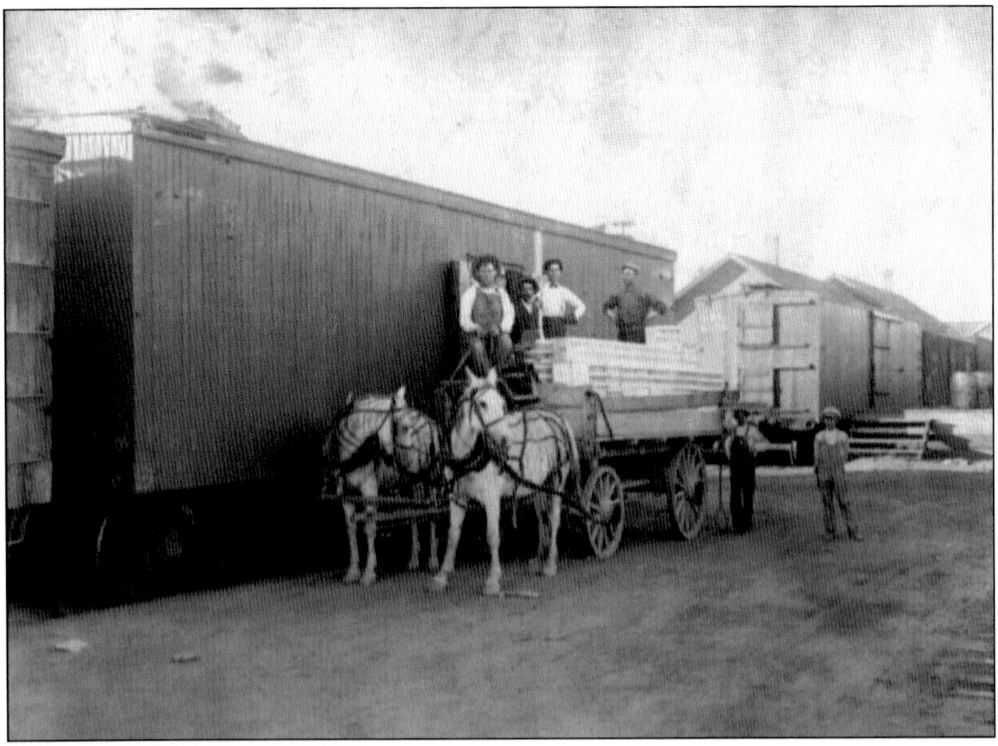

Eugene Rock and his horses, Maude and Molly, are shown in front of a train car. Other men in the picture are unidentified. Though this picture is not dated, it must be from the early part of the century, as it was when the term "freight wagon" still meant freight was loaded into a horse-drawn wagon. (Courtesy Overland Trail Museum.)

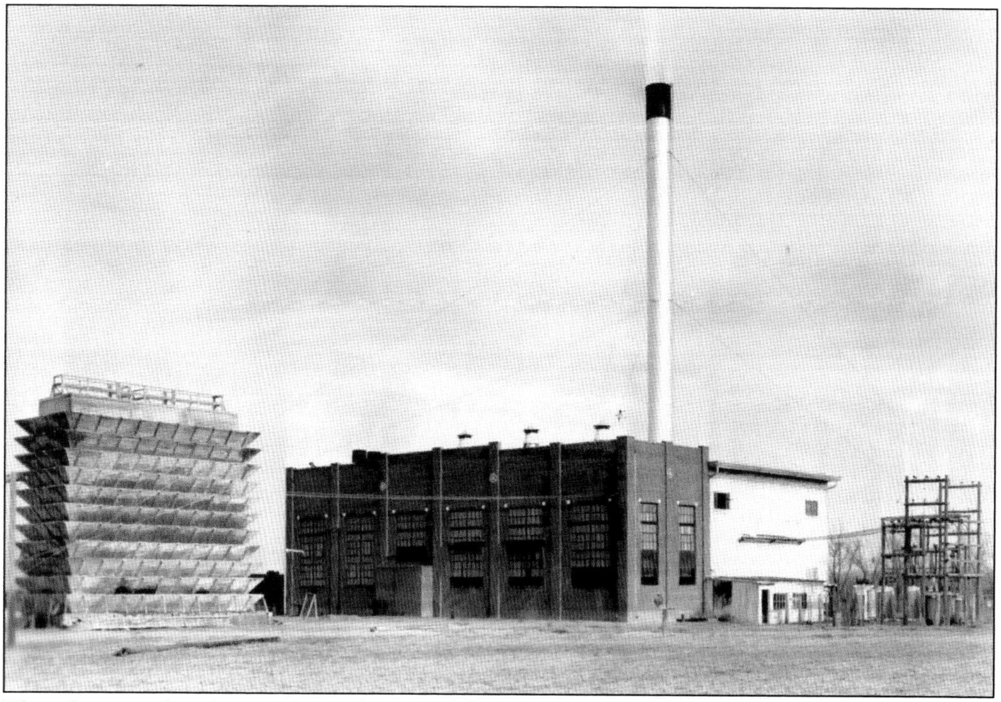

This photograph, taken in the early part of the 20th century, is of an electric power plant then located east of Sterling. It is possibly the second light company built in 1908 and 1909. It was first known as the Sterling Consolidated Electric Company. The company purchased the first Sterling Public Service Company, owned by O. P. Sells. This company was purchased in 1916 by the Colorado Power Company. In 1924, it merged with Public Service. The remains of the power plant can still be found north of Chestnut Street east of the railroad lines. (Courtesy Overland Trail Museum.)

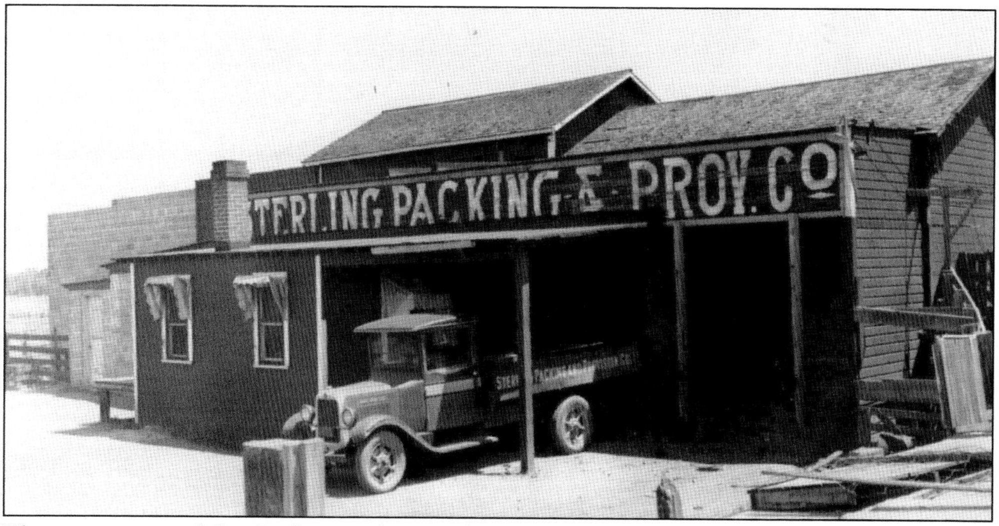

This is a picture of the Sterling Packing and Provision Company, where baby beef and buffalo are being cooled for a banquet on June 8 at the annual convention of the Colorado Livestock Growers and Feeders Association. The exact year of the photograph is unknown. (Courtesy Overland Trail Museum.)

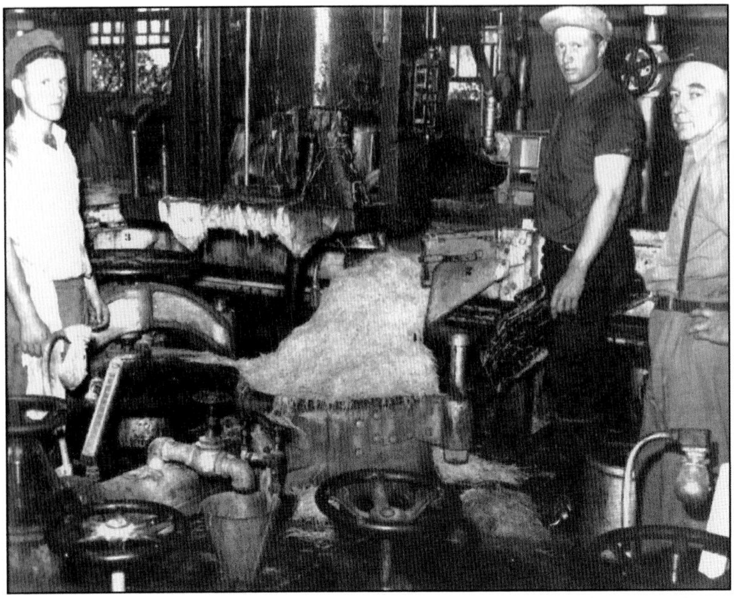

This 1940s picture shows workers at the Sterling sugar beet factory, where sugar beets were processed for their sugar and pulp. The pulp can then be used for feed. (Courtesy Overland Trail Museum.)

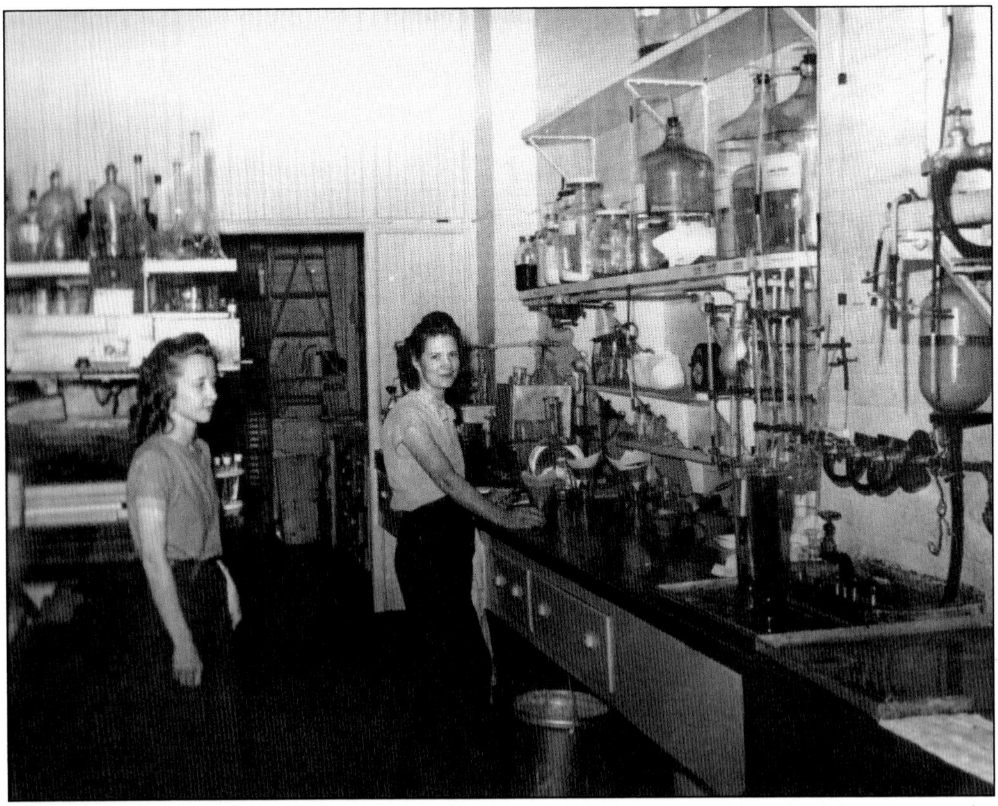

This 1947 photograph is of Annabell Dill (left) and Gladys Reinhardt in the laboratory at the Sterling sugar beet factory. This picture shows the true purity station in the laboratory. Lon Edwards was the lab technician, Perry Jackson was the lab foreman on this shift, Willard Zimmerman worked the beet station, Gladys Reinhardt at the sugar station, and Annabell Dill at the purity station. (Courtesy Overland Trail Museum.)

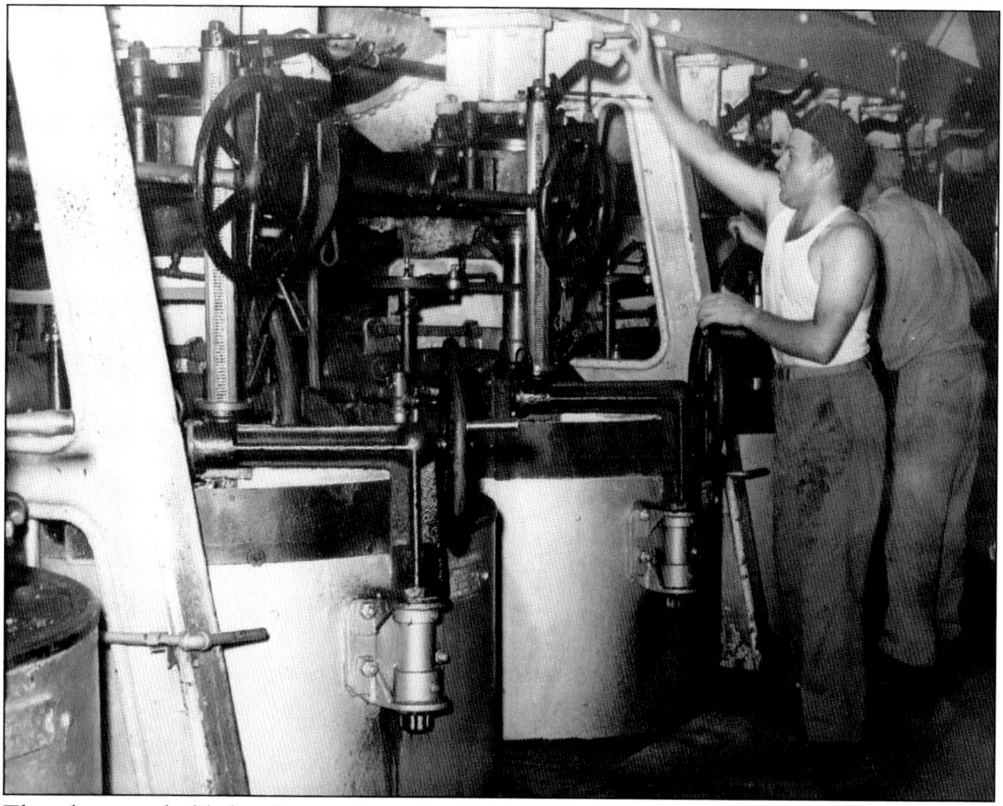

This photograph, likely taken in the mid- to late 1940s, shows how physically demanding it was to work at the Sterling sugar beet factory. (Courtesy Overland Trail Museum.)

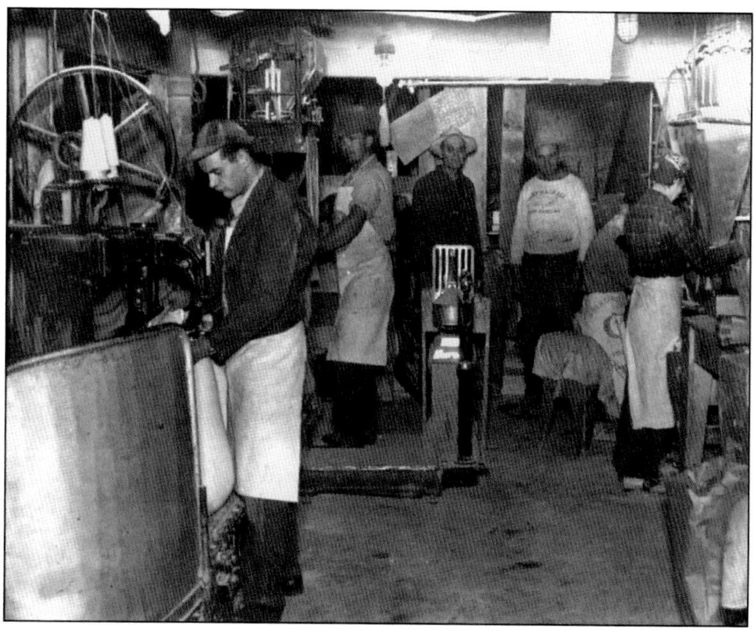

Factory workers sack newly processed sugar beet sugar in this photograph. The sugar factory provided jobs for many residents of the Sterling community, from its opening in the early 1900s through the 1980s. (Courtesy Overland Trail Museum.)

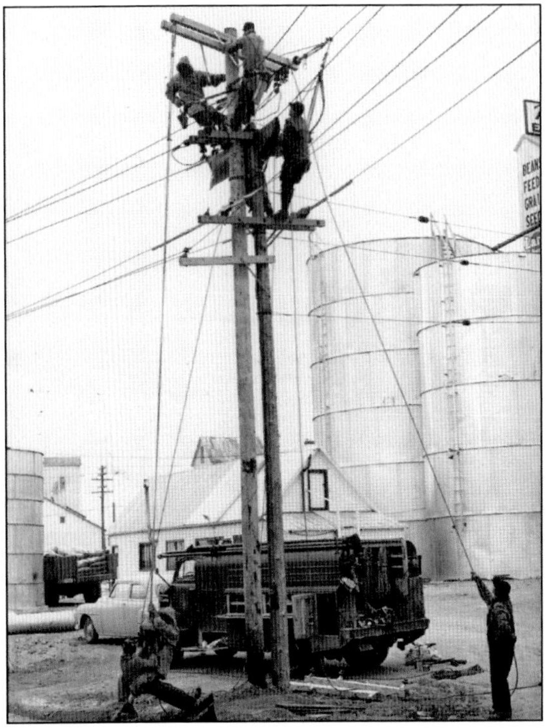

This photograph, taken February 25, 1953, shows Public Service Company employees expanding electrical power to Sterling on a pole near the railroad tracks and Chestnut Street. On the pole are Harold Seeley, Larry Hunt, Dean VanDyle, and Albert Green (hidden from view). On the ground are Bill St. John, Ed Anderson, and Ray Mecham. Public Service evolved into Xcel Energy in the 1990s. (Courtesy Overland Trail Museum)

Thought to be taken around 1953, this photograph is of Public Service Company employees. From left to right are Ray Mecham, Earl Steinhauer, Harvey Wade, Bill Drefke, Larry Hunt (in truck), Orville Grover, Cecil County (in truck), and Pete Seeley. (Courtesy Overland Trail Museum, Larry Hunt photograph.)

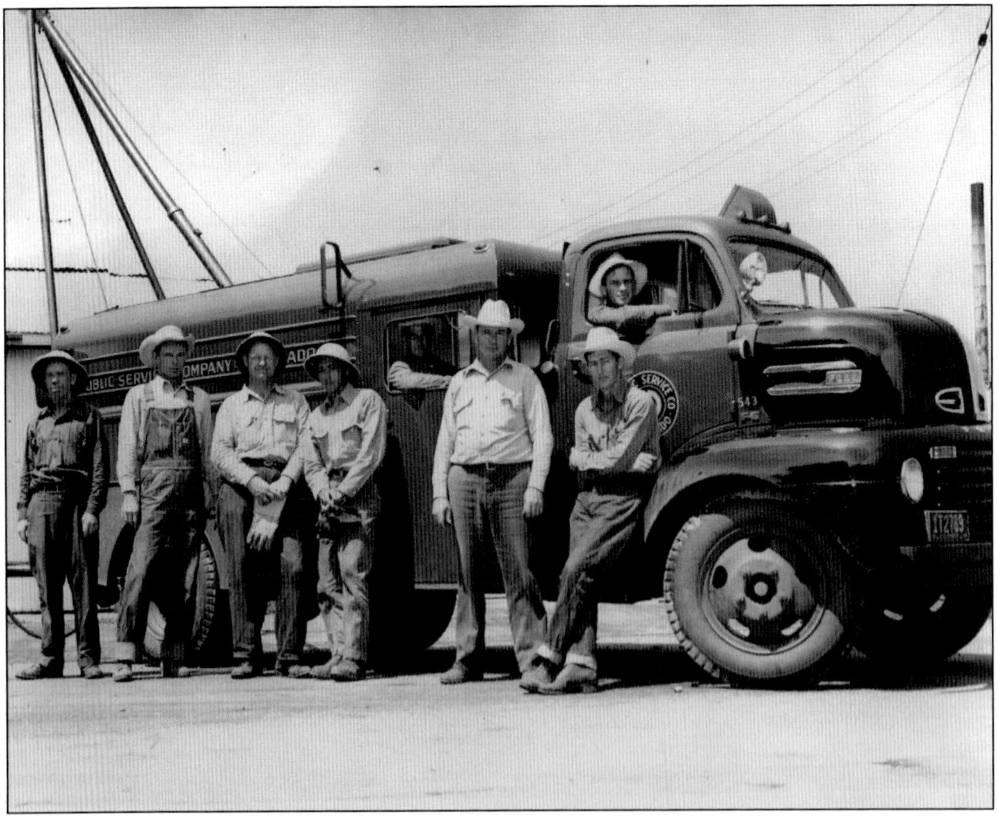

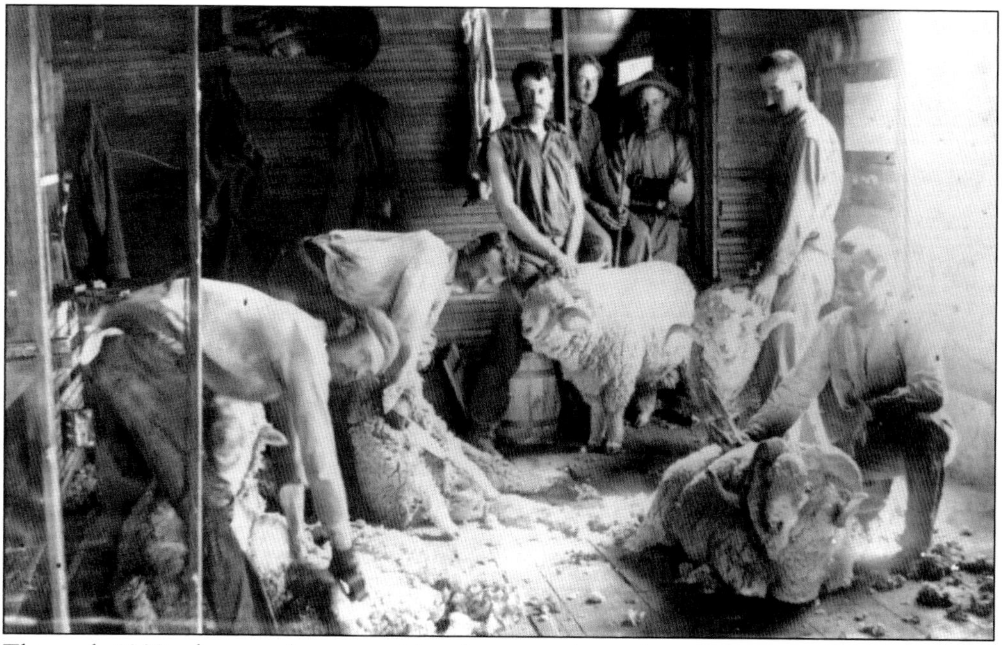

This early-1900s photograph, presumably taken near Atwood, is of the sheepshearing process. During the period of the open range, the cattlemen and sheepherders are rumored to have had little love for each other, although there is no record of actual physical clashes in Logan County. The largest sheep operations in the early 1900s were on the Blair and Dillon Ranches between Proctor and Iliff. L. P. Cheairs ran sheep near Atwood. The scene pictured could have been on his ranch. (Courtesy Overland Trail Museum.)

This photograph, estimated to be from the mid-1980s, is likely of an award to Sterling's Great Western Sugar Factory. The four men are pictured in front of a Great Western Sugar plaque. The man second from right is J. B. Powell, and Lester Garner, longtime manager of the Sterling factory, is at the far right. (Courtesy Overland Trail Museum.)

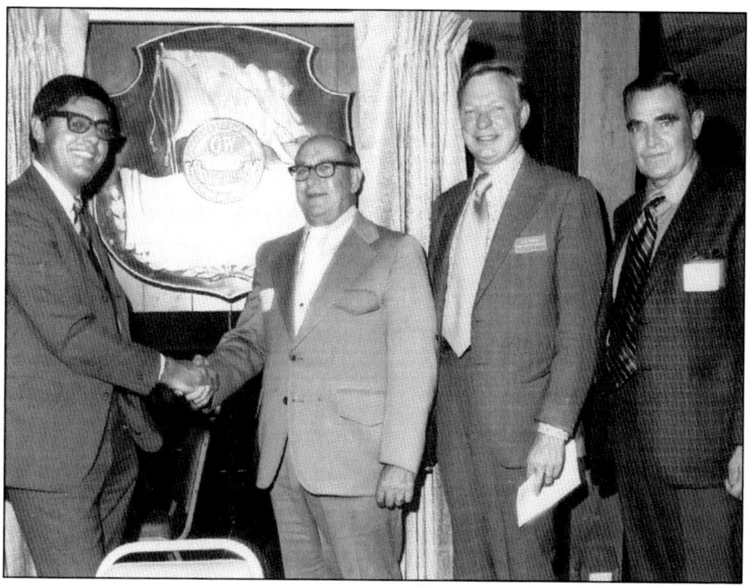

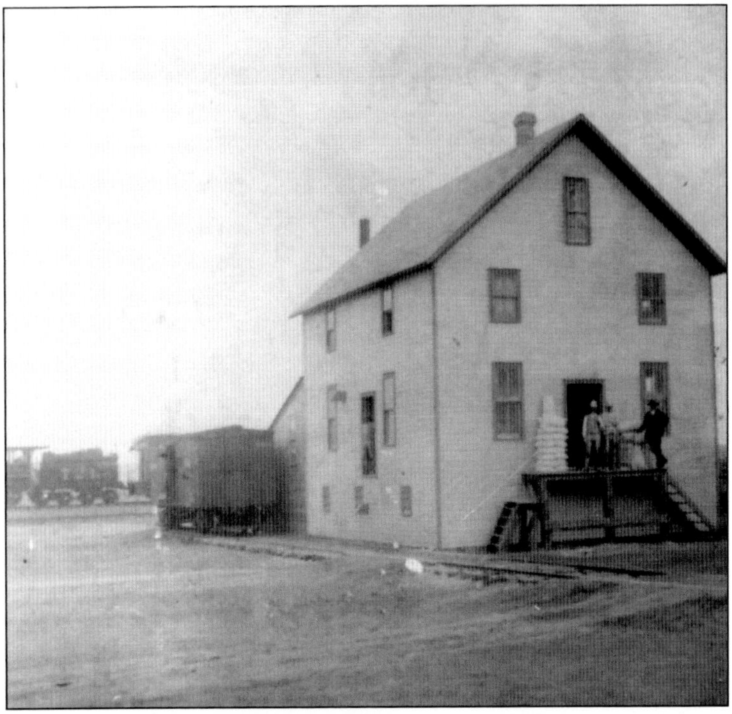

This 1890 photograph is of the Robuck S. B. Flour Mill. The Robuck family moved to Sterling in 1877. The flour mill was located on Front Street. (Courtesy Overland Trail Museum.)

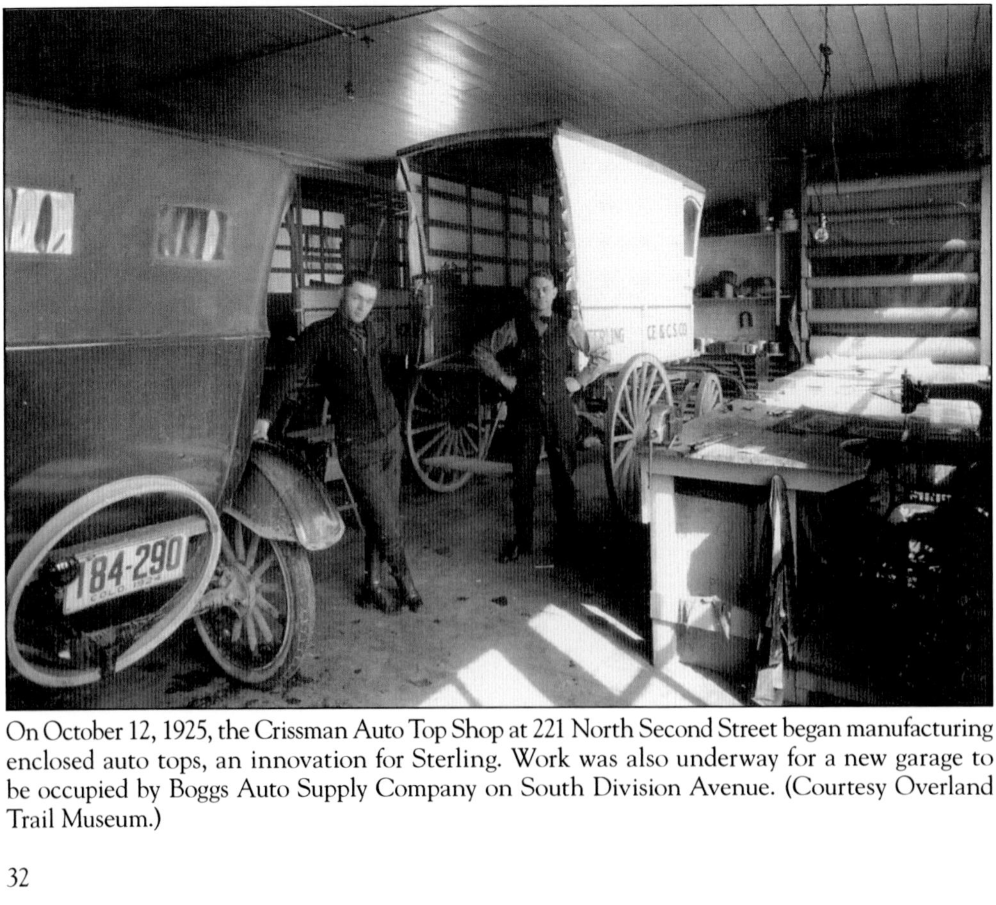

On October 12, 1925, the Crissman Auto Top Shop at 221 North Second Street began manufacturing enclosed auto tops, an innovation for Sterling. Work was also underway for a new garage to be occupied by Boggs Auto Supply Company on South Division Avenue. (Courtesy Overland Trail Museum.)

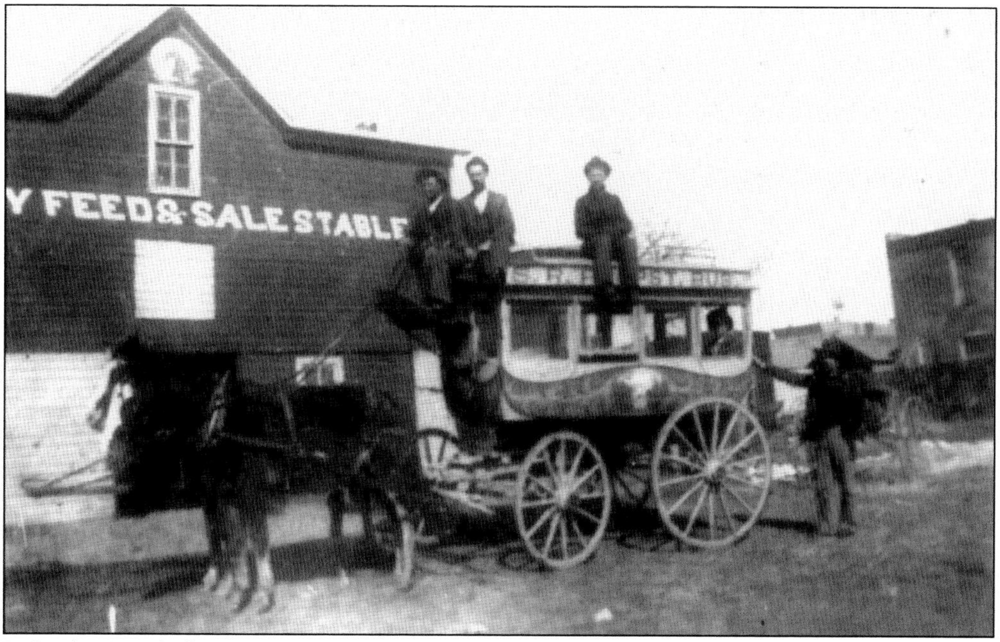

In Sterling's early days, transportation was horse-drawn. This photograph, taken sometime between 1892 and 1896, is of the S. R. Propst stagecoach bus at either the 100 block of South Second Street or the corner of Second and Poplar Streets. The bus service started in 1876 and went to Sidney, Nebraska; Sterling; and Greeley. Pictured from left to right are driver Charley Burt, Milt McKay, V. B. Watts, Art Hudspeth (inside coach), and Dan Gilbert (standing). (Courtesy Overland Trail Museum.)

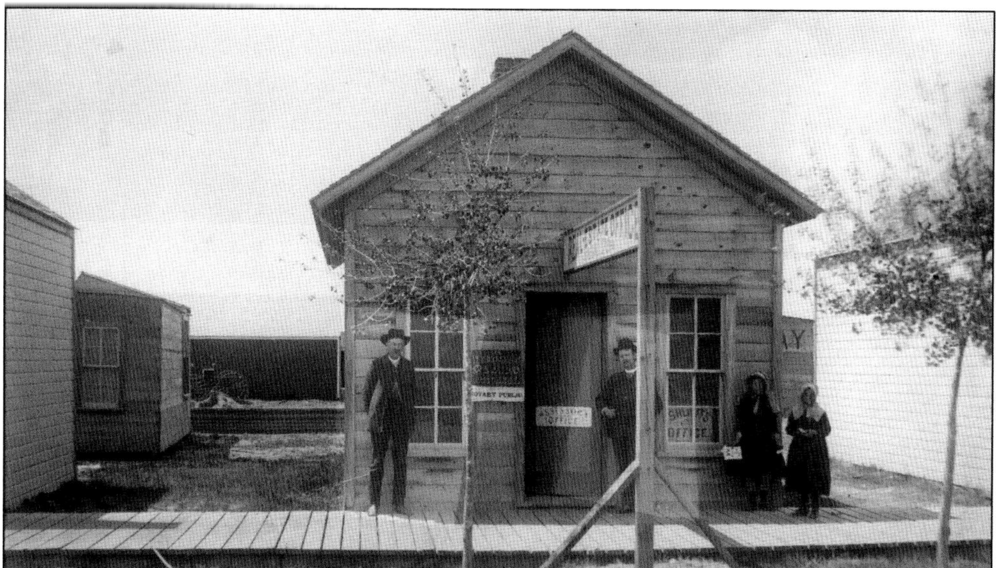

This is a picture of the W. E. Crissman Law Office. Crissman died in 1899, and the firm was bought by Halley and Thomas Munson. Others continued to operate the firm after the Munsons died. It was once believed to be the longest continuous law firm in the state in Colorado. (Courtesy Overland Trail Museum.)

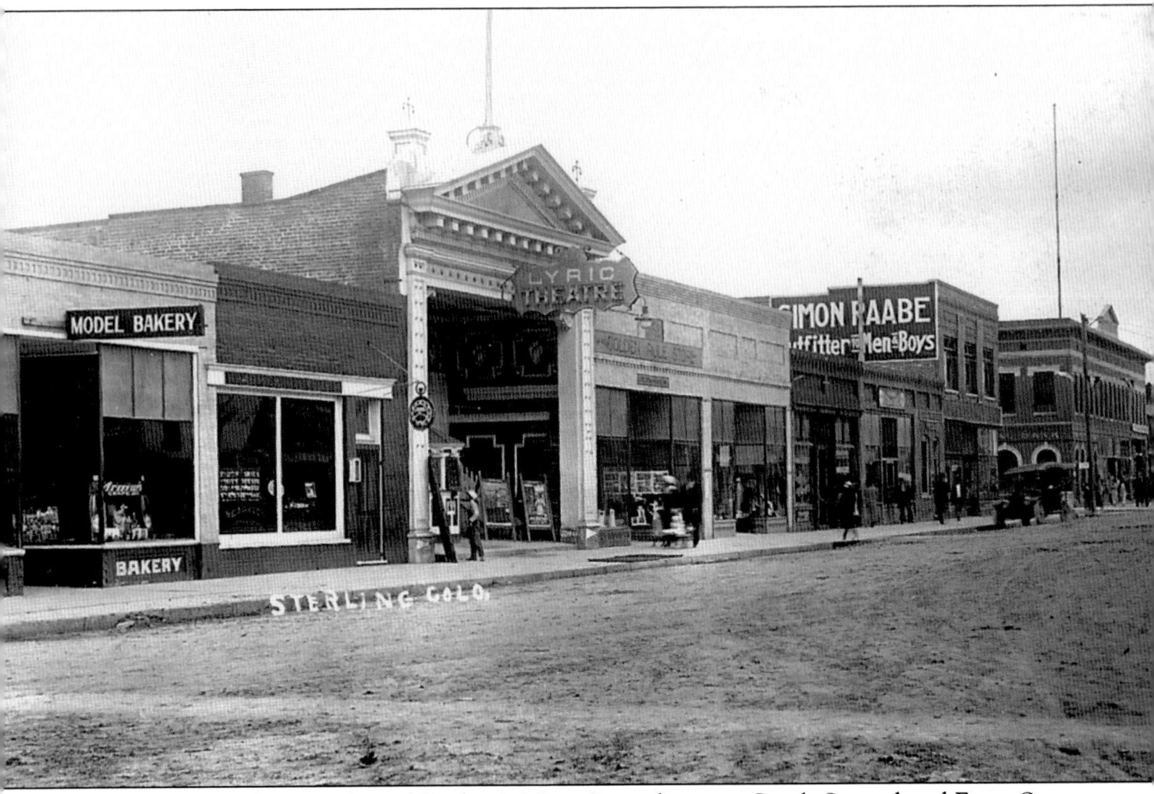

This c. 1915 photograph is of Sterling's Main Street between South Second and Front Streets. The city block includes a bakery and the Lyric Theatre. Information available indicates that the Lyric Theatre was formerly known as the Sterling Theatre. It was operated by Earl Smith. John Headrick was employed as a projection machine operator as a young man, and Jear Dalglish played the piano there for some time. The area was later used as storage for Stickney's store. It is presently divided into several businesses and offices. (Courtesy Overland Trail Museum.)

Three

City Buildings
Great and Small

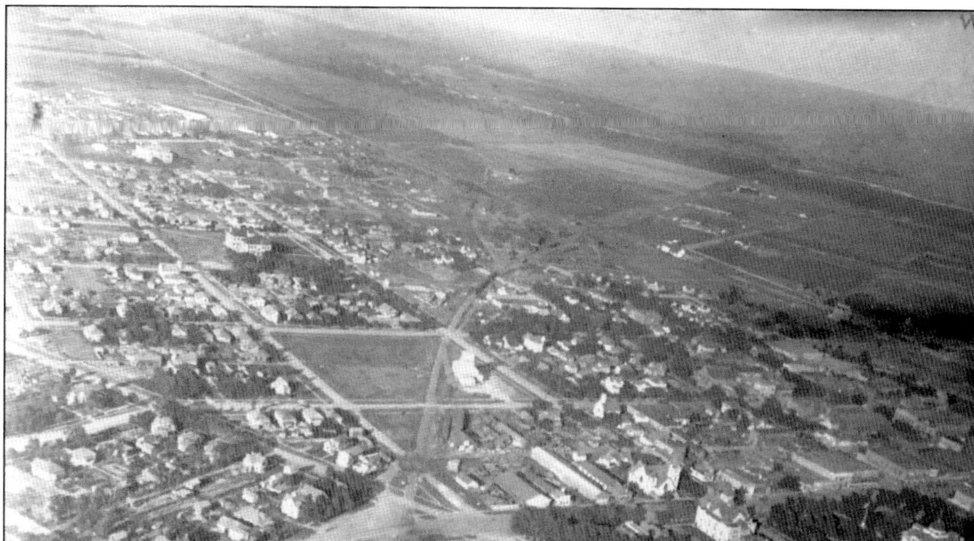

Pictured is a view of Sterling in 1919 taken from an airplane flying over the town. In the center of the photograph is the intersection of Division and Main Streets. To the right, the Logan County Courthouse can be seen. On the left are the street corners that are currently occupied by a drugstore, coffee shop, and a muffler repair shop. (Courtesy Overland Trail Museum.)

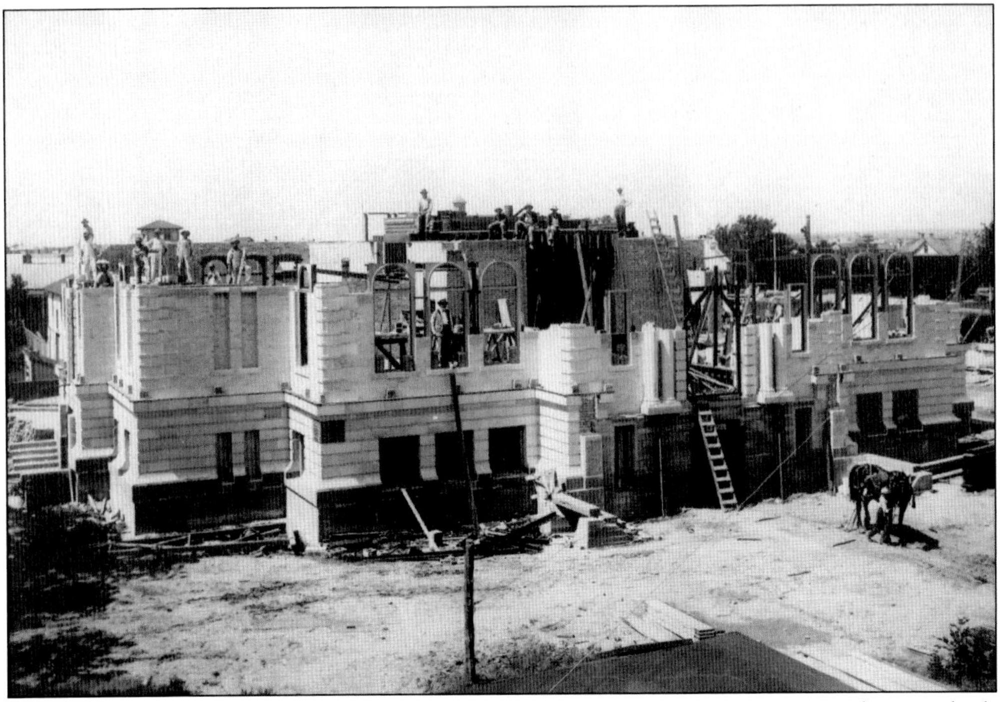

Workers posed for this picture during construction of the new Logan County Courthouse, which was built when the original was condemned. It faces Main Street between Third and Fourth Streets. (Courtesy Overland Trail Museum.)

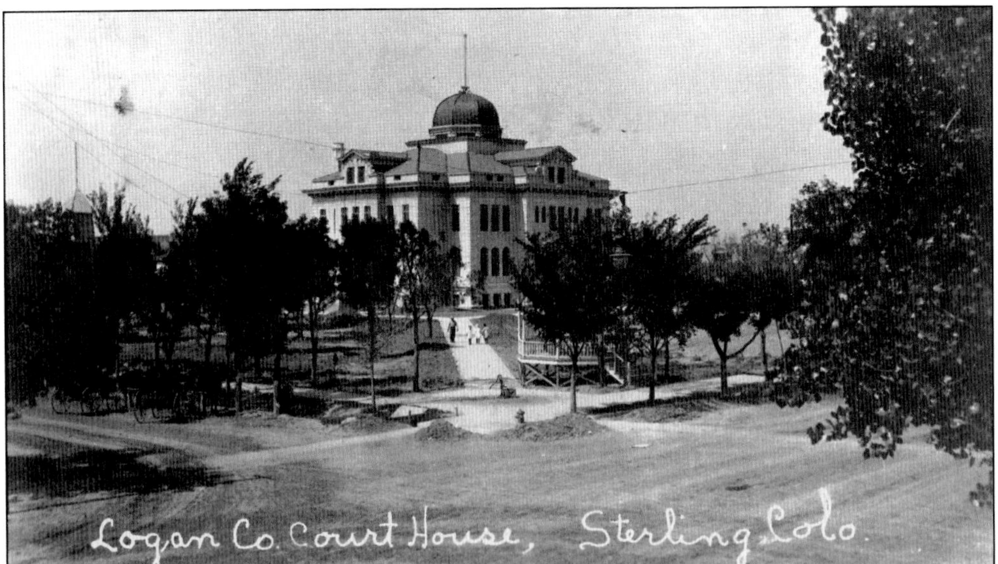

This view of the Logan County Courthouse is from the northeast at about Third and Main Streets. The sidewalk at the center of the photograph would later feature Clarence's Corner, a popcorn stand that became a landmark of its own. Just to the left is a bandstand. A gazebo was later built near the southwest corner of the grounds. (Courtesy Overland Trail Museum.)

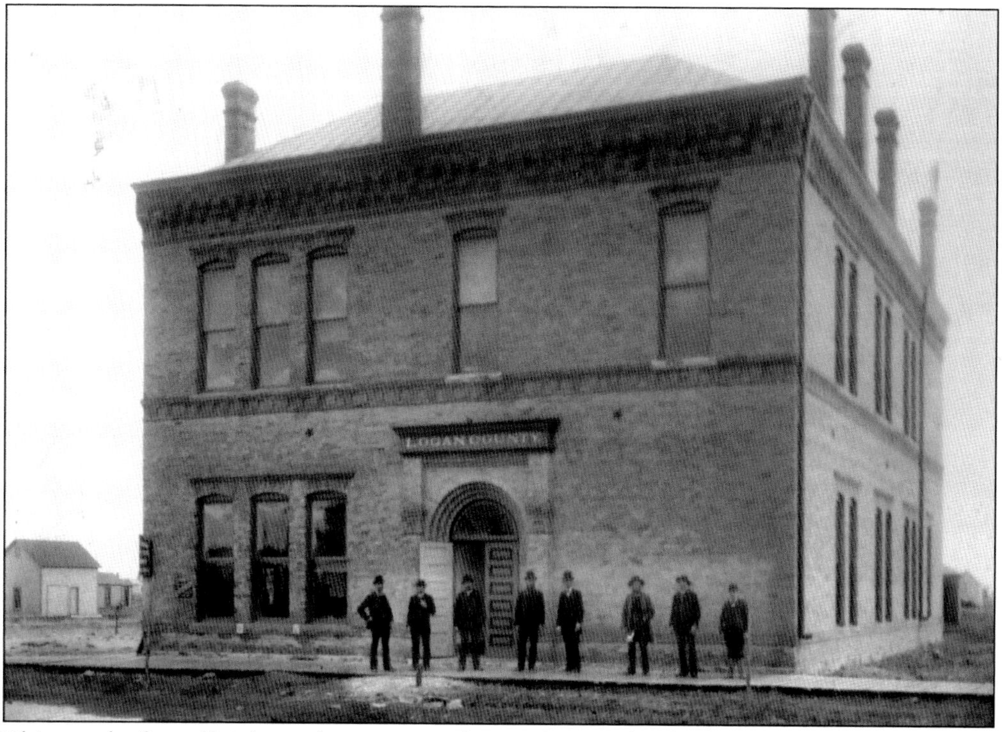

This was the first official courthouse serving Logan County, finished the year Logan County was created (1888). It was built of brick made in the proximity of Sterling. The structure was later condemned and the present courthouse erected. The boiler at the rear of the building served as the steam plant to heat the structure. The men standing in front of the building are believed to be county officials. (Courtesy Overland Trail Museum.)

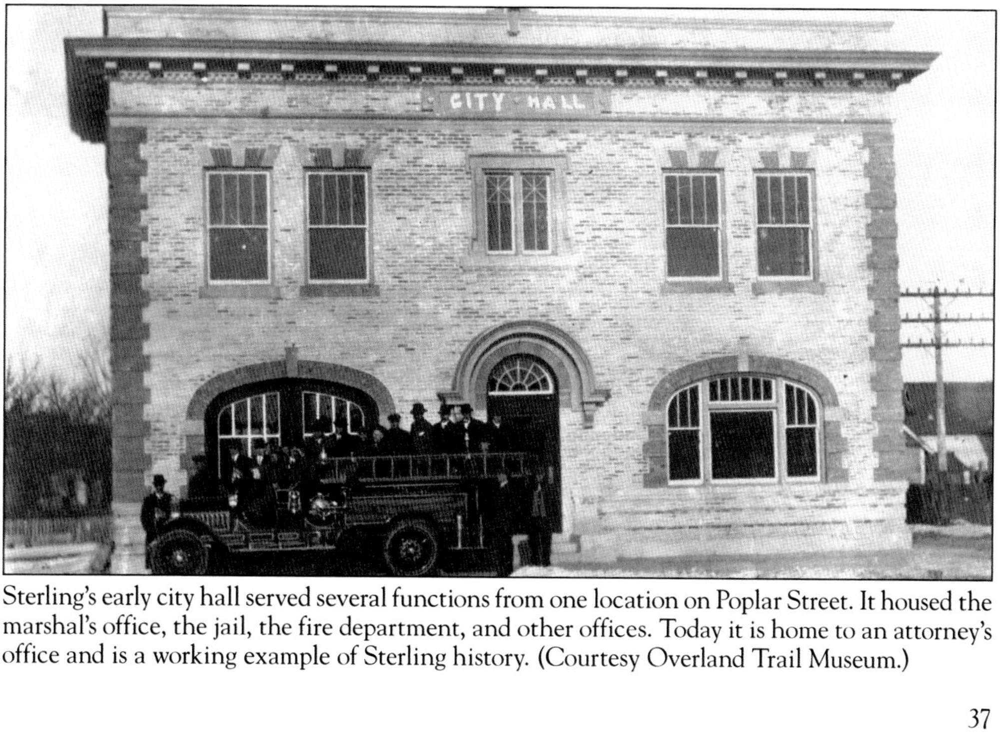

Sterling's early city hall served several functions from one location on Poplar Street. It housed the marshal's office, the jail, the fire department, and other offices. Today it is home to an attorney's office and is a working example of Sterling history. (Courtesy Overland Trail Museum.)

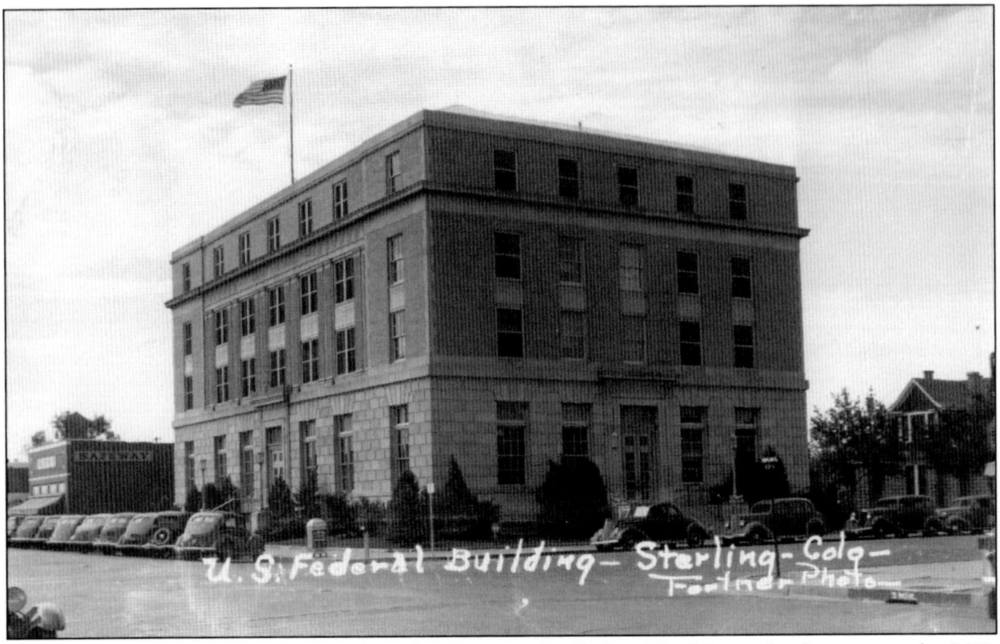

Located at the corner of Third and Poplar Streets, the Federal Building, also known as the U.S. Post Office, has been a landmark in Sterling since it opened in 1930. This picture dates from before 1940. A handicap ramp was added, and the entrance was updated in the 1990s, and the building still serves as a post office in 2010. (Courtesy Russell Johnson.)

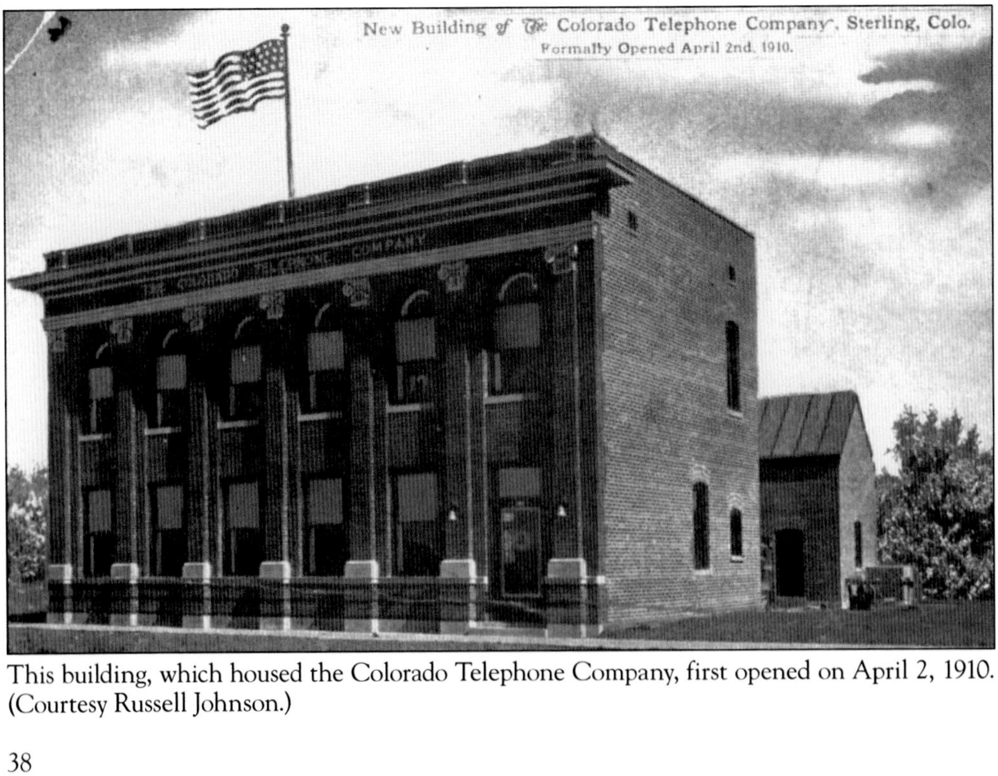

This building, which housed the Colorado Telephone Company, first opened on April 2, 1910. (Courtesy Russell Johnson.)

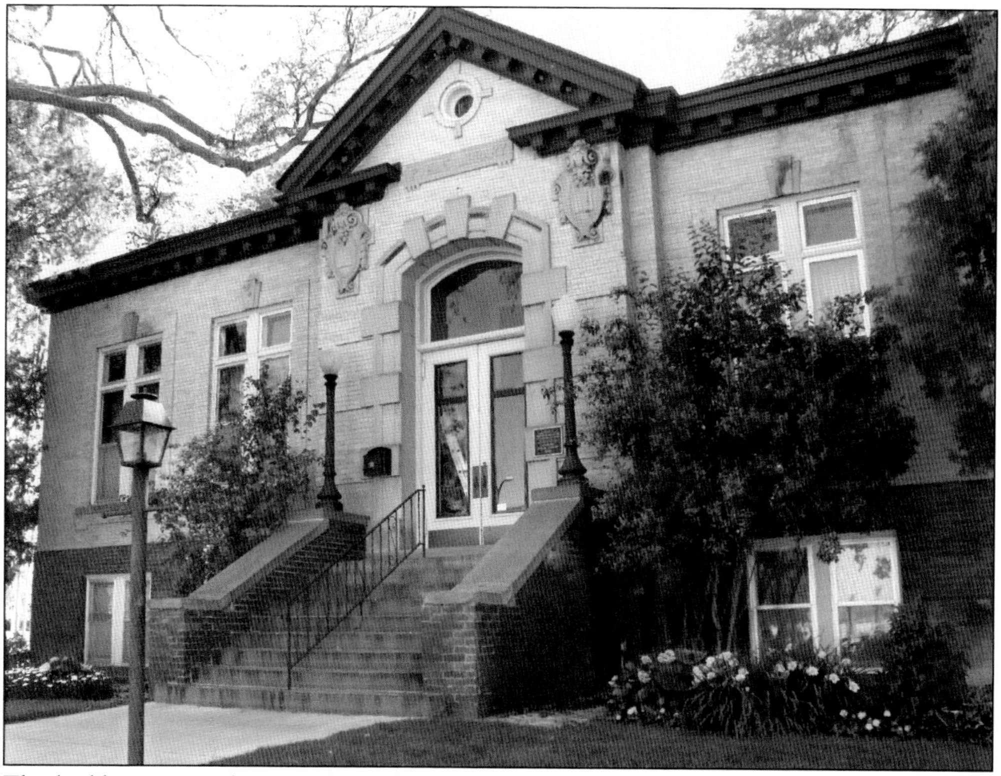

This building, pictured in 2007, housed the Carnegie Public Library. Erected in 1916, it was one of more than 2,500 such public libraries built around the United States through grants provided by businessman and philanthropist Andrew Carnegie and local funds. In recent years, the building was renovated and converted into a bed-and-breakfast called the Old Library Inn. Some of the building's many other uses have been as a counseling center, a probation office, and a private residence. (Courtesy *Sterling Journal-Advocate.*)

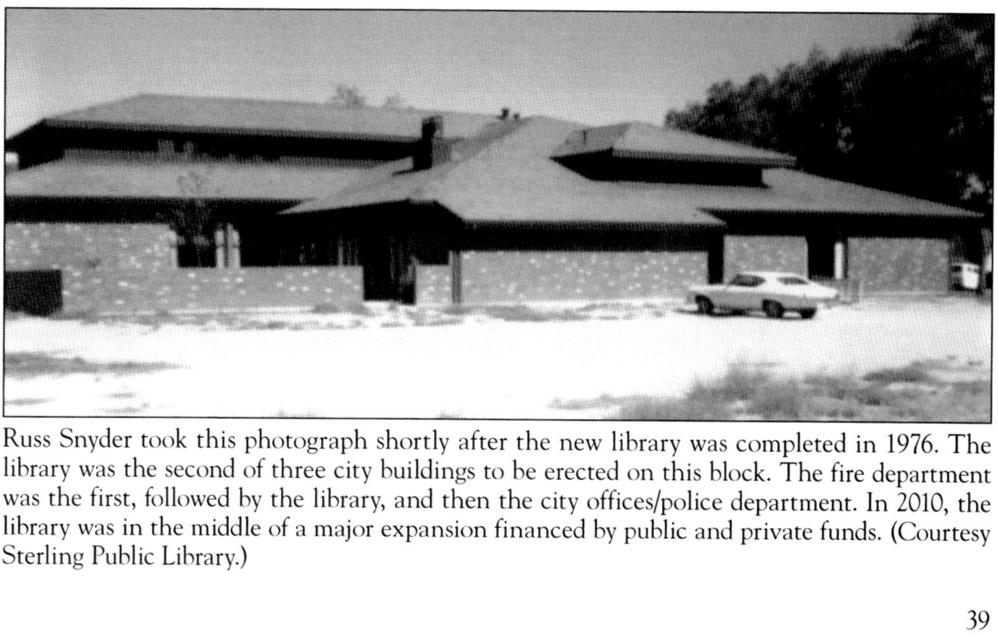

Russ Snyder took this photograph shortly after the new library was completed in 1976. The library was the second of three city buildings to be erected on this block. The fire department was the first, followed by the library, and then the city offices/police department. In 2010, the library was in the middle of a major expansion financed by public and private funds. (Courtesy Sterling Public Library.)

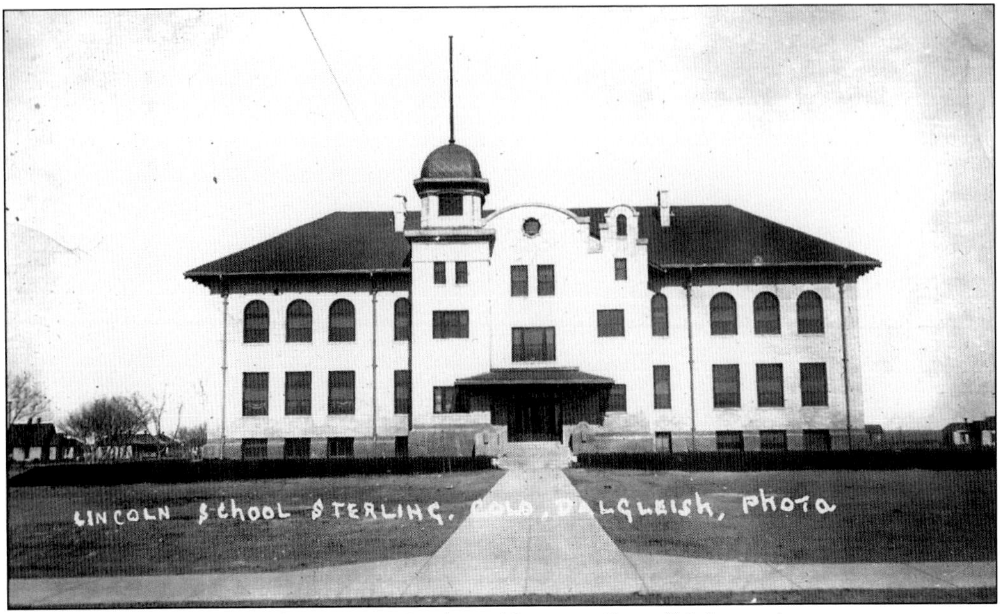

This is the Lincoln School in 1918 in Sterling. (Courtesy Russell Johnson.)

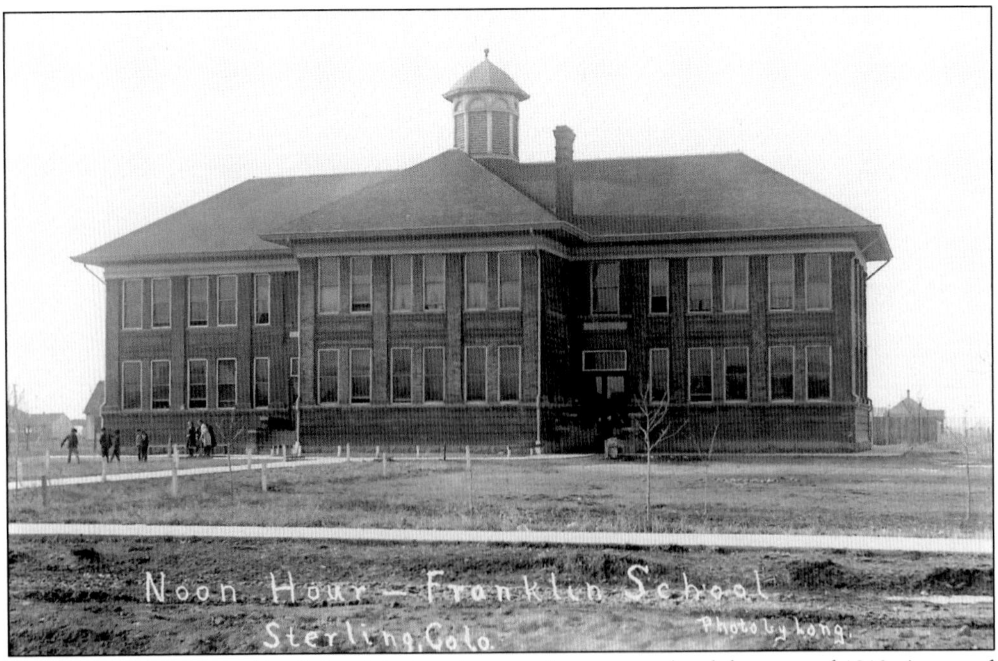

Pictured is the first Franklin School during the noon hour on a school day around 1910. A second Sterling school was later named Franklin Elementary School. (Courtesy Russell Johnson.)

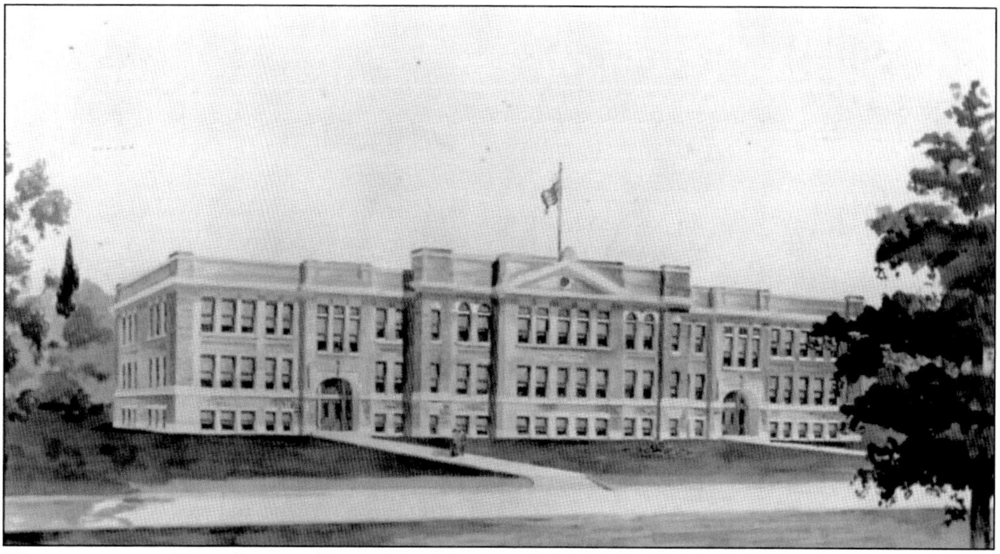

This is an artist's rendering of Logan County High School. Built in the early 1900s, the high school was later converted into the junior high school. Students attended classes in the building until the 1980s, when Sterling Middle School was built. (Courtesy Russell Johnson.)

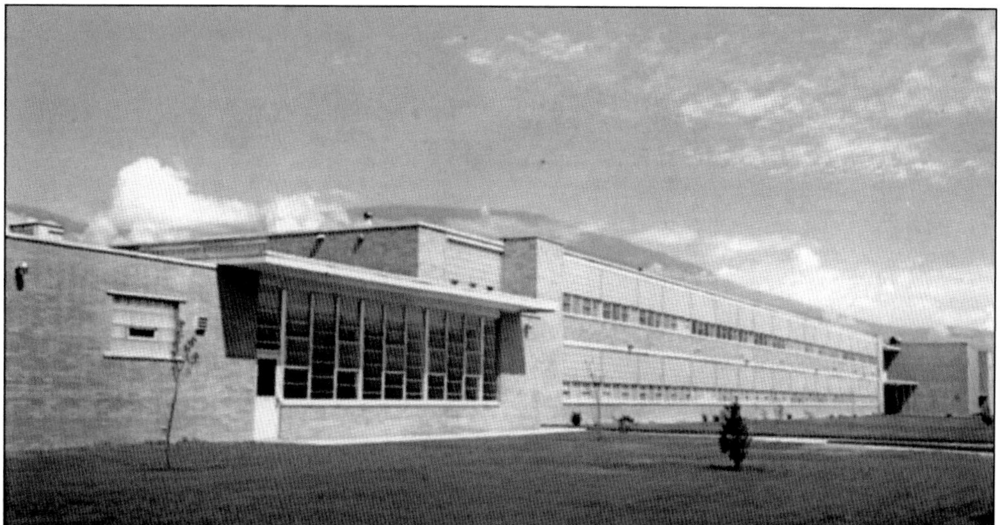

Pictured is the newly built Sterling High School in the mid-20th century. The school was renovated and expanded in 2007. (Courtesy Russell Johnson.)

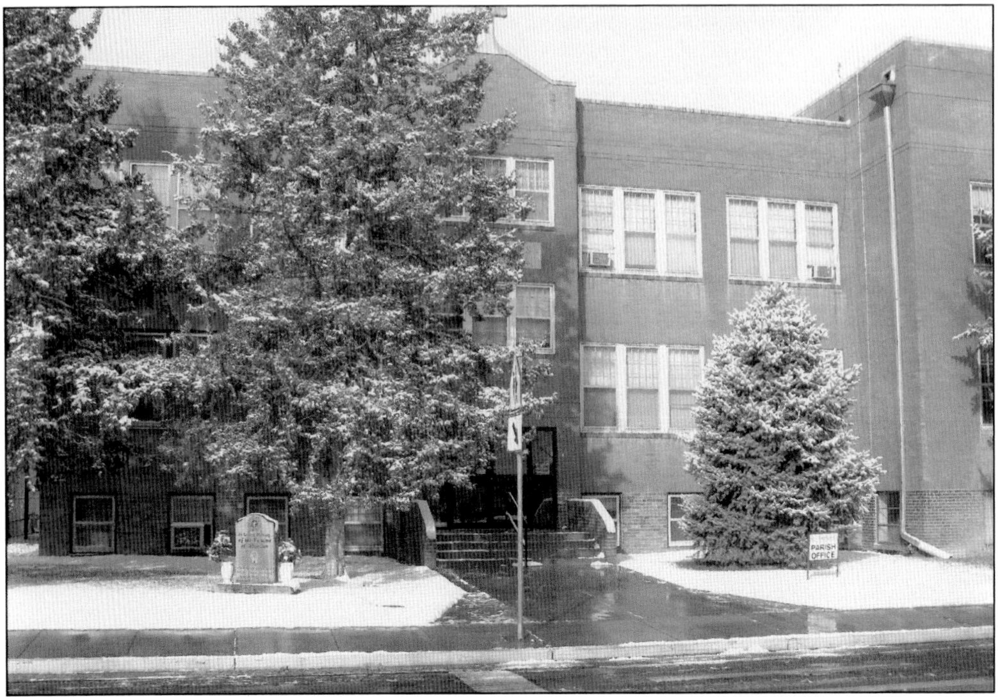

Pictured is St. Anthony Catholic School in 2009. The private parochial school, which once educated students in grades 1 through 12, now enrolls students in preschool through eighth grades. (Courtesy *Sterling Journal-Advocate*.)

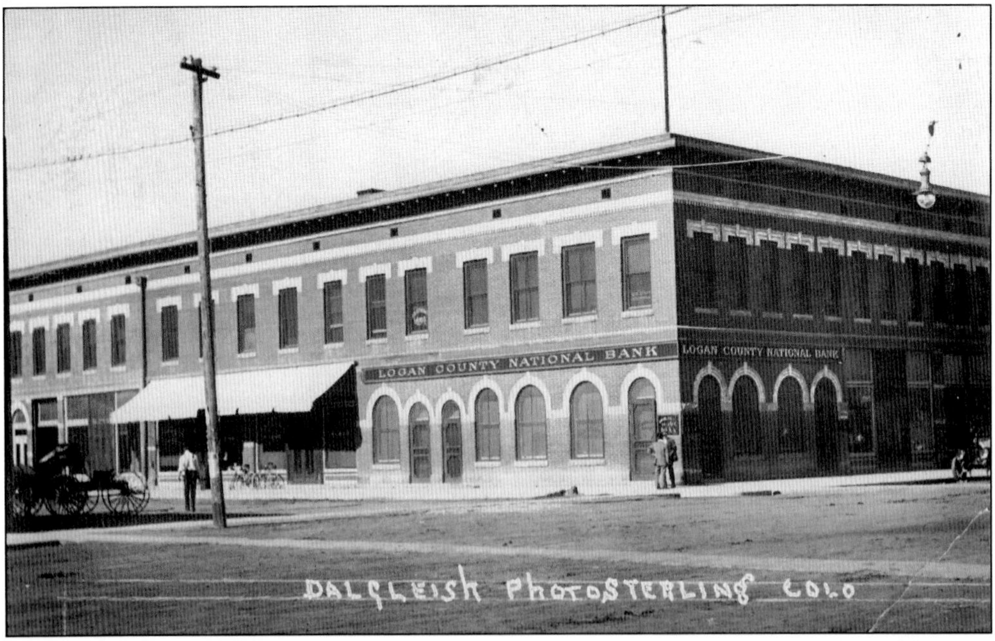

This photograph is of Sterling's Main Street between Second and Front Streets. The building still stands and was used by Stickney's for a warehouse. It is now subdivided into several businesses and offices, including an alternative education setting for the RE-1 Valley School District. (Courtesy Overland Trail Museum.)

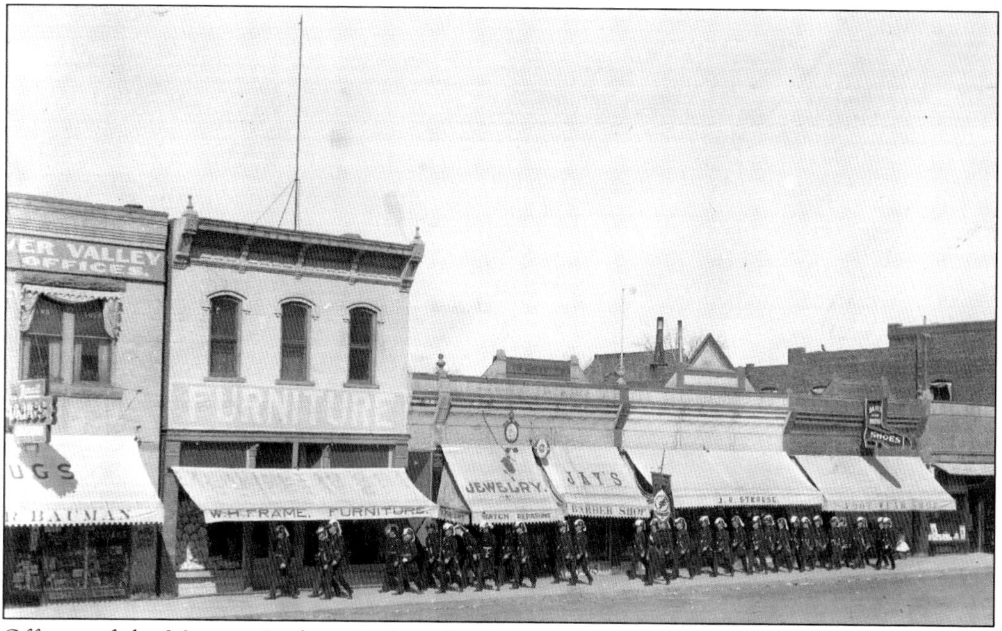

Officers of the Masonic Lodge march in formation and formal attire from Second and Main Streets. (Courtesy Overland Trail Museum.)

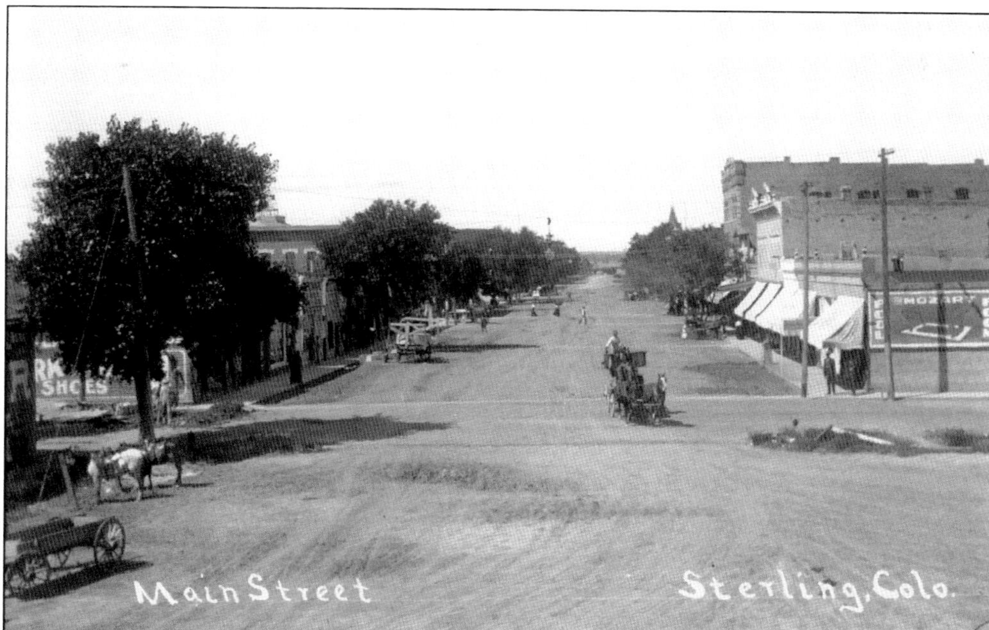

Main Street is pictured here in the pre-automobile era. (Courtesy Overland Trail Museum.)

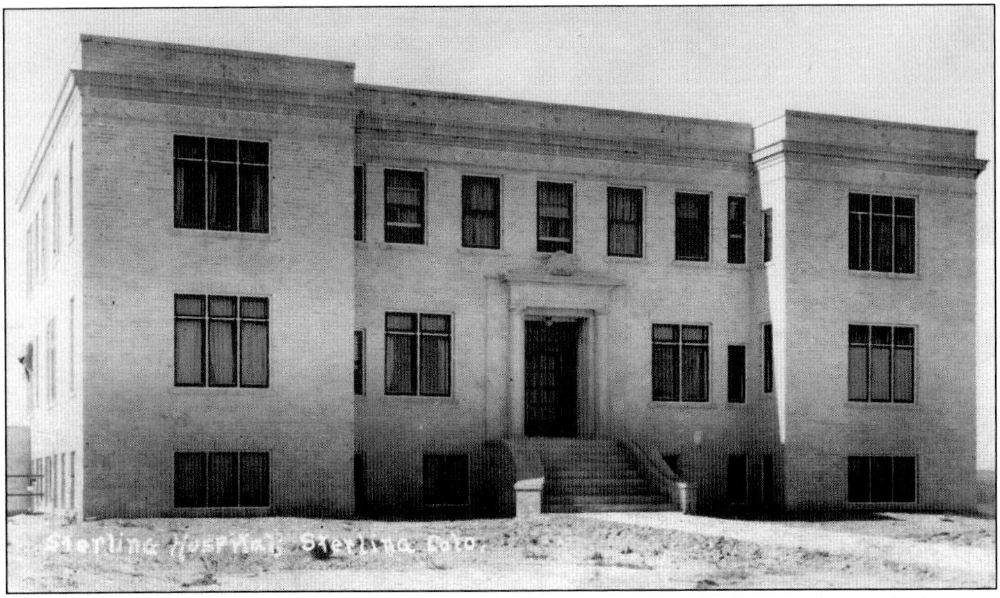

Pictured is the Good Samaritan Hospital in 1922. Opening in 1921, the hospital boasted 30 rooms and seven wards. The construction cost of $80,000 was largely funded through community donations solicited by the Sterling Hospital Association. In 1938, the facility was leased to Lutheran Health Systems. The hospital closed in 1954 with the construction of Logan County Hospital, which has since been replaced with Sterling Regional MedCenter. The Good Samaritan building still stands near Seventh Avenue and Beattie Street. (Courtesy Russell Johnson.)

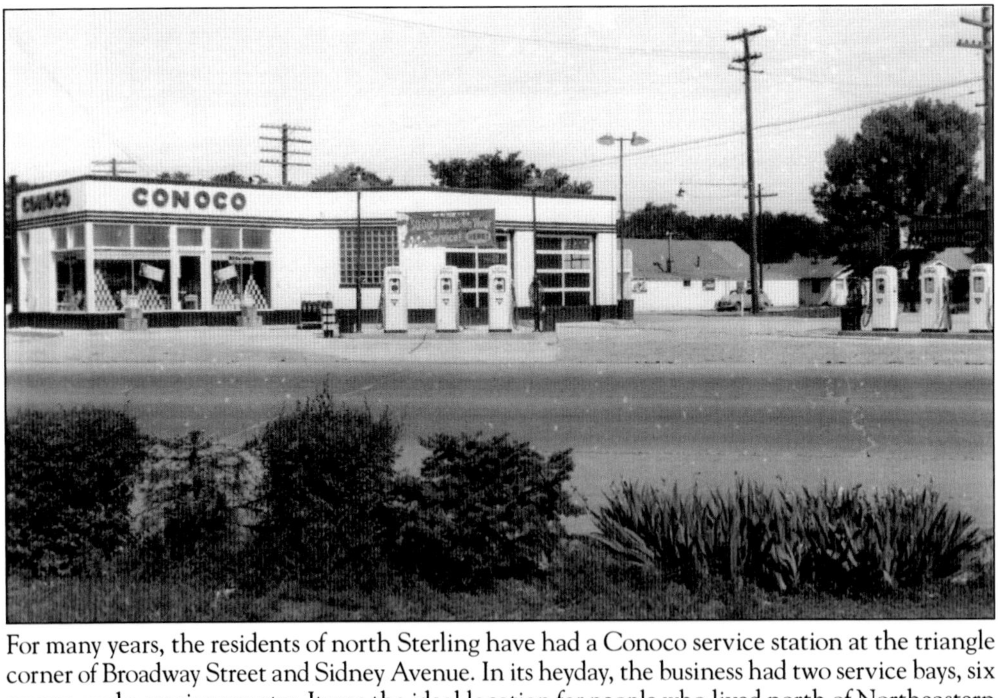

For many years, the residents of north Sterling have had a Conoco service station at the triangle corner of Broadway Street and Sidney Avenue. In its heyday, the business had two service bays, six pumps, and a service counter. It was the ideal location for people who lived north of Northeastern Junior College, students at the college, or people commuting northeast on Highway 138. (Courtesy Overland Trail Museum.)

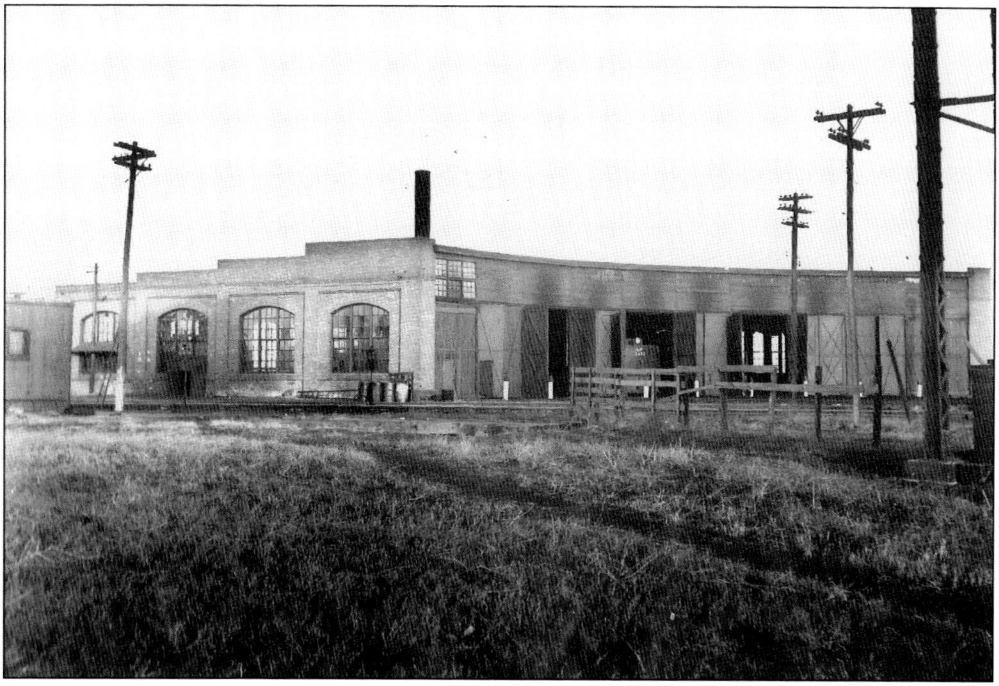

The pictured roundhouse was given to the city of Sterling in 1959. It was used as the location for city shops until 1998 when a new service center was built. The roundhouse was razed in April 2000. (Courtesy McCoy/Collman Collection, Overland Trail Museum.)

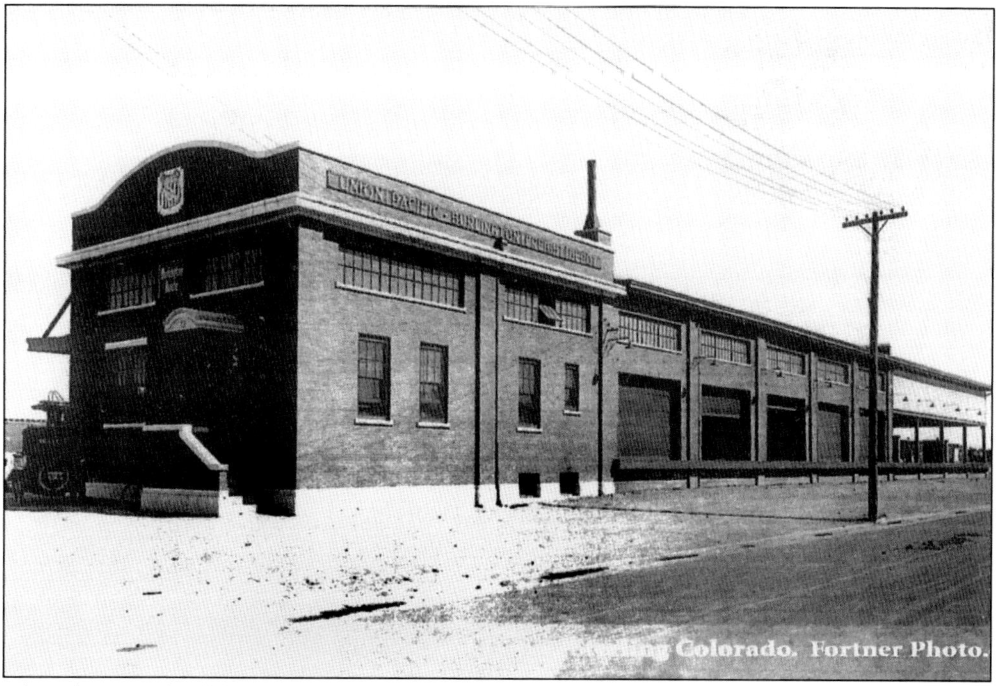

This photograph of the freight depot was taken in 1930. It shows the brick freight depot that was located on Front and Main Streets. It was used by both the Union Pacific and Burlington Northern railroads. (Courtesy Overland Trail Museum.)

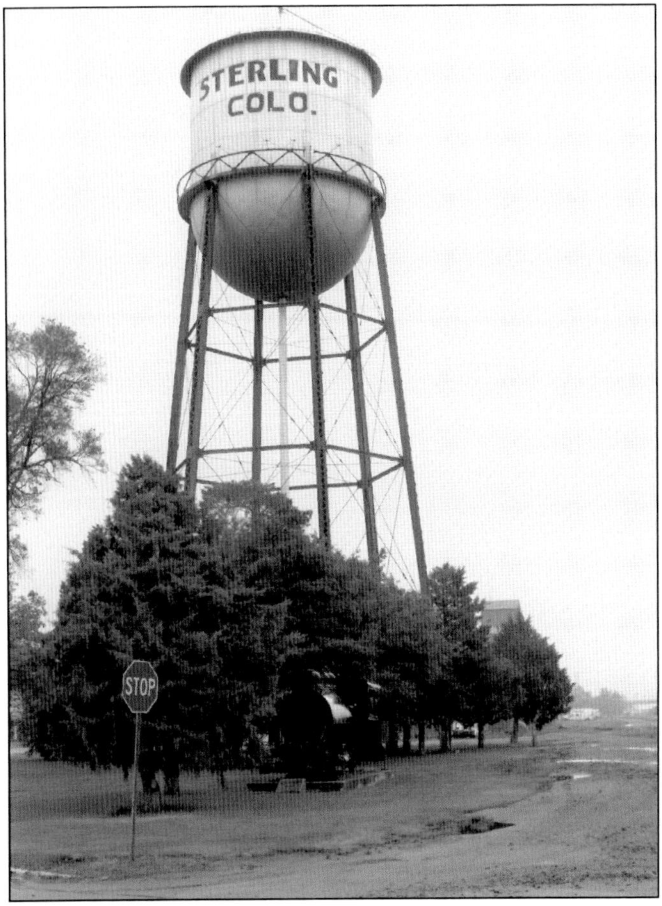

Pictured is the south water tower. Below it sits the engine that once serviced the sugar beet factory. (Photograph by Forrest Hershberger.)

This is the view from Sterling's first water tower in the early 20th century. (Courtesy Russell Johnson.)

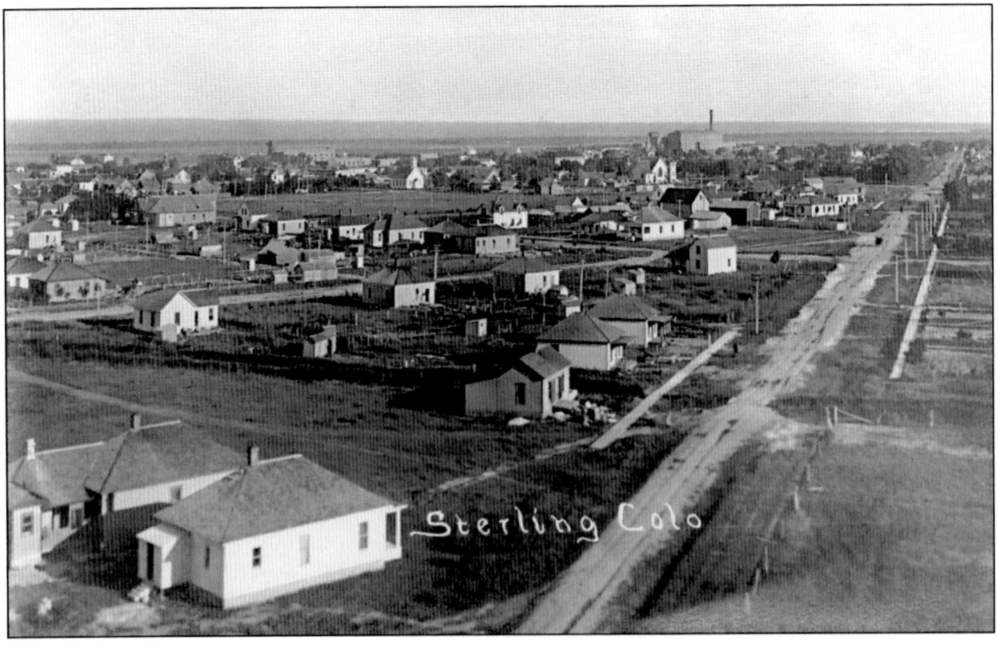

Four

Homes and Churches

As Diverse as the Community

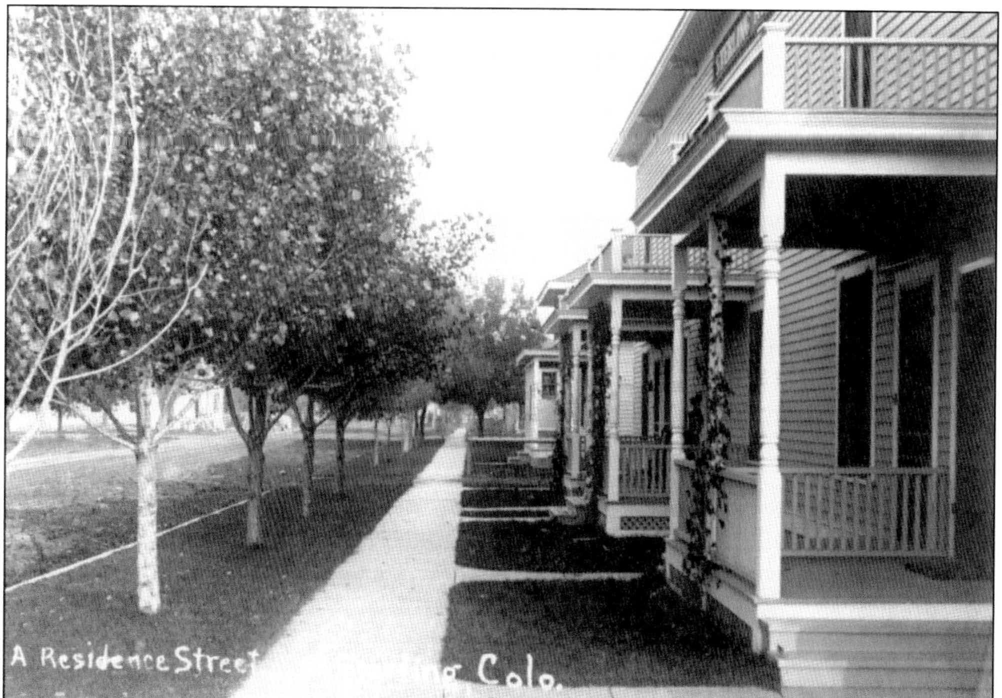

In the early part of the 1900s, Poplar Street was primarily a residential area, as pictured here, populated with homes complete with front porches. This area between Third and Fourth Streets was known as Lutin Terraces on the south side of the street. The area later became today's Fox 5 Theatre. (Courtesy Overland Trail Museum.)

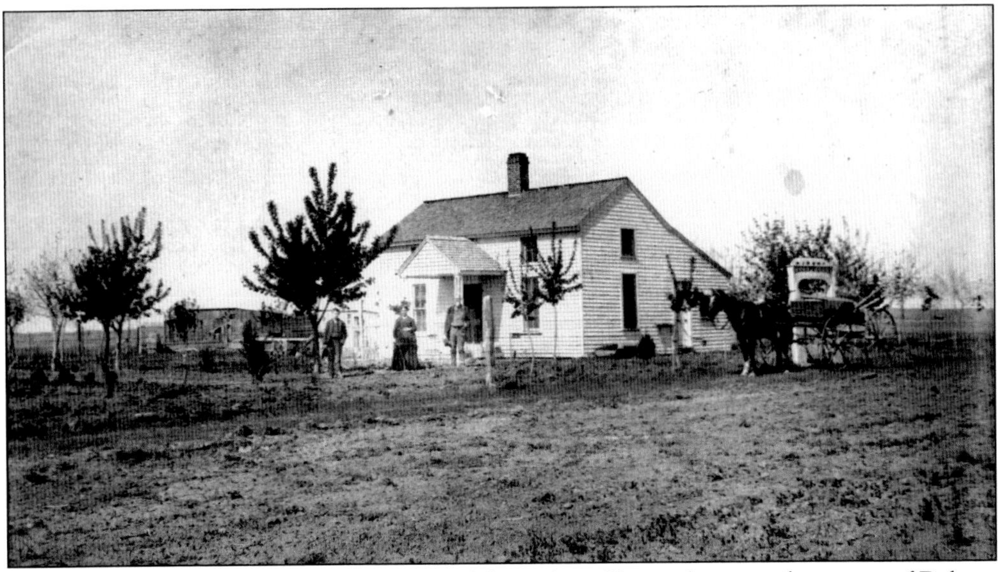

This photograph, taken in 1881 or 1882, is of the Calvin Cheairs home at the corner of Delmar and South Division Streets. The home was built with the first carload of lumber brought by the Union Pacific railroad. The home was at the north end of Columbine Park. The Cheairs family owned the land where the park is now. Mrs. Calvin Cheairs is pictured at the center, with Calvin to the right. (Courtesy Overland Trail Museum.)

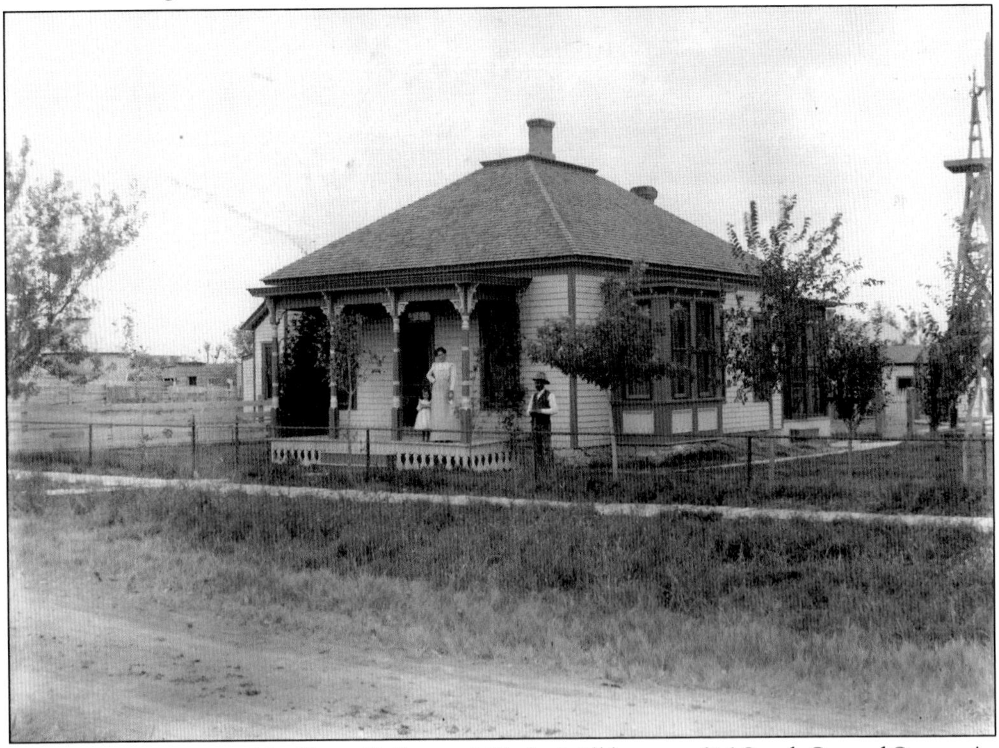

This is a 1900 picture of the Dave, Nellie, and Gladys Mill home at 316 South Second Street. As of the mid-1970s, the house was still standing in the same location, but it had an addition and had been painted. The house could still be seen in 2010. (Courtesy Overland Trail Museum.)

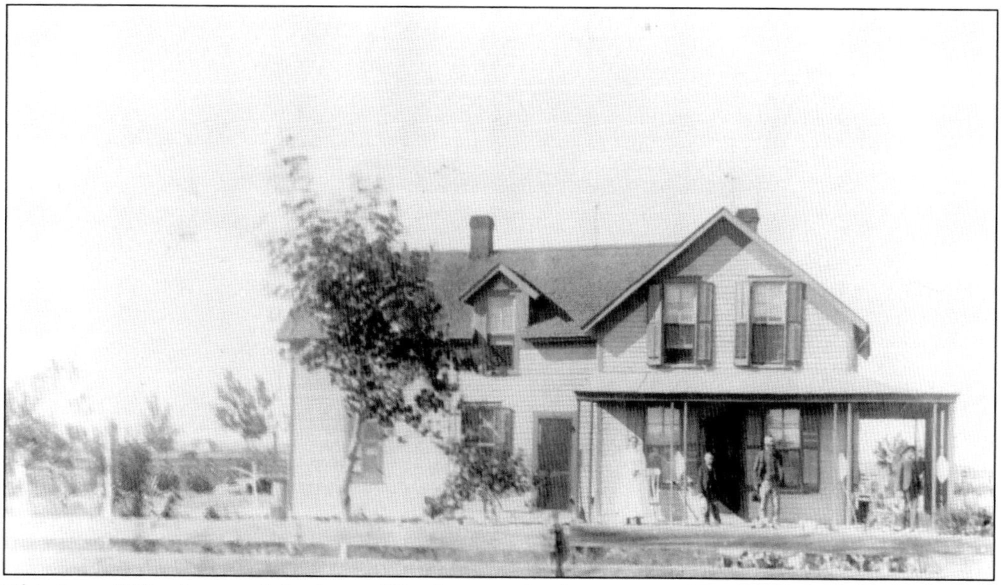

This is an 1881 picture of the James Weir home, which was moved from Julesburg to Sterling in two sections. It was located on Chestnut Street, just east of Section House, facing south and close to the railroad. (Courtesy Overland Trail Museum.)

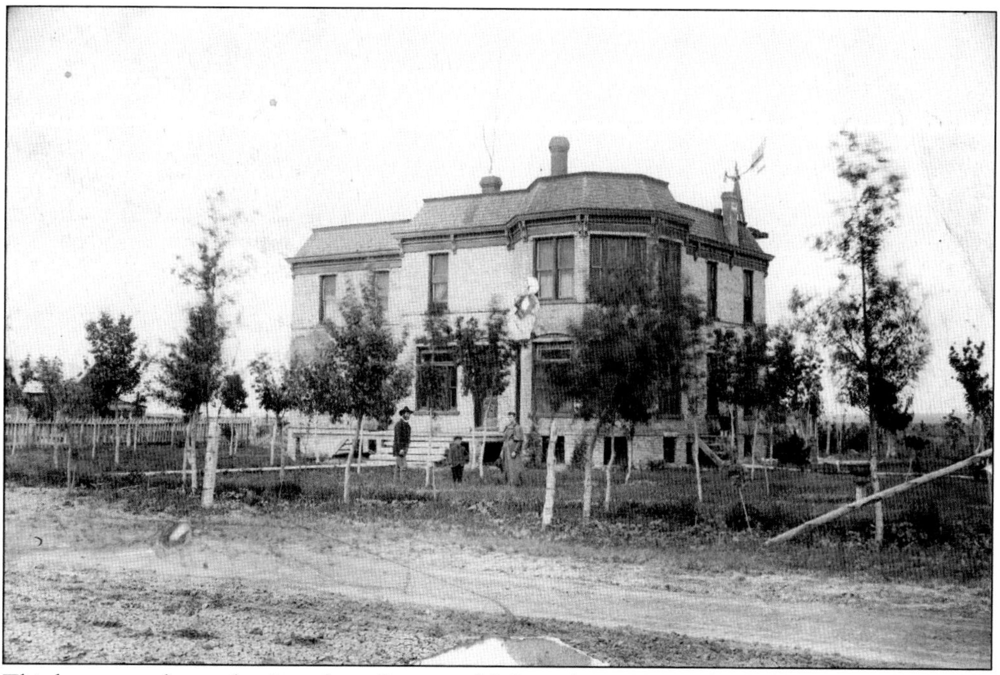

This house was located at Broadway Street and Sidney Avenue near the early county fairgrounds. The house was built by a Mr. Schenk. It became the home of S. R. Propst. Pictured are S. R. Propst, Myron Propst, and Della Propst. The fairgrounds have since moved west of this location. The site of this house later became a shopping center adjacent to Sterling's junior college. (Courtesy Overland Trail Museum.)

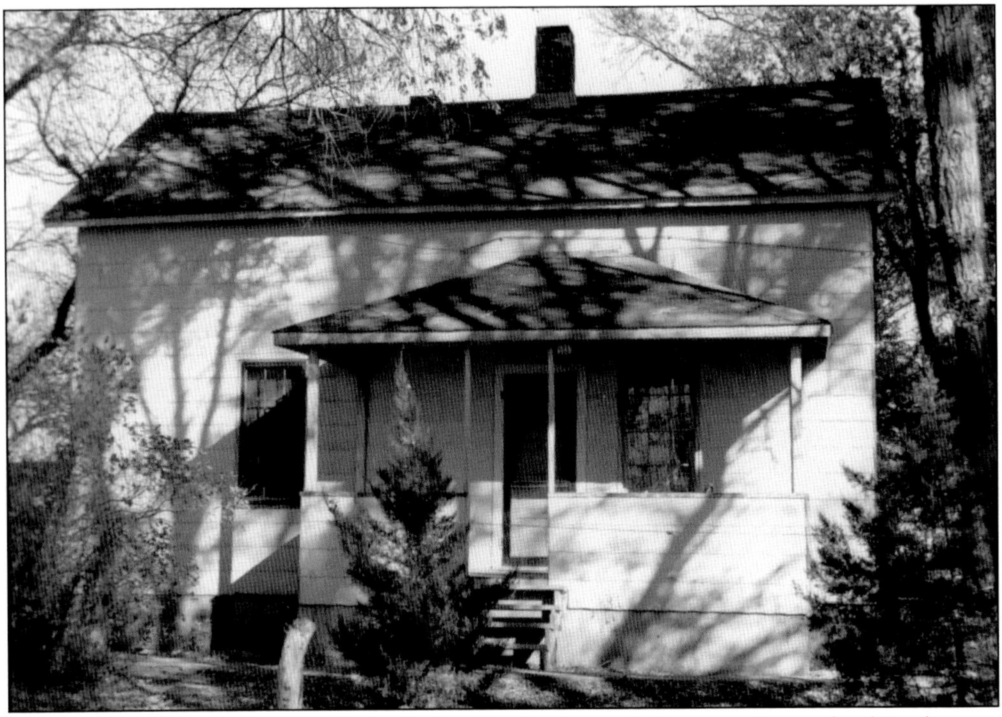

This is a picture of the home of Mrs. L. R. Cheairs, located about a mile north of Sterling on Sidney Avenue. This house was originally located between South Sixth and Seventh Avenues and was a Burlington Northern section house. (Courtesy Overland Trail Museum.)

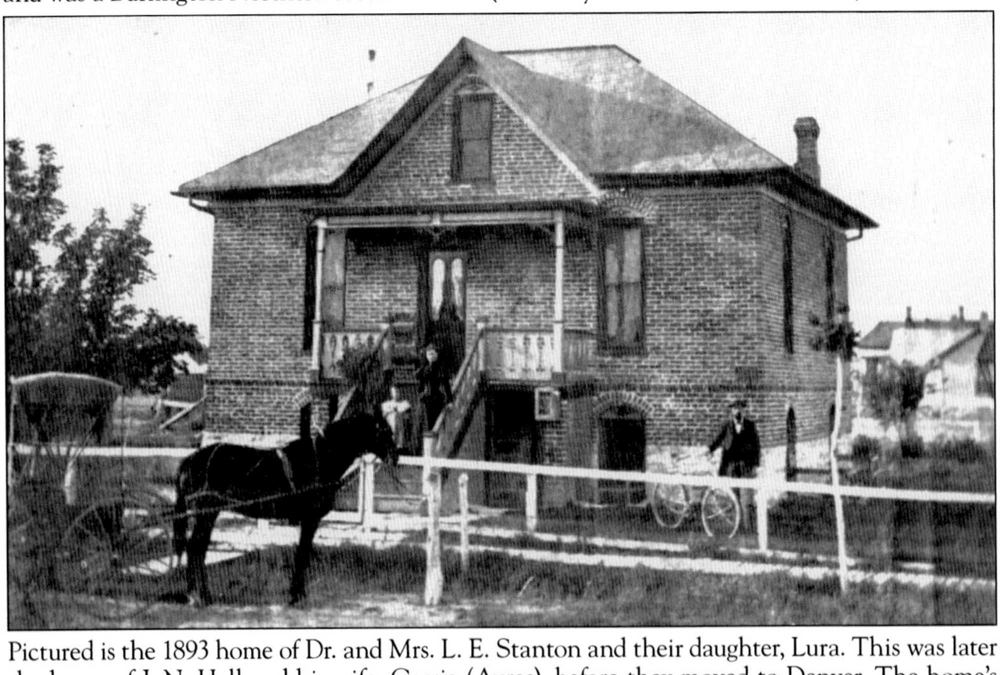

Pictured is the 1893 home of Dr. and Mrs. L. E. Stanton and their daughter, Lura. This was later the home of J. N. Hall and his wife, Carrie (Ayres), before they moved to Denver. The home's location, Second and Ash Streets, later became the site of Sterling's Veterans of Foreign Wars (VFW) Hall. (Courtesy Overland Trail Museum.)

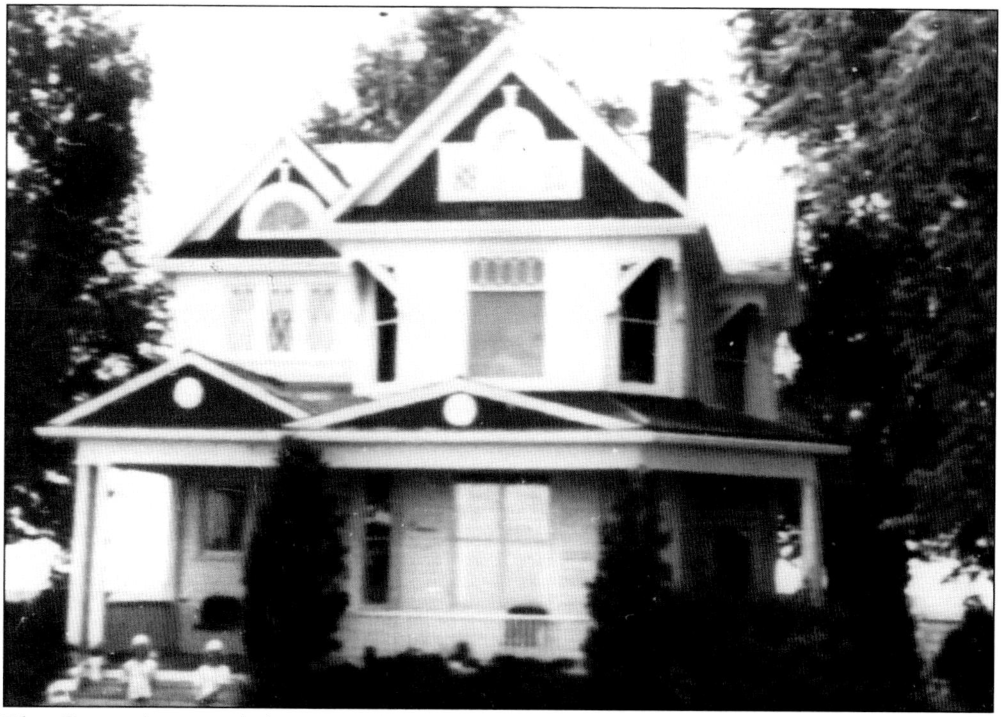

This Queen Anne–style house was built around 1906 in the 300 block of Poplar Street. It was moved to what was then west of Sterling on Highway 14 to be the home of the Conrad Luft Sr. family in the 1920s. Luft family members have resided in this home continually since then. Although there is some research claiming the home was once used as a mortuary, family members say this is not the case. (Courtesy Overland Trail Museum.)

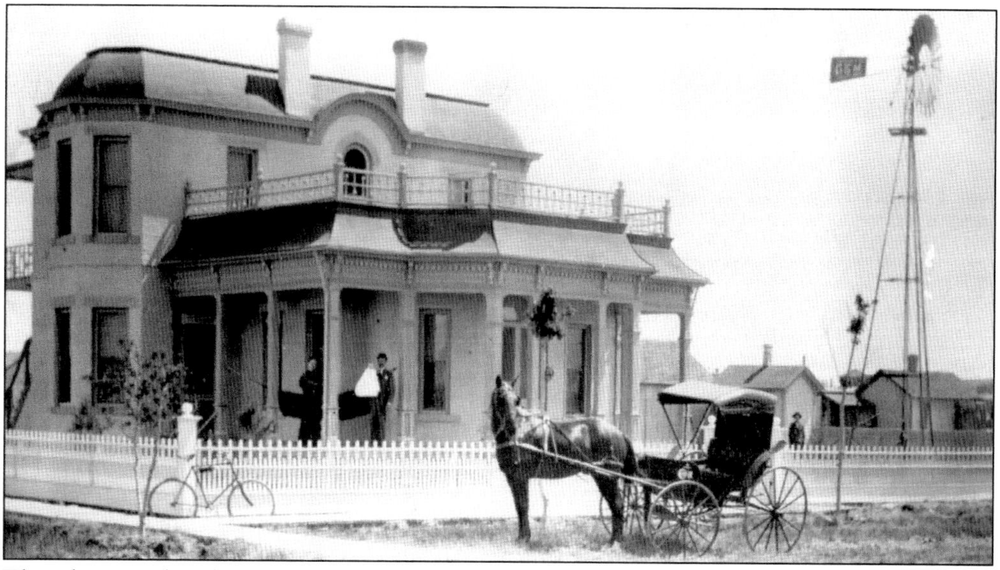

This photograph, taken in 1895, is of the George Henderson house. The house had five marble fireplaces. Henderson moved in around 1885. The house was torn down to build the new Security State Bank. It has since been called several other names and is currently the Wells Fargo Bank branch in Sterling. (Courtesy Overland Trail Museum.)

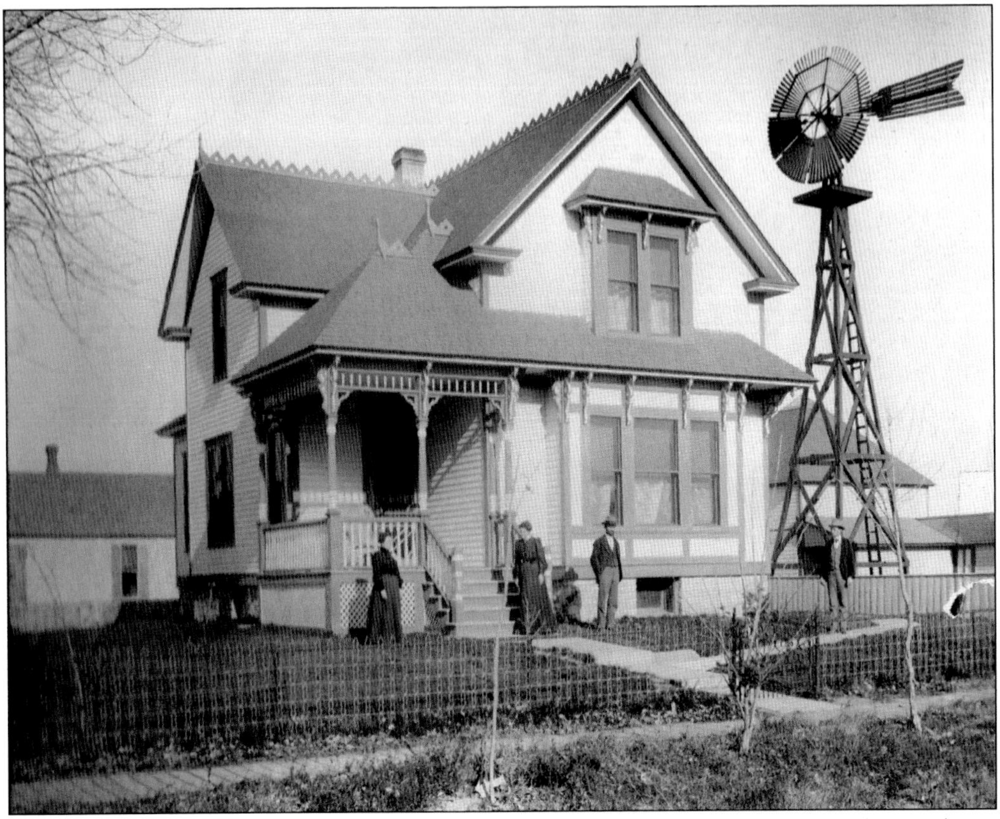

This photograph, taken in the late 1890s, is of the W. H. Conklin residence at the northeast corner of Third and Chestnut Streets. The corner is now the location of the Sonnenberg Agency. (Courtesy Overland Trail Museum.)

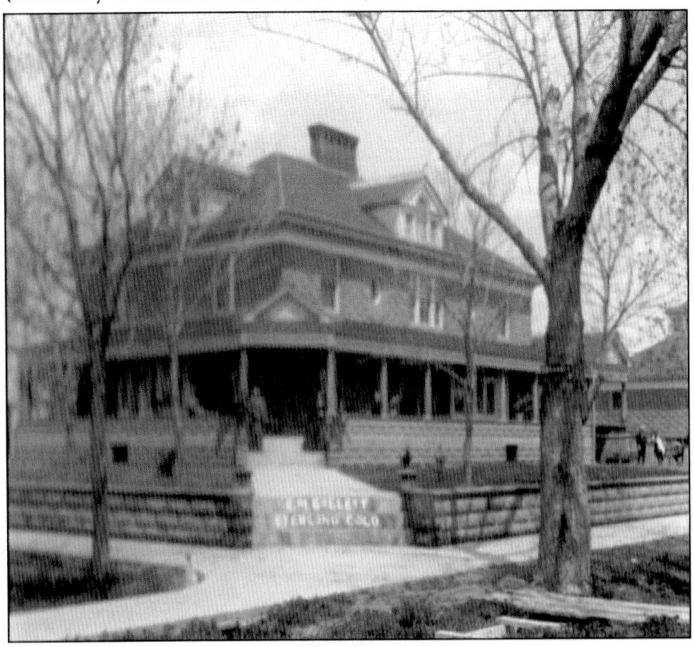

The exact date of this photograph is not known, but the house was built by 1908. It was the home of E. M. Gillett, a banker and businessman in Sterling. It was located at the corner of Third and Chestnut Streets, where a self-service Sinclair station is now located. The house was eventually torn down for a garage business. The barn was used as a workshop. Later the garage and barn were torn down to make way for the service station at the base of an overpass. (Courtesy Overland Trail Museum.)

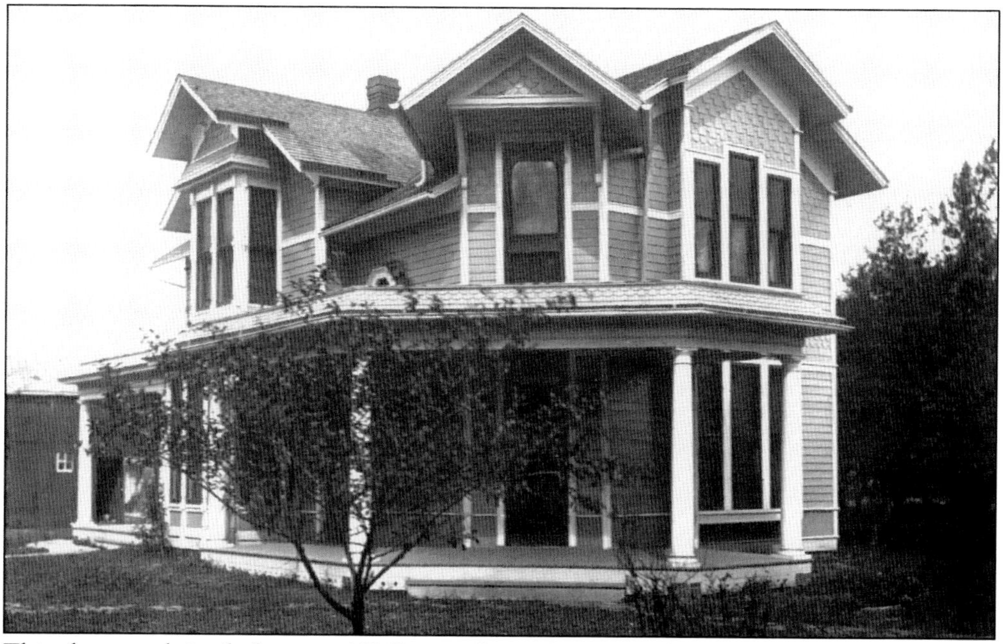

This photograph is of a home at 128 Denver Street. In 1917 and 1918, it was the home of Louis and Ouida Davenport. Louis was a stockman and rancher. Ouida was the daughter of Mrs. Horace B. Davis (from a former marriage). Both Louis and Ouida were well known in the community. (Courtesy Overland Trail Museum.)

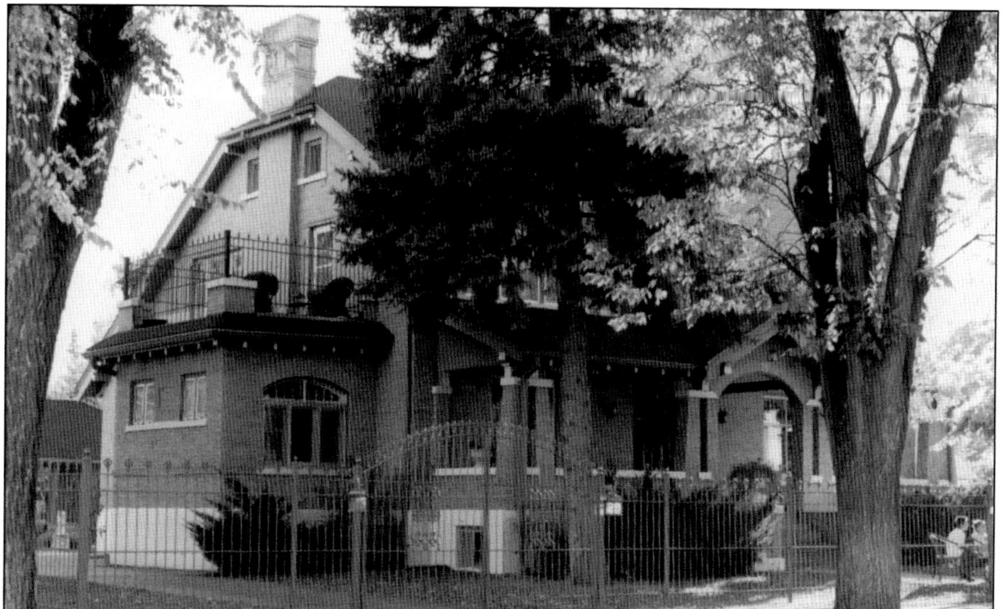

This picture, taken by Vickie Schure in 2002, is of a home built in 1914 by C. F. "Fred" Lutin at 129 Denver Street. Fred, a young man at the time, came to Colorado with his brother John in 1872. They ran a successful freighting and ranching operation. John built his home at 102 Denver Street. At the time of this photograph, Fred's home belonged to Stan and Bonnie Kloberdanz. (Courtesy Overland Trail Museum.)

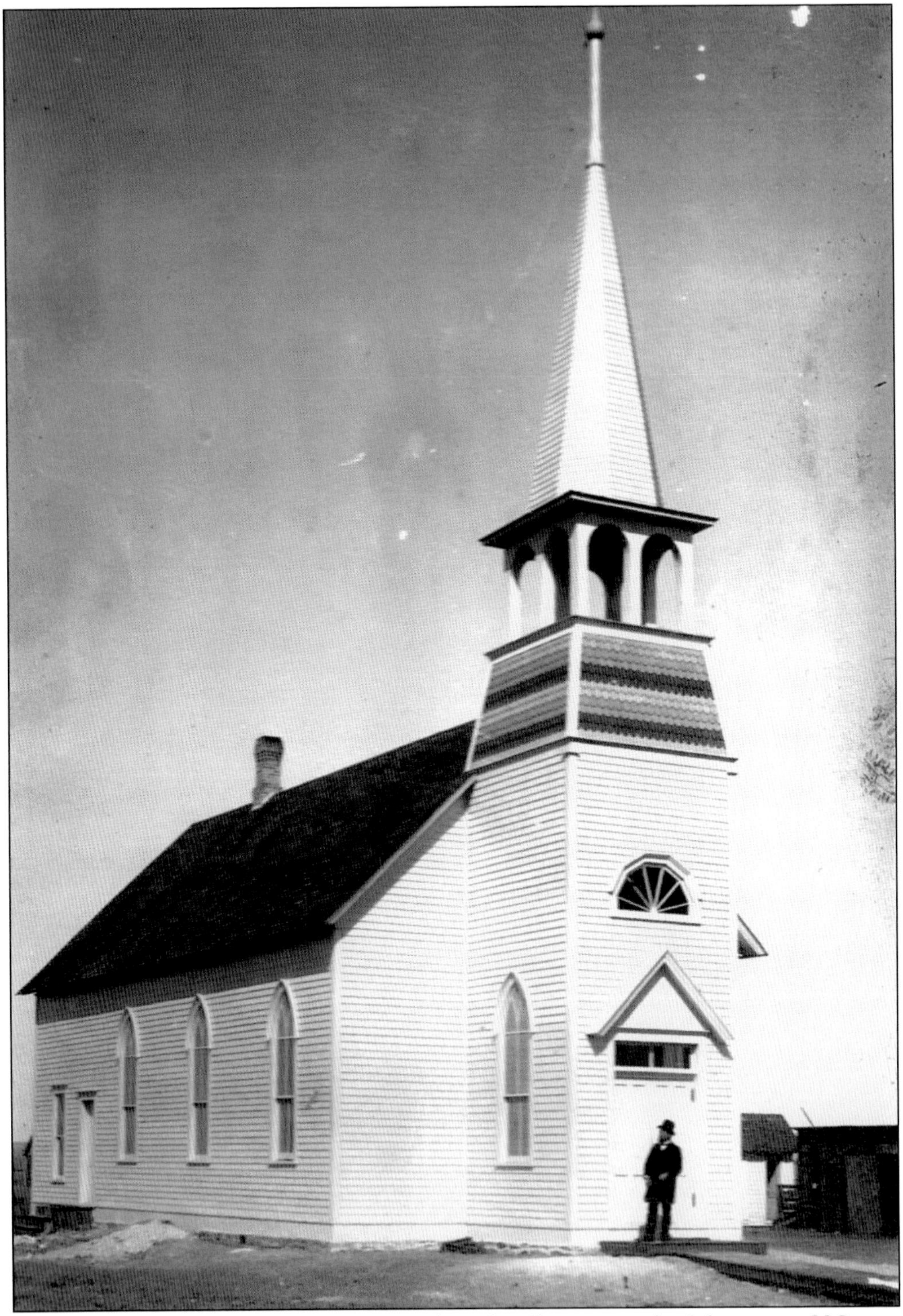

Built in 1889, this Baptist church was erected on the alley just north of the present U.S. post office on Third and Poplar Streets. It was located approximately where the present-day Equitable Savings and Loan office can be found. (Courtesy Overland Trail Museum.)

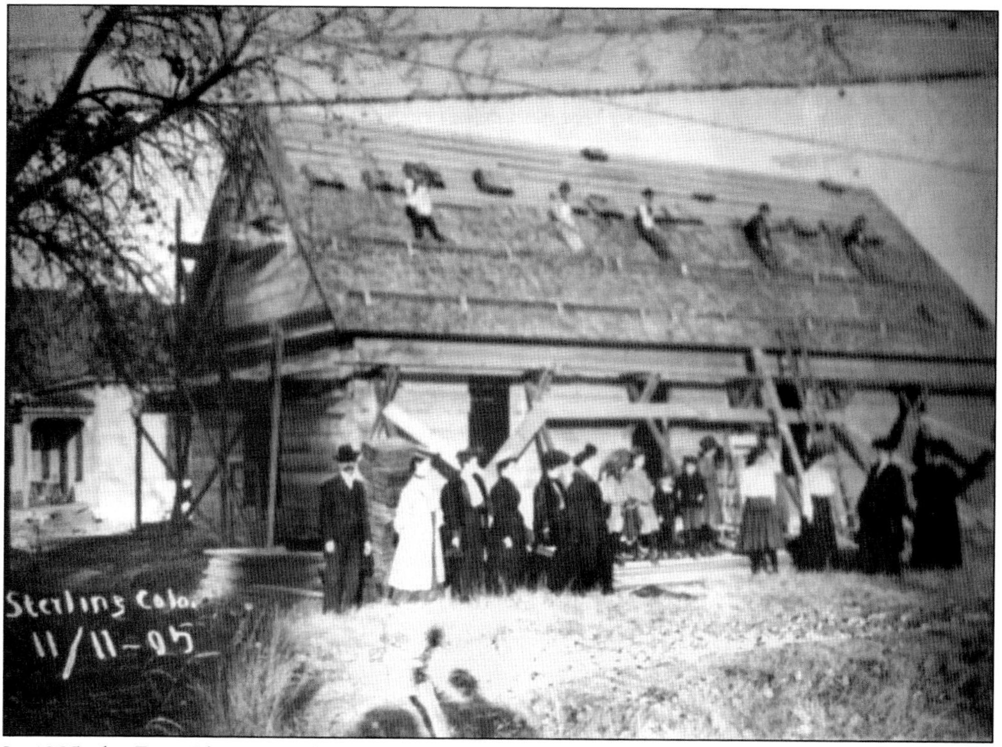

In 1905, the First Christian Church was located on the 100 block of North Fourth Street. This November 11, 1905, picture shows women of the church gathering while men are working on the roof. (Courtesy Overland Trail Museum.)

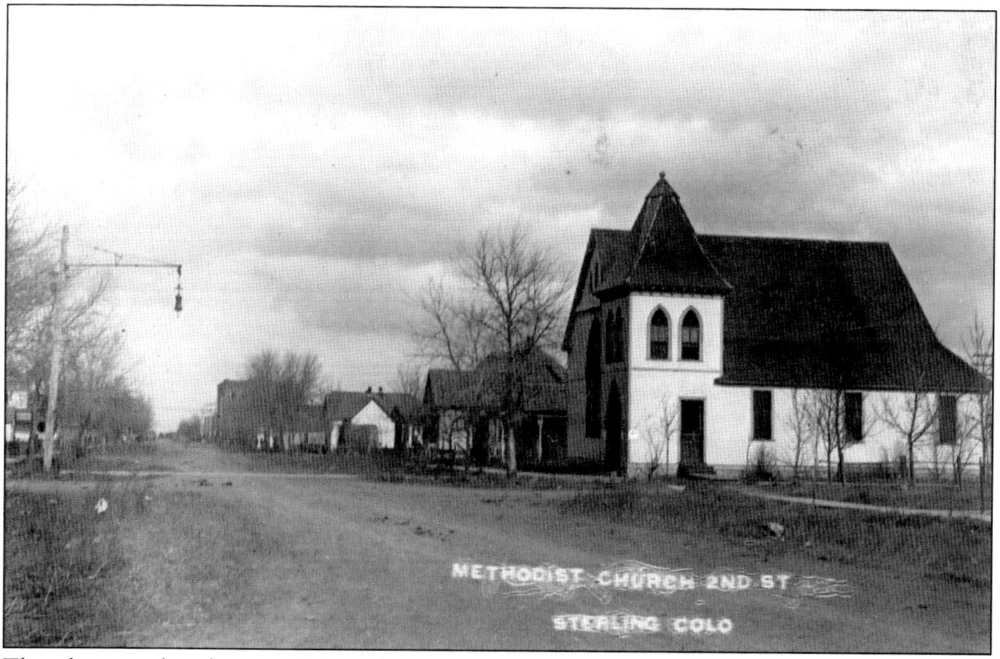

This photograph, taken in 1897, is of the Methodist church at South Second and Beech Streets. The building was sold to the Baptist church in 1913. (Courtesy Overland Trail Museum.)

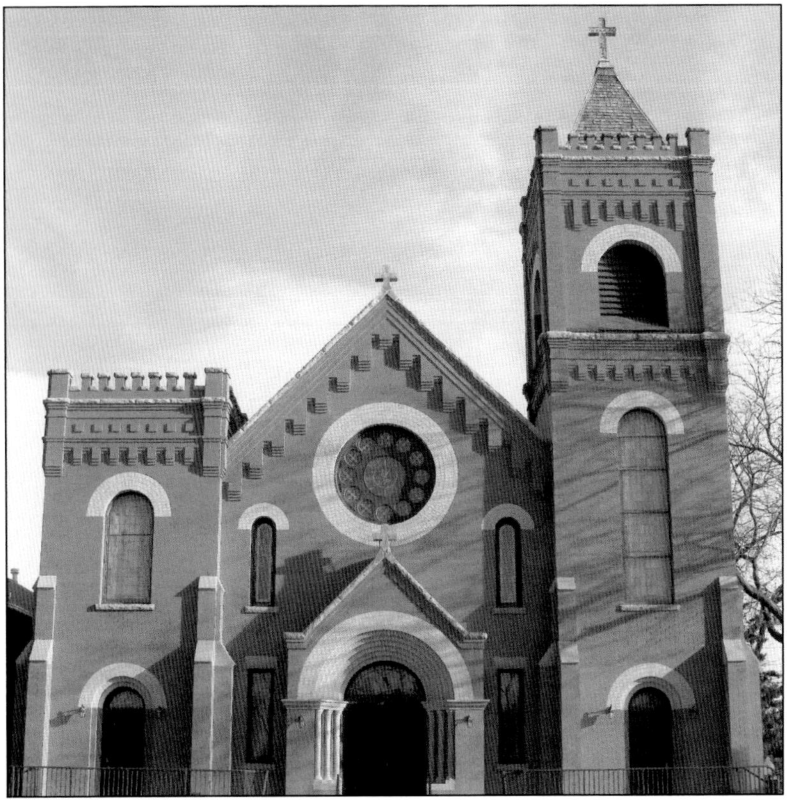

Pictured is St. Anthony of Padua Catholic Church, which was built in 1911. The parish was established in 1908. Now part of a tri-parish with churches in the nearby towns of Peetz and Iliff, St. Anthony celebrated the parish's centennial in 2008 with a special Mass at the Logan County Fairgrounds. (Courtesy *Sterling Journal-Advocate*.)

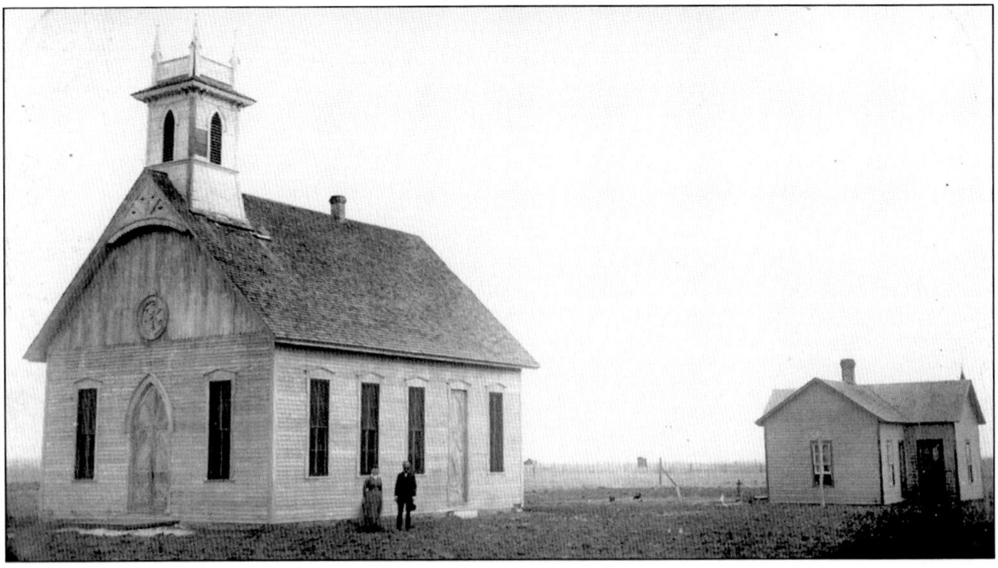

This 1880s photograph is of the first church structure built in Sterling. It was located at Beech and Second Streets, the site of the present-day Delgado's restaurant. The church served from 1883 to 1898. The first church, in what became Logan County, was built of sod and located in old Sterling about 4 miles north of present-day Sterling. This church was shared by the Methodists, whose members helped to construct it. The manse at the right was occupied by the Reverend and Mrs. S. R. Shull, who are pictured in the photograph. (Courtesy Overland Trail Museum.)

Five

Pioneers and Other Notable Folks

From Fields to Offices

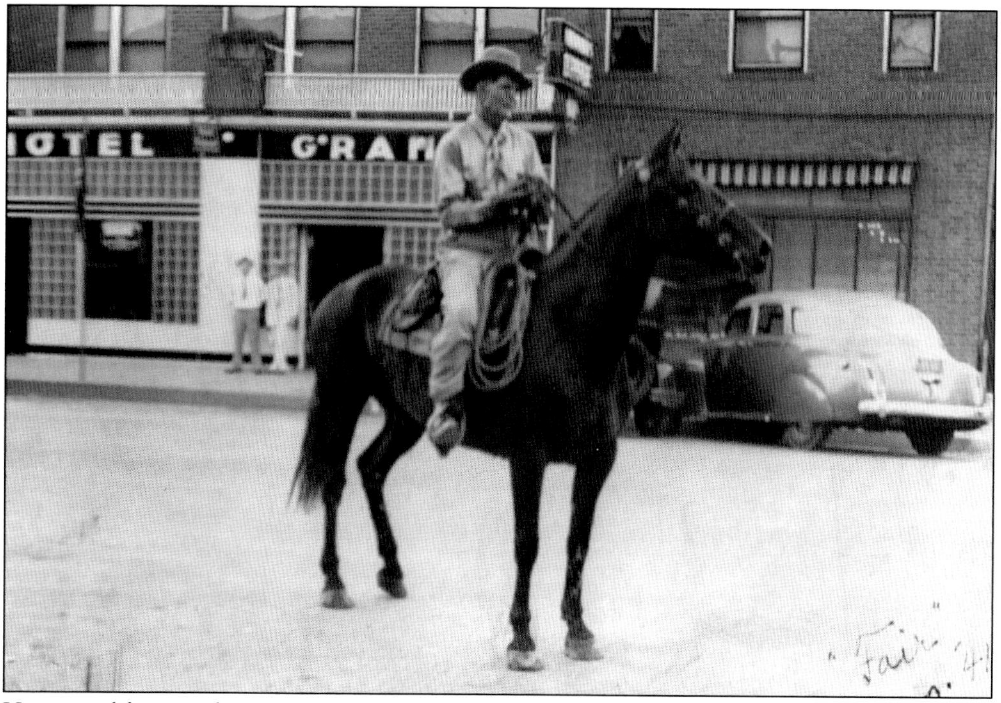

Horses and fair time have gone together since the beginning of Sterling and Logan County. This photograph, taken in August 1941, is of Arch Monroe on horseback in front of the Graham Hotel at fair time. (Courtesy Overland Trail Museum.)

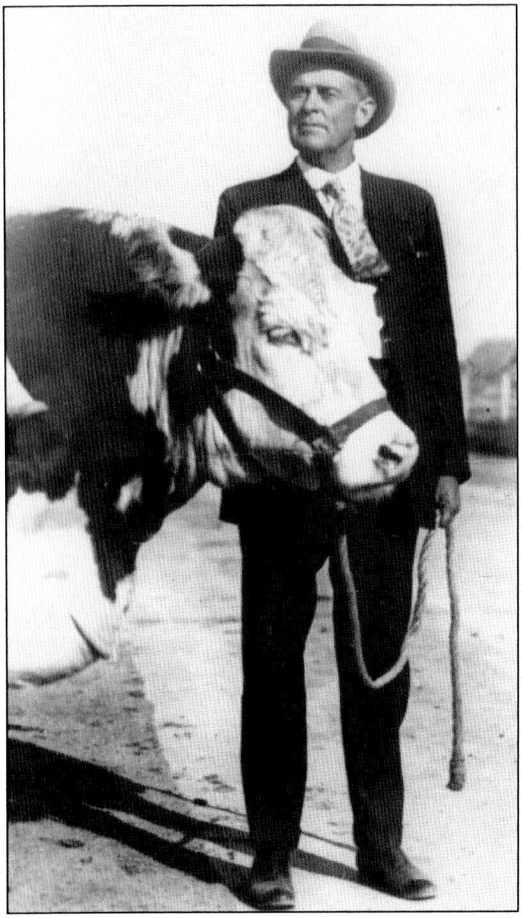

W. C. Harris is pictured at left with a prize steer. Harris is one of 10 businessmen who helped oversee the North Sterling Reservoir project become reality. The organization, known as Ten Men Company, conducted a survey in 1905 from the South Platte River near Union to Pawnee Creek. In addition to his work in the Sterling business community, W. C. Harris was also elected to office. He is pictured below in 1900 as a member of the Colorado General Assembly. (Both, courtesy Overland Trail Museum.)

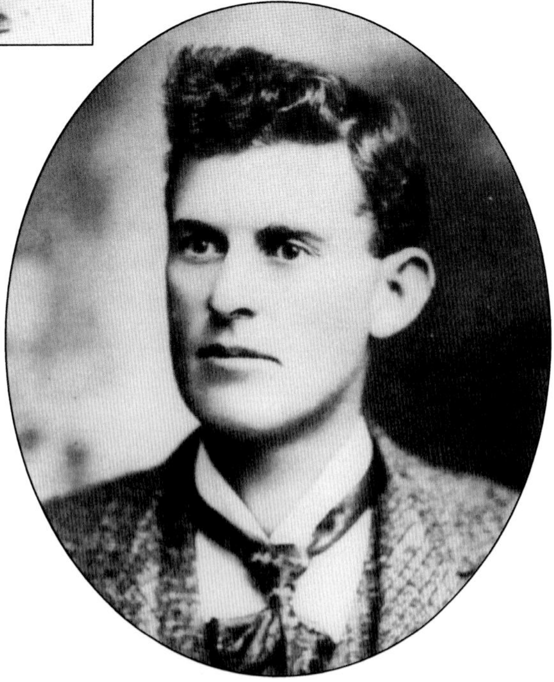

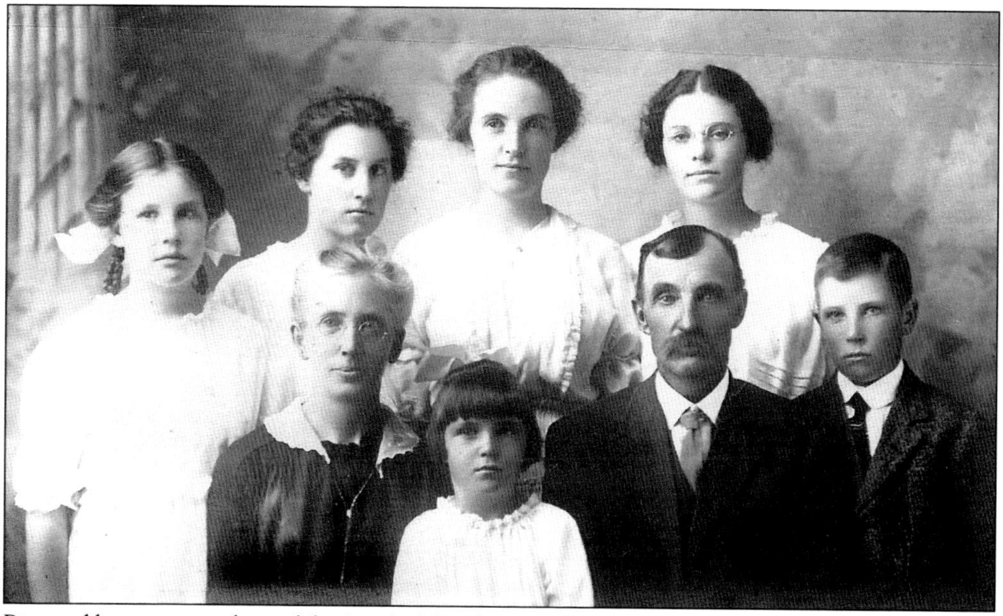

Pictured here are members of the Jim Ard family. From left to right are (first row) Mrs. Jim "Silver" Ard, Erma Ard, Jim Ard, and Norman Ard; (second row) Thelma Gilhem, Myrna Roberts, Hazel Fulfurt, and Freida Lippett Goff. (Courtesy Overland Trail Museum.)

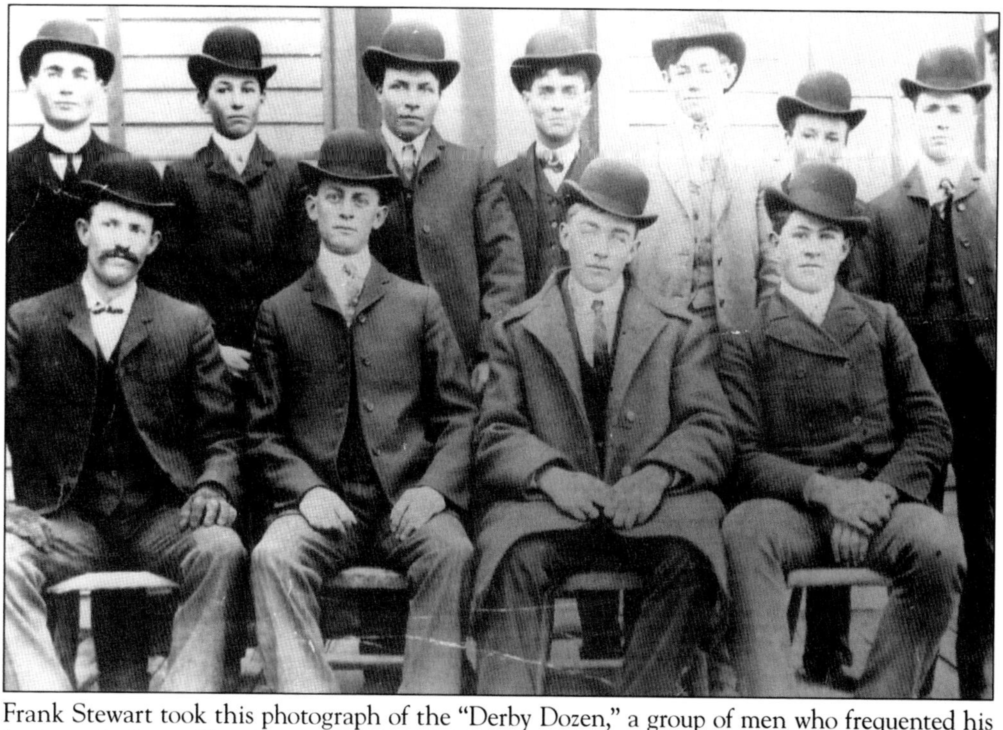

Frank Stewart took this photograph of the "Derby Dozen," a group of men who frequented his business, in front of his shop at approximately 322 Main Street in 1904. Pictured from left to right are (first row) H. D. Robuck, Guy Brownell, W. H. "Billy" Armour, and Len Sherwin; (second row) Sam Cheairs, Sammy Mathews, Sam Brownell, Frank Propst, Howard Simpson, Vernon Robuck, and Myron Propst. (Courtesy Overland Trail Museum.)

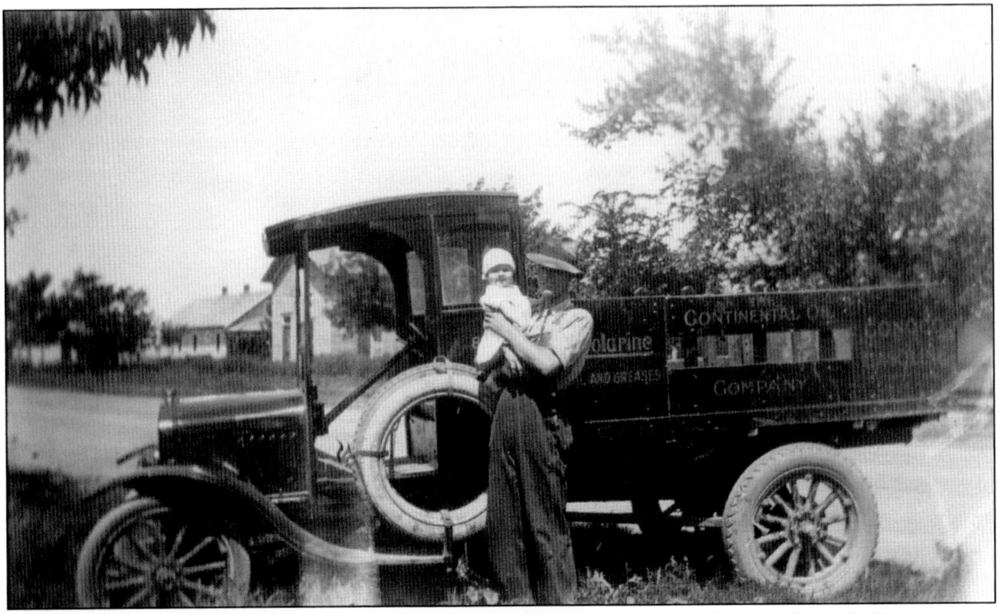

Pictured in 1923 are J. C. McCarthy and his son, Harold. They are standing at a Continental Oil Company Conoco service truck. (Courtesy Overland Trail Museum.)

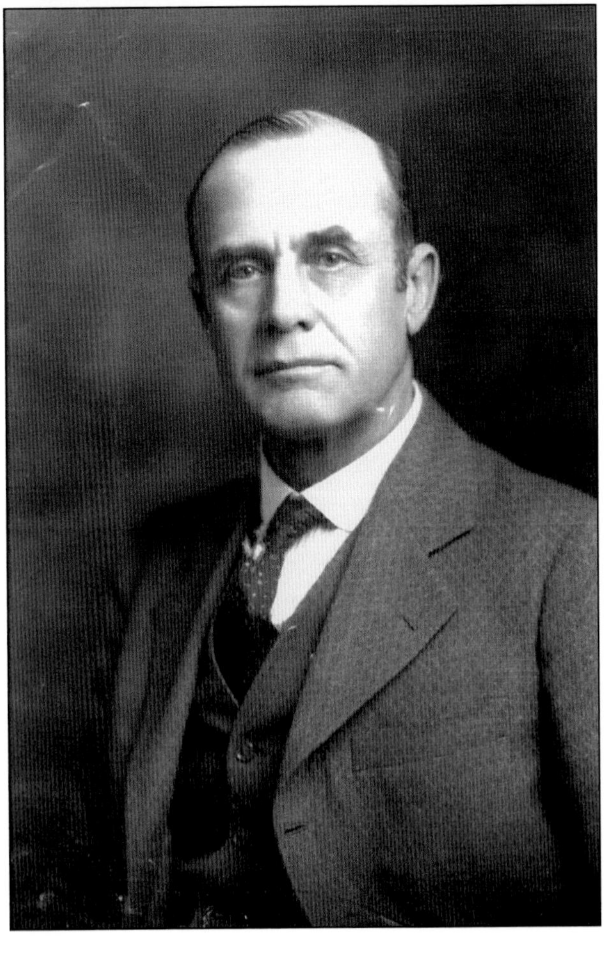

Frank Howard Blair came to Sterling from South Dakota in 1891. He was born in Elk Point of the Dakota Territory on August 12, 1870. He was principal of the high school for six years and married Virginia Powell, one of his pupils. Later he went into ranching with his father-in-law, William J. Powell. The Blairs had two children, William J. Blair and Harrison D. Blair. William retired from the military as a colonel, and Harrison served in the U.S. Army at Long Island, New York. (Courtesy Overland Trail Museum.)

While the date on this photograph is unknown, it shows William S. Hadfield and Charity Sanders in what is likely their wedding picture. The Hadfields were some of the first white people to live in Logan County. (Courtesy Overland Trail Museum.)

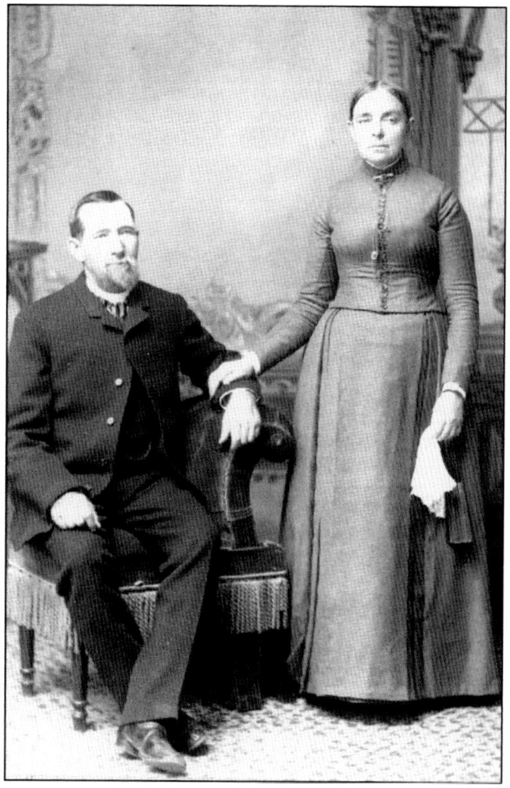

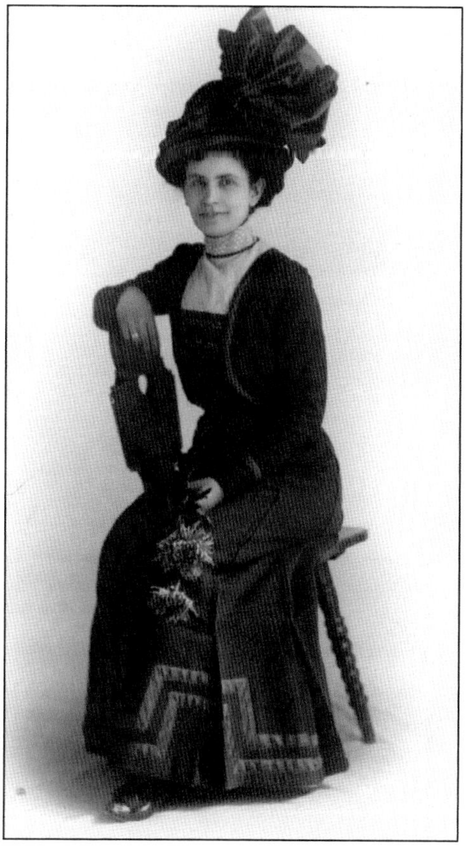

This is an 1880s photograph of Clara Bascom. She may have been the wife of L. H. Bascom, president of School District No. 34 in the 1880s, or possibly the wife of D. C. Bascom, the first agriculture specialist in Logan County. (Courtesy Overland Trail Museum.)

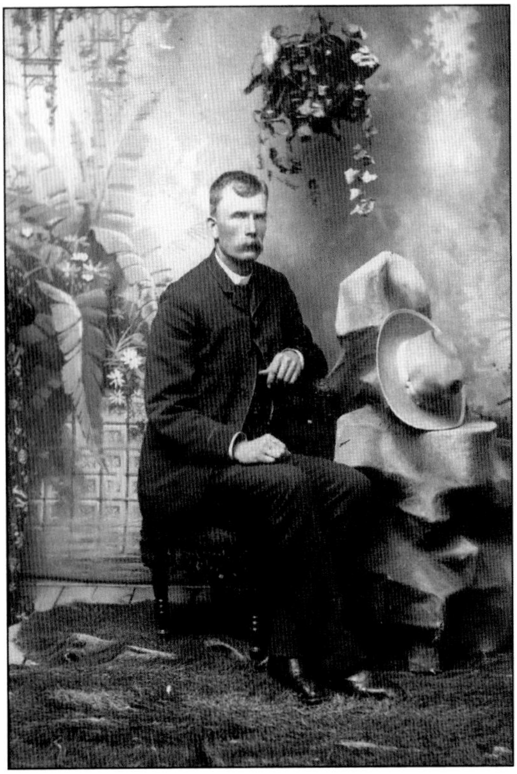

This is a picture of Robert D. Sanders, father of Myrtle Sale. He is one of the A. H. Sanders early settlers. (Photograph by John S. Legerton, courtesy Overland Trail Museum.)

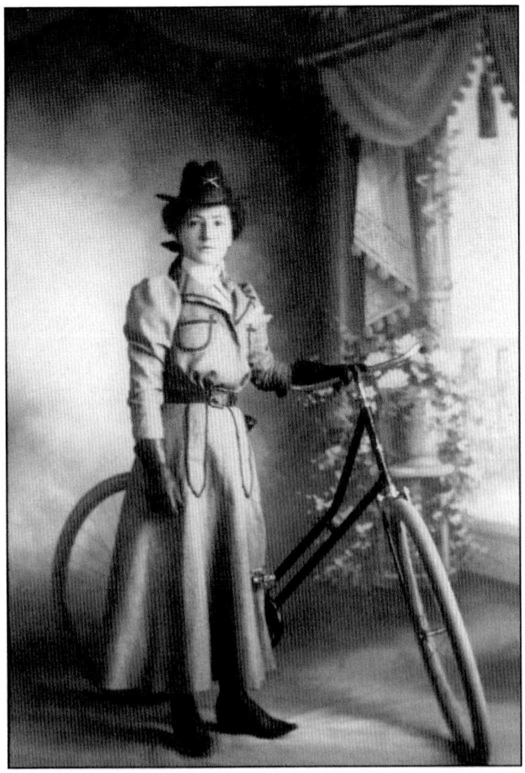

Patty McEndaffer is dressed for a bicycle ride during the late 19th century or possibly the early part of the 20th century. Motorized automobiles, motorcycles, and bicycles arrived in Sterling before paved streets. (Courtesy Overland Trail Museum.)

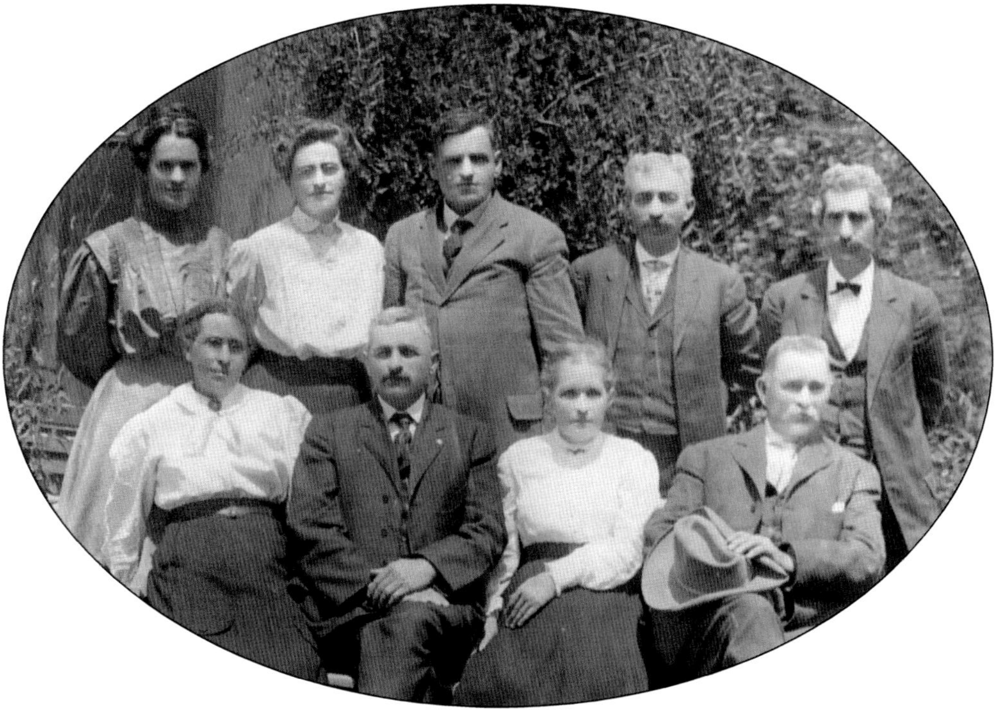

This 1910 photograph of the Propst family shows those who made their way from Alabama to Colorado. From left to right are (first row) Mary J. Propst Weis, John H. Propst, Bell Propst Clanton, and S. R. Propst; (second row) Lena Propst Woolman Emery, Edna Propst Weir Westlake, Thomas Koger Propst, William Cathey Propst, and Wiley Ferd Propst. The migration started with S. R. Propst in about 1873. Belle Propst Clanton moved here in 1874; William Cathey Propst in 1875; Mary J. Propst Weir, Wiley F. Propst, Thomas K. Propst, Edna Propst Weir Westlake, and Lena Propst Woolman Emery in 1876; Allen H. Propst in 1876; and John H. Propst in 1877. (Courtesy Overland Trail Museum.)

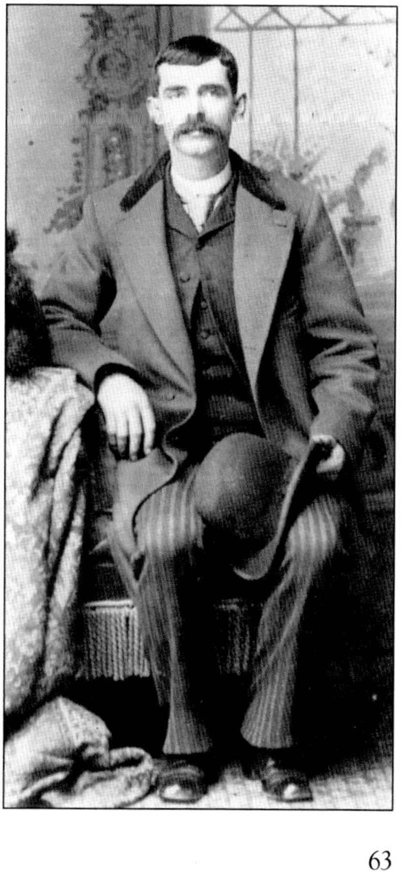

This 1892 picture is of Allen H. Propst, the sixth son of M. V. and J. S. Propst. He was born in Alabama on January 15, 1861, and came to Buffalo (later called Merino), Colorado, on April 1, 1876. He died in Sterling on August 20, 1894. He was known as a joyous, happy cowboy. (Courtesy Overland Trail Museum.)

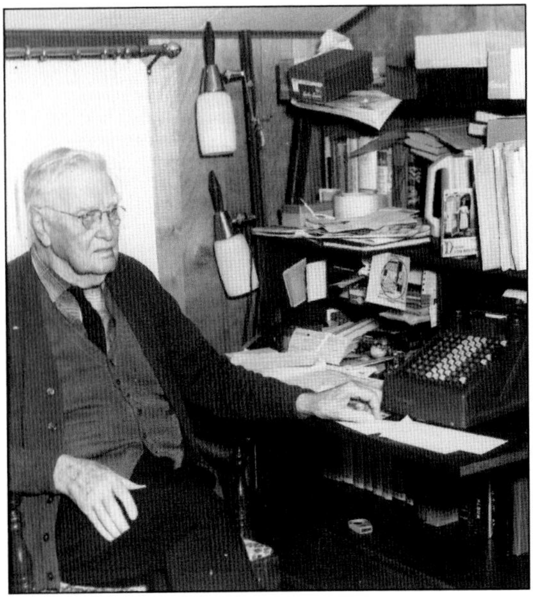

Dr. D. D. Monroe was born October 12, 1873, and died February 6, 1975, at the age of 101. He came to Sidney, Nebraska, by train and travelled to Sterling by Propst stagecoach in 1880. He graduated from Sterling High School, is credited as the first student from Sterling to go to college, and graduated from Rush Medical School in Chicago in 1901. He practiced medicine in France during World War I. While there, he attended the University of Paris. He was with the Veterans Administration at Edwardsville, Illinois, until 1927. He was the superintendent of the Madison County Tuberculosis Sanitarium. He had five sons by his first wife and a daughter by his second wife. Medicine was his first love, travel his joy, and his children his greatest concern. (Courtesy Overland Trail Museum.)

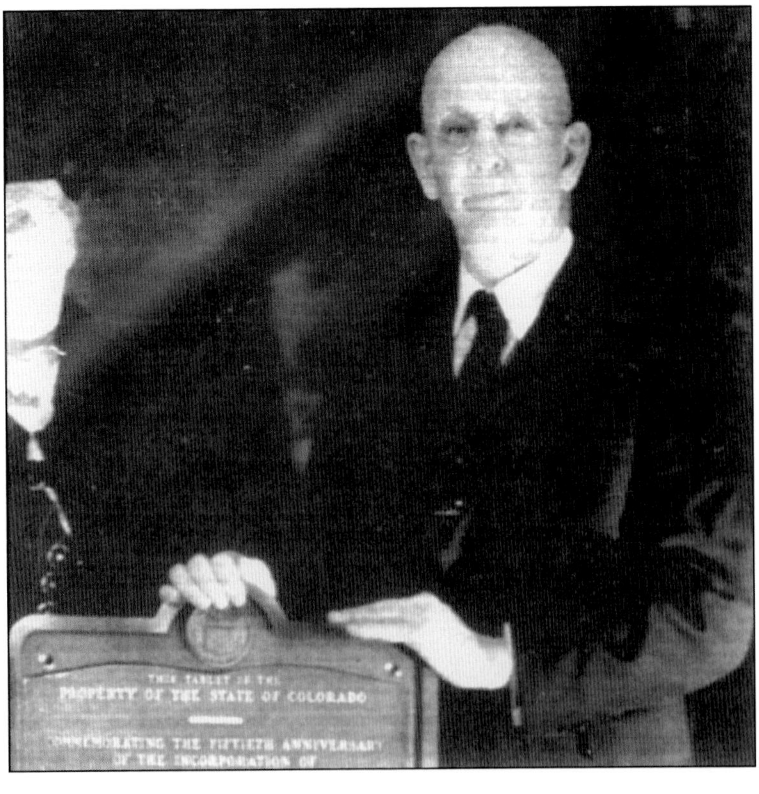

Harvard graduate Dr. J. N. Hall was one of Sterling's earliest and finest physicians. He married Carrie Ayres, and they later moved to Denver, where he had a thriving medical practice. He established the Mrs. J. N. Hall Foundation, which erected historical markers throughout the state. Several are in Logan County, including one in front of the Overland Trail Museum. (Courtesy Overland Trail Museum.)

Pictured is the first school superintendent for the area, H. M. Day, who then was overseeing all Logan County schools. The county's schools have since separated into four districts, with students also attending schools in nearby Sedgwick and Phillips Counties. (Courtesy Overland Trail Museum.)

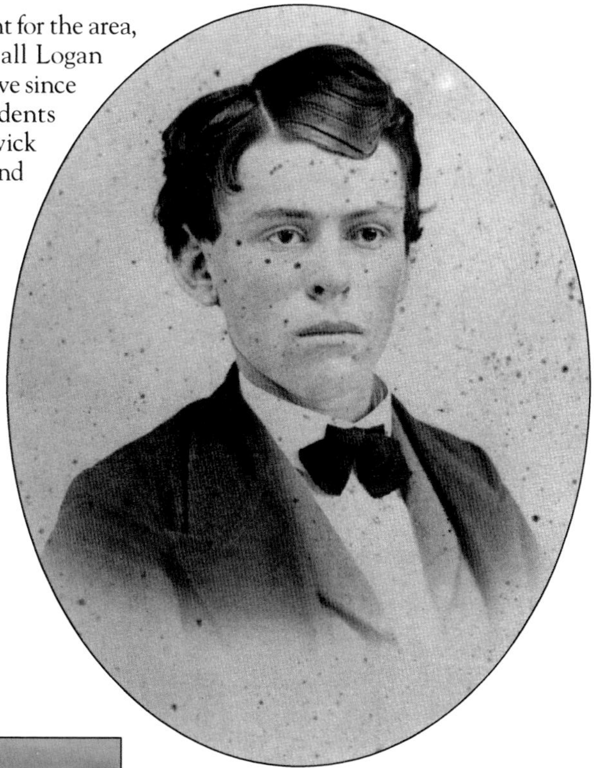

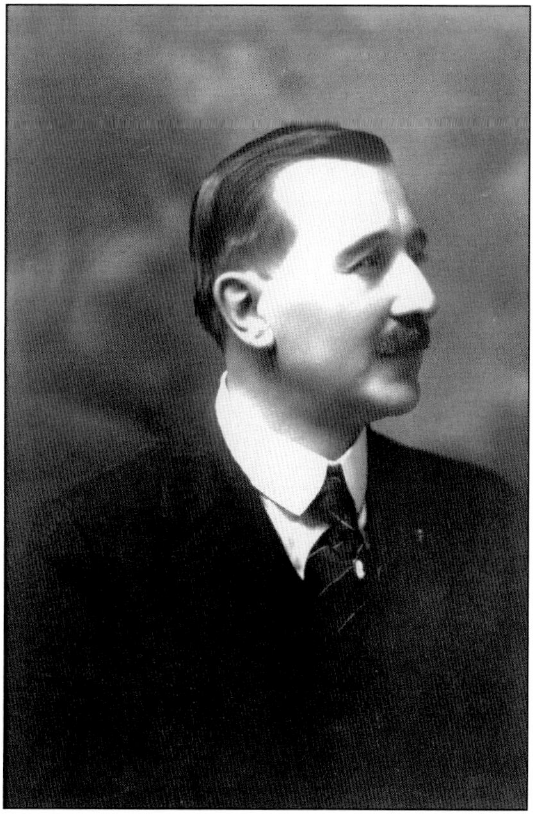

Pictured is Charles Bauman, a druggist in Sterling's early years. He lived in the Sterling community for many years, and he was also an amateur photographer. Sterling has drawn many medical professionals during its history. It has had several hospitals, which later combined into today's Sterling Regional MedCenter, and several doctors who frequently operated clinics from their homes. (Courtesy Overland Trail Museum.)

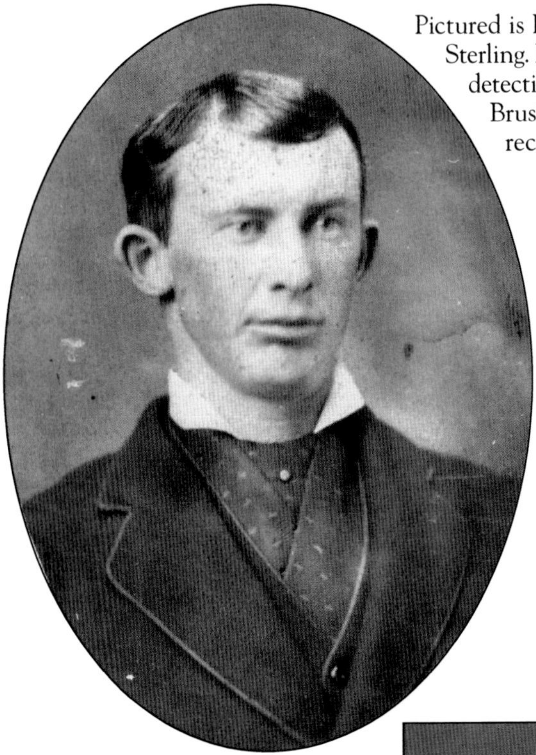

Pictured is Dixon Buchanan, the first elected sheriff in Sterling. He was known as a nemesis of cattle rustlers, a detective with bulldog courage, manager of the Jared Brush cattle ranch, and later, a U.S. land office receiver. (Courtesy Overland Trail Museum.)

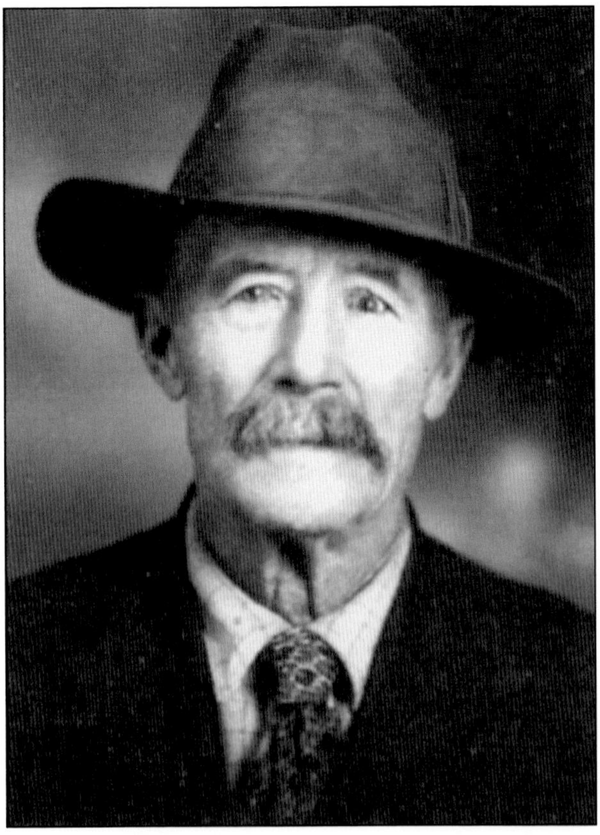

Manassas "Nass" Litch, last of the buffalo hunters, came to Julesburg on the train from Ohio. He walked to Buffalo, which was later named Merino. His brother had come earlier to hunt buffalo. The buffalo were mostly gone in a year or two, so he raised sheep, farmed, and ran various other business enterprises. He was the first marshal in Sterling and was wearing a peace officer badge when he died in 1945 at the age of 92. (Courtesy Overland Trail Museum.)

Alexander Majors was a member of freighting firm Russell, Majors, and Waddell, which did business in and around Sterling. (Courtesy Overland Trail Museum.)

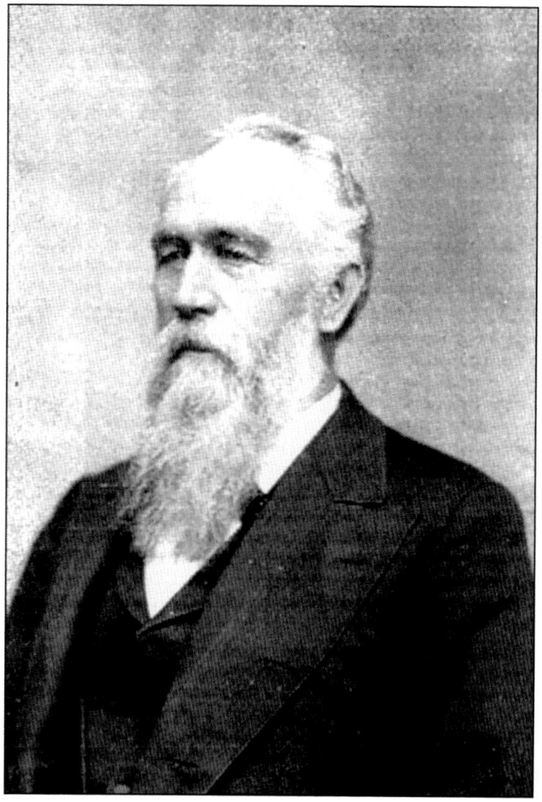

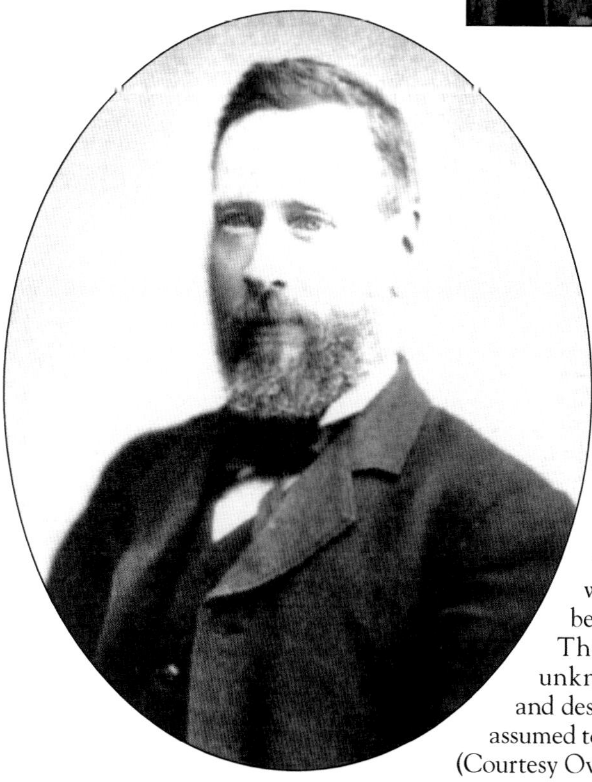

This is a photograph of A. F. Spoor, who was the first train master in Sterling for the Union Pacific railroad. Naming the town of Sterling for him was a consideration at one time. He was the father of Ethel (Spoor) Johnson, benefactor of the Overland Trail Museum. The exact date of this photograph is unknown. However, by the composition and design of the photograph, it can be safely assumed to be early 19th century, possibly earlier. (Courtesy Overland Trail Museum.)

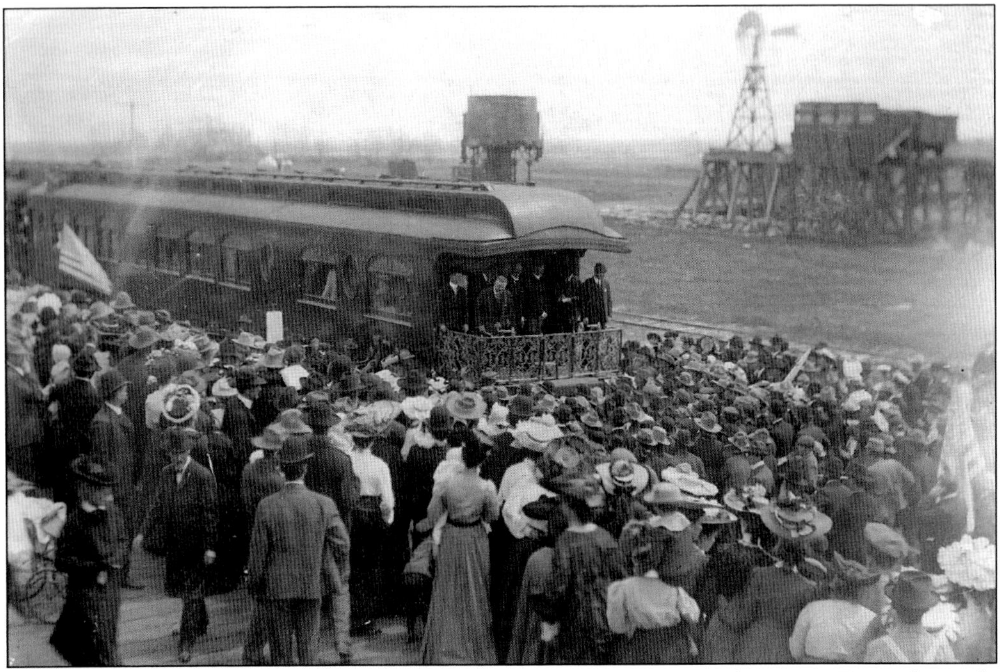

Sterling has had its share of celebrities visit the community over the years. From the early days, politics have played an important part in the local who's who photographic record. Pres. Theodore Roosevelt was one politician who made a whistle-stop in Sterling in May 1905 (above). In a May 9, 1905, picture (below), Roosevelt sits down for a meal with members of his hunting party during a stop on the way east after a hunting trip in Glenwood Springs. (Both, courtesy Overland Trail Museum.)

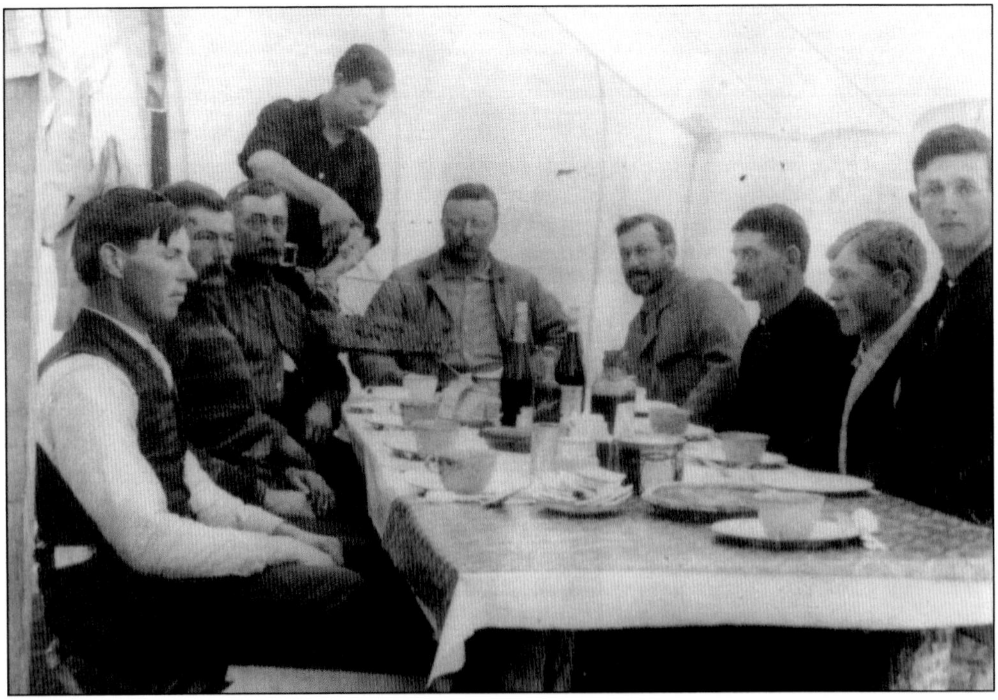

In October 1948, Gov. Thomas Dewey (in the dark suit with his back to the camera) arrived in Sterling for a whistle-stop campaign visit in his race for the presidency. Just a small portion of his train car is visible in this photograph by Russell Collman. (Courtesy McCoy/Collman Collection, Overland Trail Museum.)

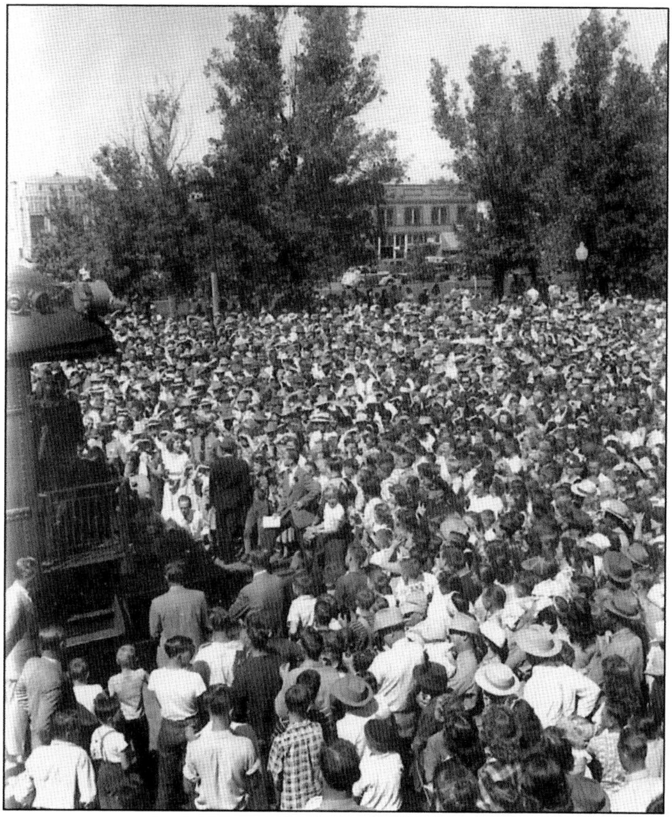

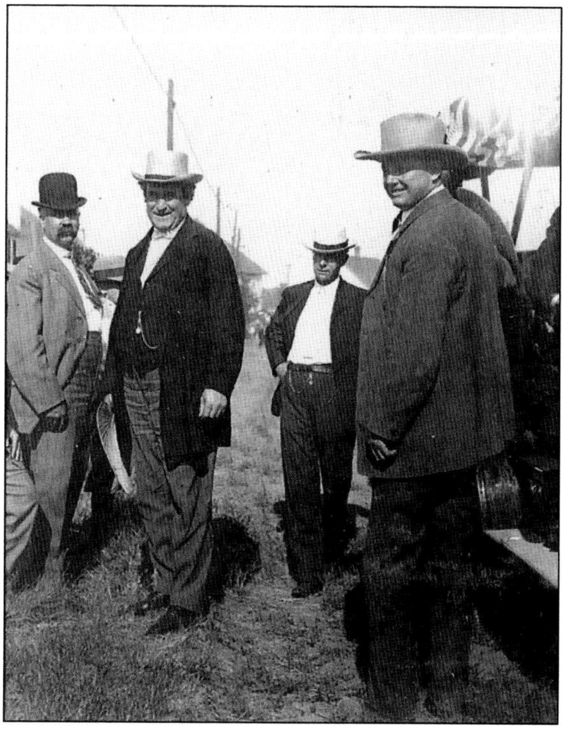

On the list of celebrities to visit Sterling in the early years is then secretary of state William Jennings Bryan, pictured second from left. Once a congressman from Nebraska and a three-time Democratic presidential candidate, he visited Sterling on July 16, 1910. (Courtesy Overland Trail Museum.)

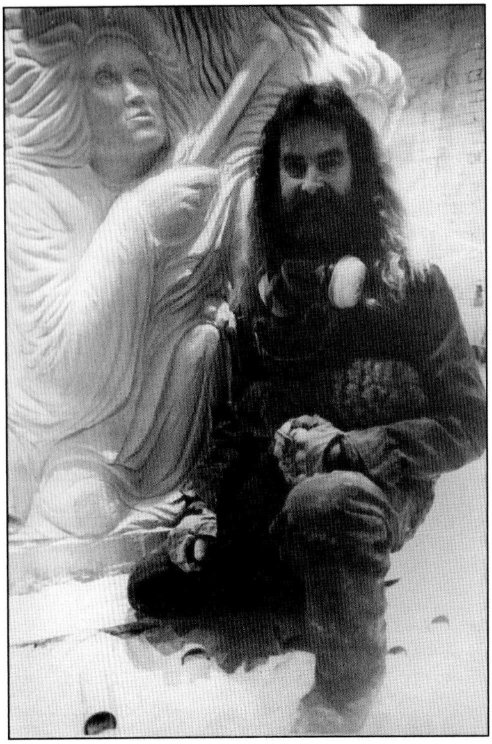

Area sculptor Bradford Rhea is pictured separately next to two of his later sculptures, *Seraphim* (left) and *Dream Redeemer*, both of which can be found in Sterling. Rhea achieved a certain celebrity when he carved the branches of an old elm tree in Columbine Park to look like the necks and heads of giraffes. That sculpture, *Skygrazers*, has since been bronzed, like many of Rhea's other carved-tree artworks, to protect it. Rhea lives in Merino but creates art that makes its way around the world, including a cane Rhea carved for Pope John Paul II upon the pontiff's visit to Denver in 1993. (Both, courtesy Overland Trail Museum.)

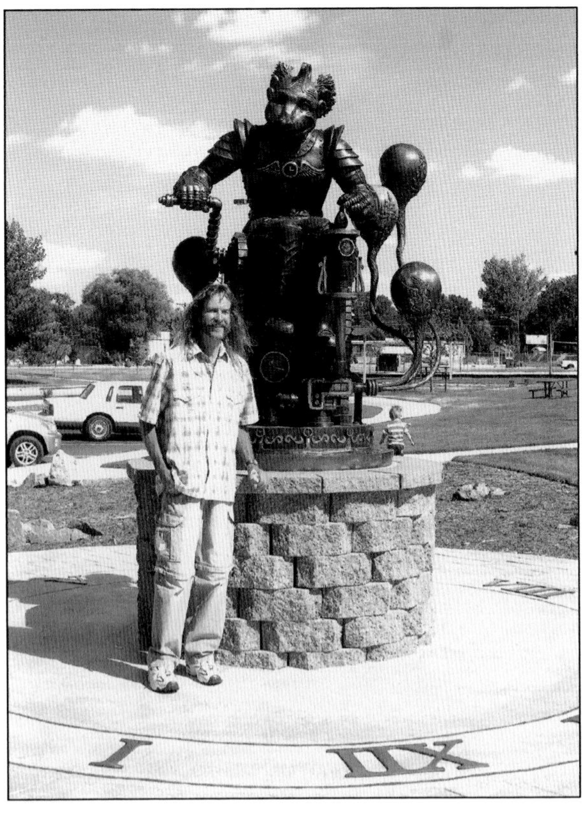

Six

Daily Life and Special Events
Something to Celebrate

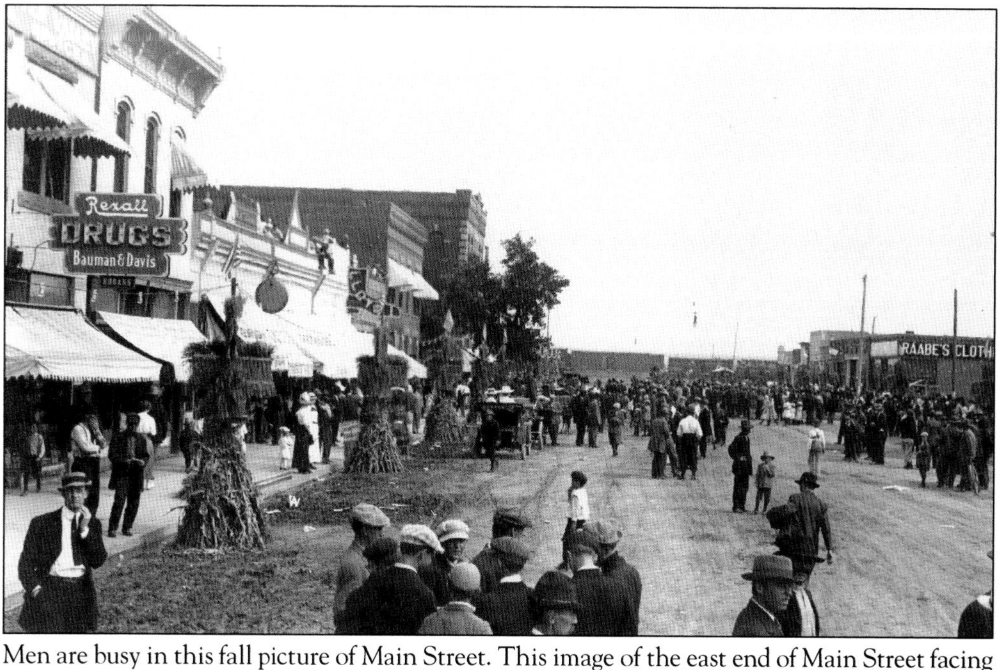

Men are busy in this fall picture of Main Street. This image of the east end of Main Street facing the railroad yard shows Bauman and Rexall Drug on the left and Raabe Clothing on the right. (Courtesy Overland Trail Museum.)

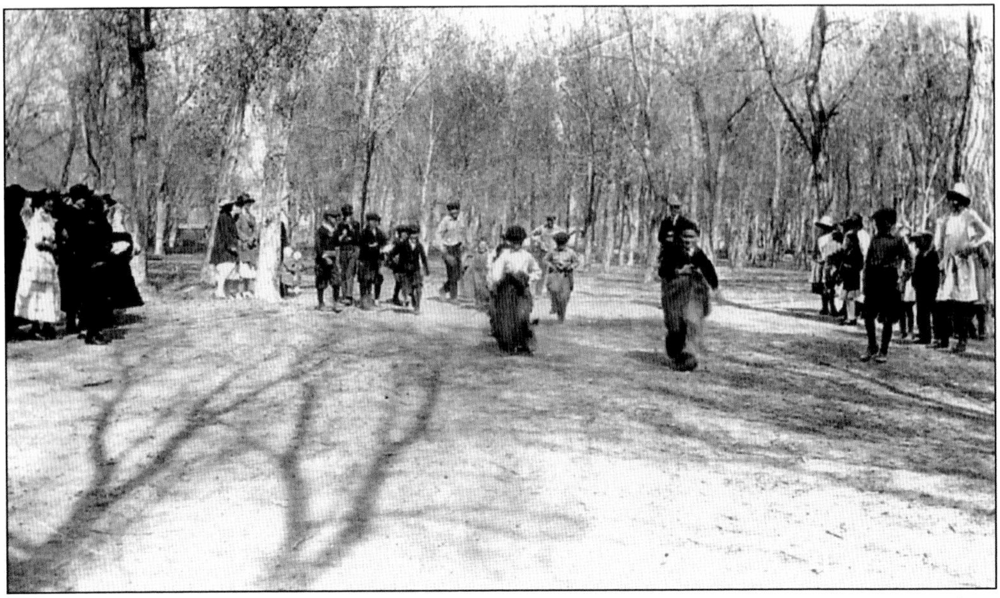

Pictured are young boys taking part in a sack race at Pioneer Park (then west of Sterling) in the early 1930s. The park has evolved from a wooded wilderness area to a combination wooded walking path, softball fields, disc golf course, tennis courts, and playgrounds. Pioneer Park also has pavilions for sheltered picnics. (Courtesy Overland Trail Museum.)

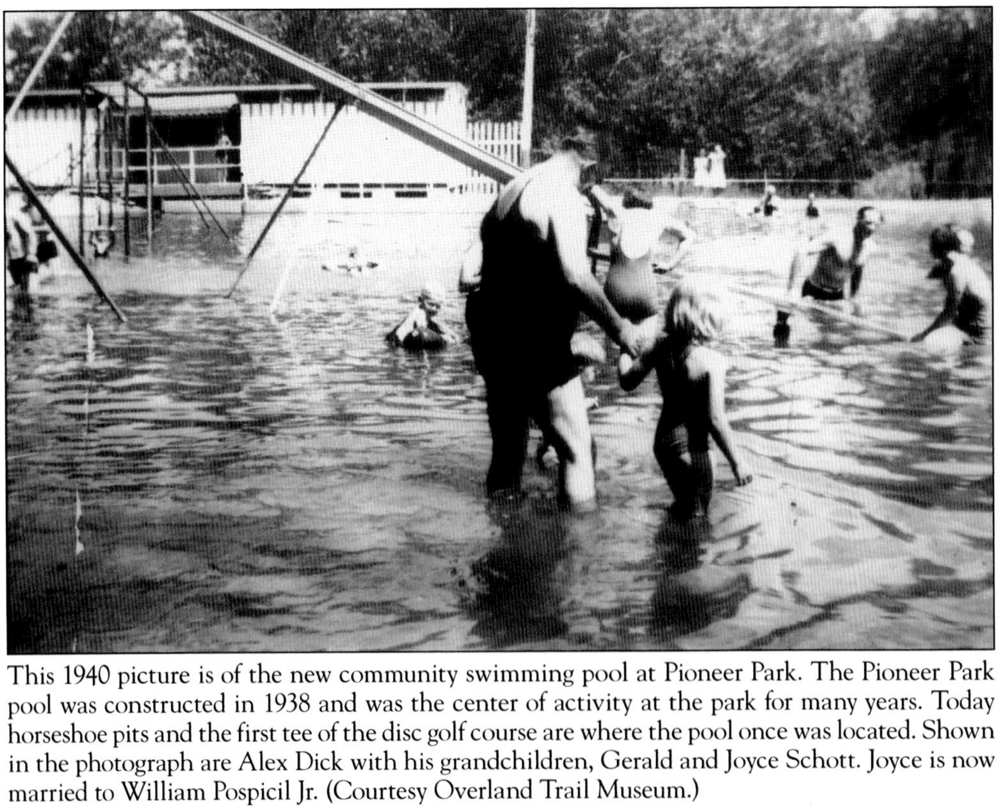

This 1940 picture is of the new community swimming pool at Pioneer Park. The Pioneer Park pool was constructed in 1938 and was the center of activity at the park for many years. Today horseshoe pits and the first tee of the disc golf course are where the pool once was located. Shown in the photograph are Alex Dick with his grandchildren, Gerald and Joyce Schott. Joyce is now married to William Pospicil Jr. (Courtesy Overland Trail Museum.)

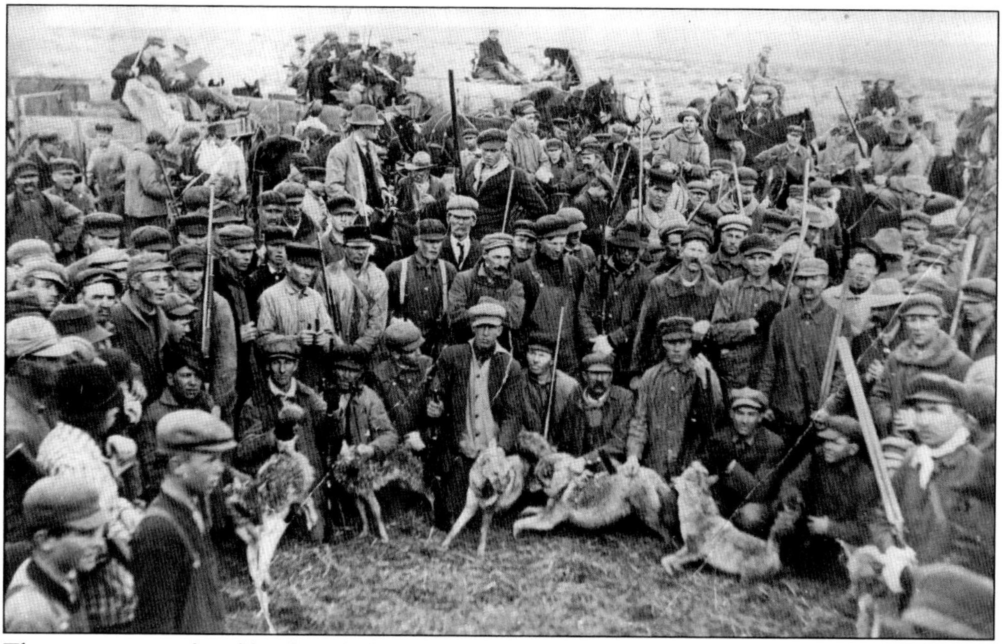

This is a picture of a rabbit drive held in Dailey in 1928. Dailey is a community in Logan County about 25 miles southeast of Sterling. (Courtesy Overland Trail Museum.)

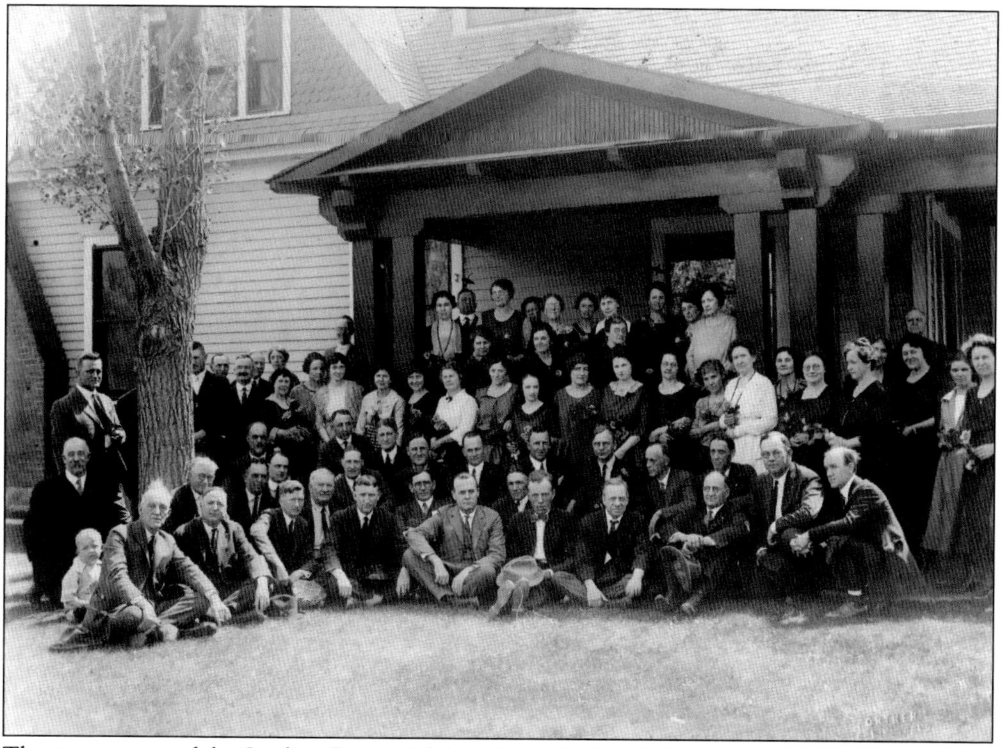

This is a picture of the Sterling Rotary Club at the S. E. Naugle home in 1922. The Rotary Club was still active in 2010, holding weekly meetings with speakers and presentations, as well as sponsoring events and youth activities. (Courtesy Overland Trail Museum.)

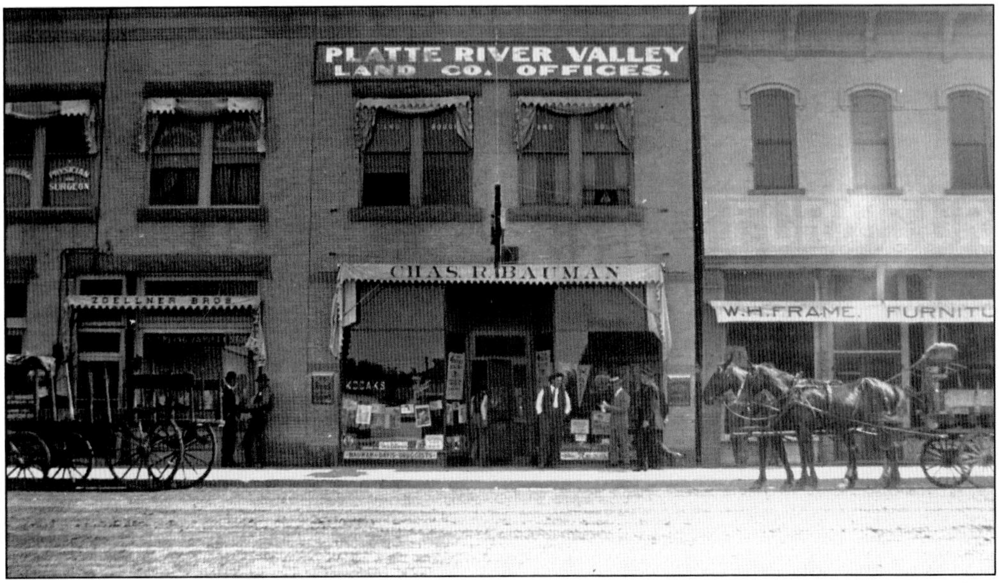

This is a 1920 photograph of the 200 block of Main Street, which is still dirt in the picture but was paved a year later in 1921. The Key Bank building is where the Platte River Land Company is located in this picture. The building then housing the W. H. Frame Furniture store is now occupied by Karousel Kids thrift store and Beau Monde bridal boutique. (Courtesy Overland Trail Museum.)

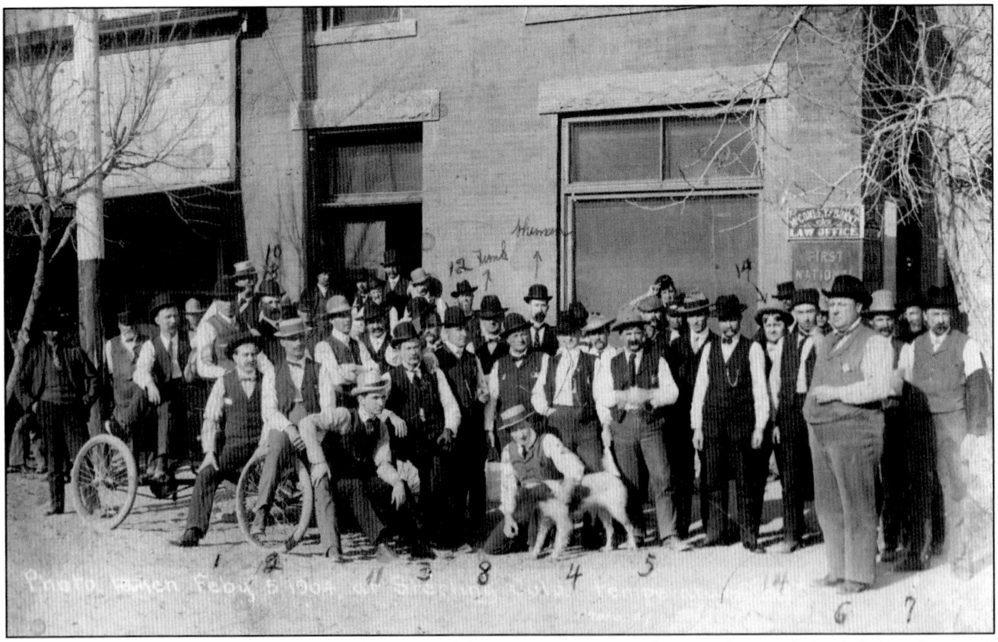

In this February 5, 1904, photograph, men of the community gather in front of the McConley and Burke Law Office and the First National Bank. Fourteen of the men in this picture were identified at one point in time, as seen by the numbering in pen. (Courtesy Overland Trail Museum.)

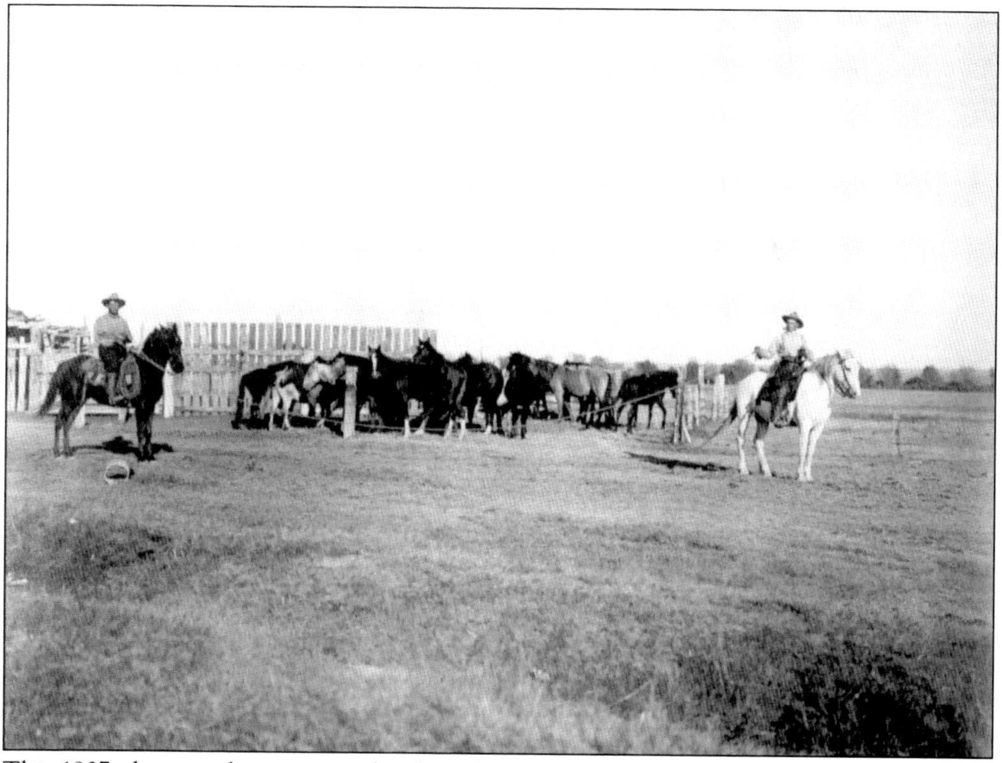

This 1907 photograph is presumed to have been taken on the J-Hook Ranch. Elgen Peer is on the horse at left, and Cuyasuta Rhoads is on the horse to the right. (Courtesy Overland Trail Museum.)

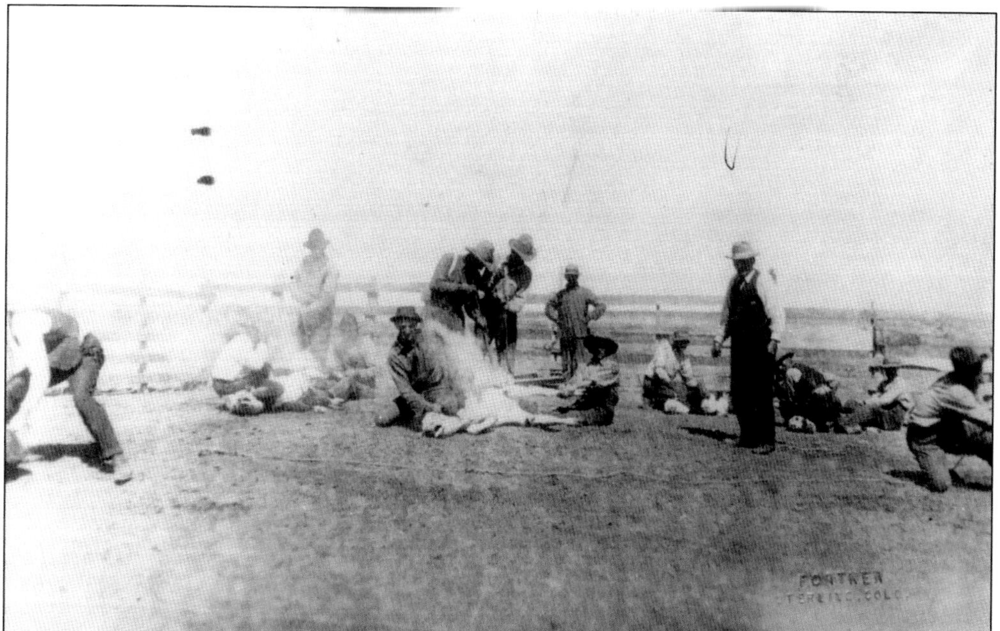

This photograph, taken by Fortner Photography in Sterling, depicts a livestock branding operation on one of Logan County's cattle ranches. (Courtesy Overland Trail Museum.)

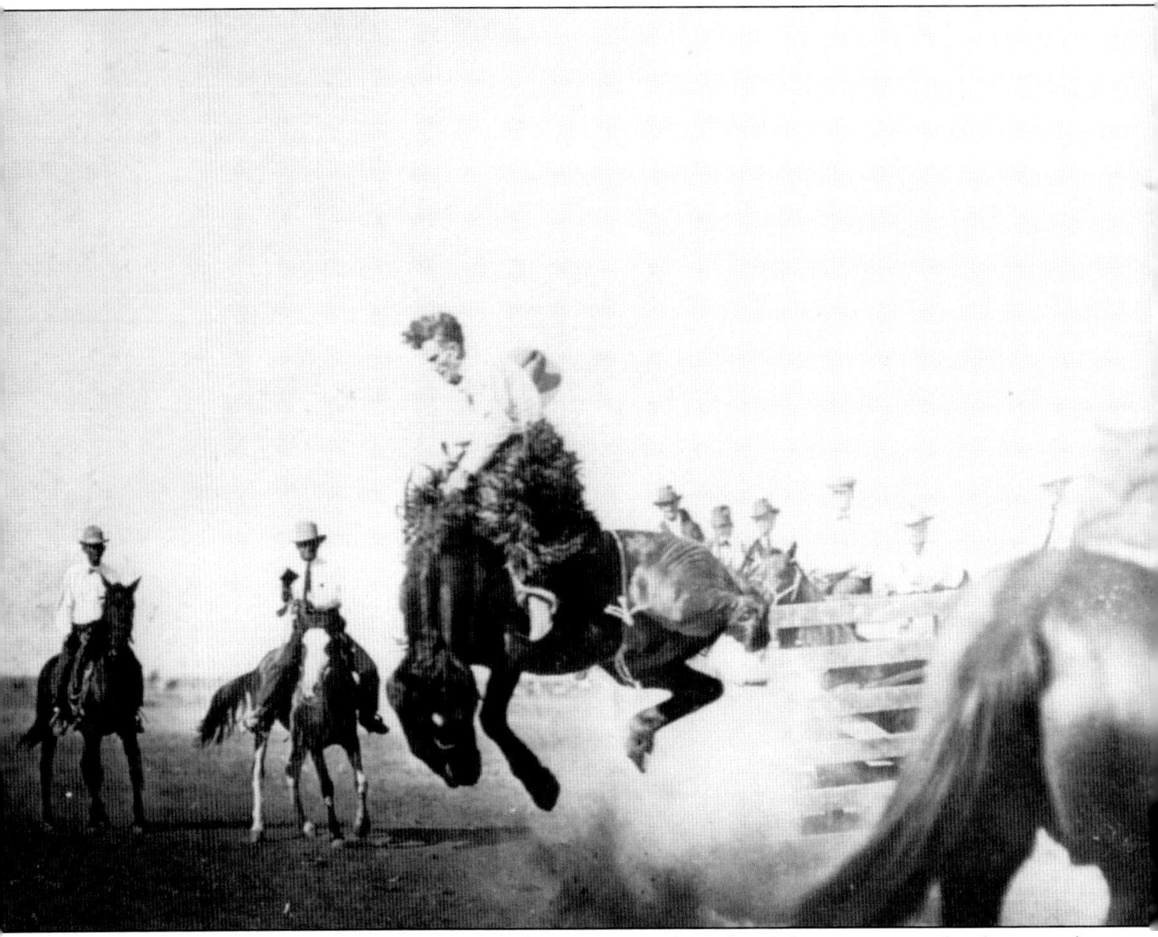

Rodeos and cowboy competitions have been a part of Sterling's history since the first ranch. In this picture, Red Sublett is riding a bucking horse named Wyoming. Several other men are watching the event as three men monitor the man-versus-horse competition within the arena. (Courtesy Overland Trail Museum.)

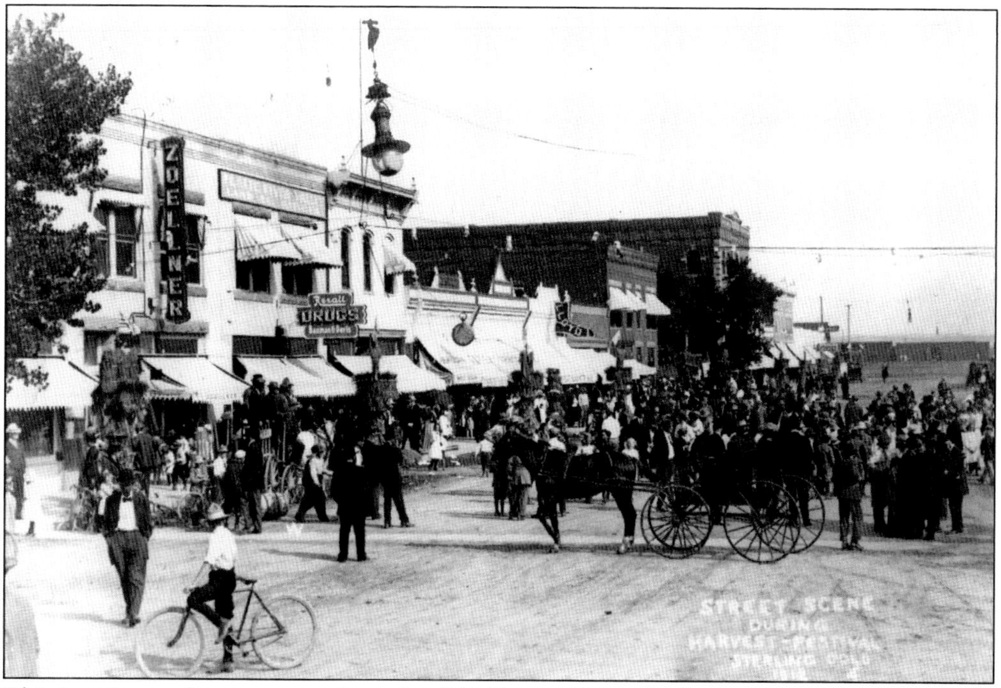

This is a picture of a street scene from the 1912 Harvest Festival. The image is from the 100 block of Main Street. (Courtesy Overland Trail Museum.)

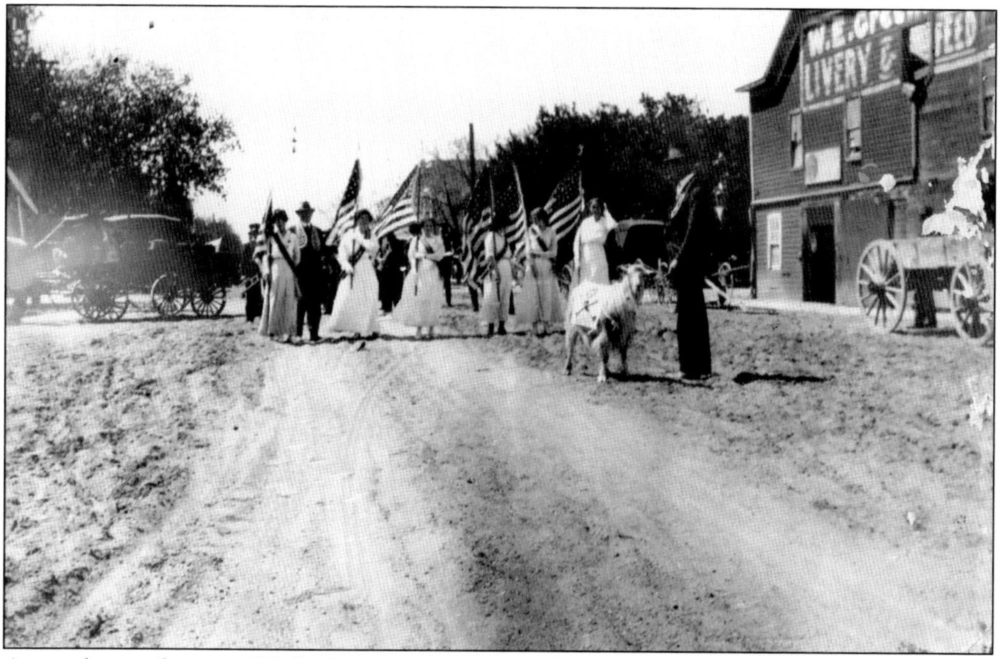

A parade marches past W. E. Greenman Livery and Feed. The dirt street indicates this event likely happened in the late 1800s. (Courtesy Overland Trail Museum.)

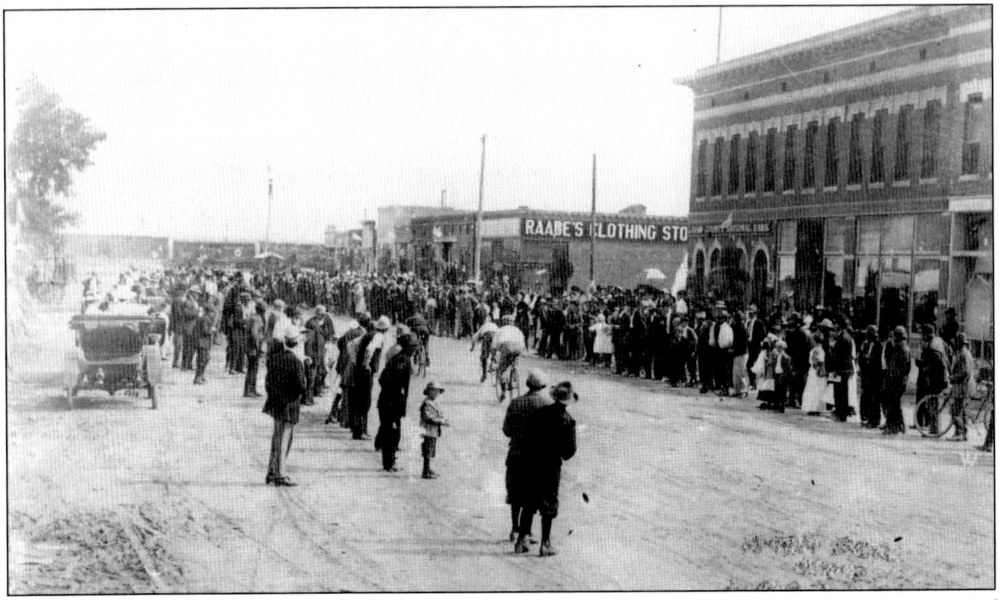

This is a photograph of a bicycle race during an early Harvest Festival. The race at the center of the street is heading east toward the Union Pacific depot. (Courtesy Overland Trail Museum.)

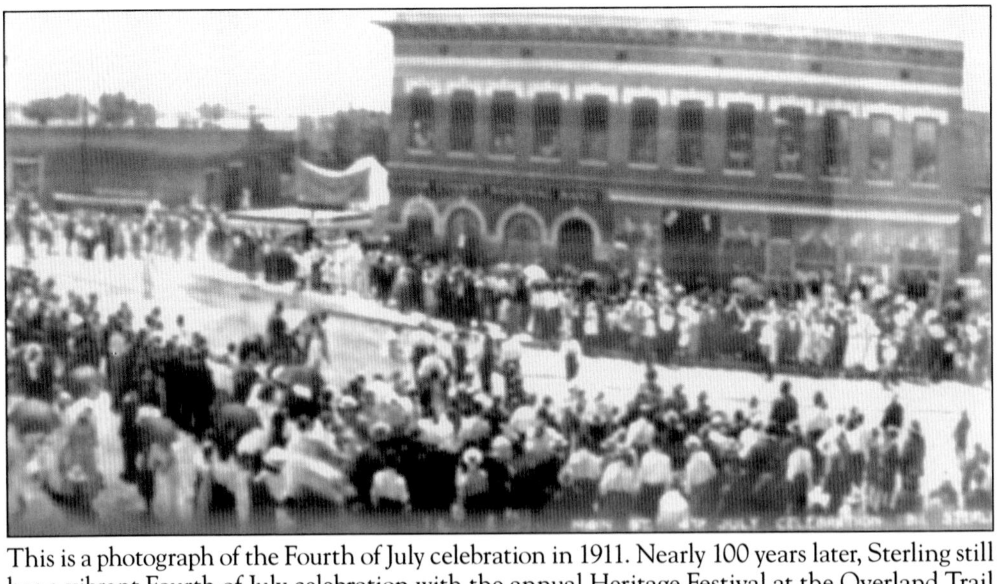

This is a photograph of the Fourth of July celebration in 1911. Nearly 100 years later, Sterling still has a vibrant Fourth of July celebration with the annual Heritage Festival at the Overland Trail Museum. An evening fireworks display is held over Pioneer Park by the Sterling Fire Department. (Courtesy Overland Trail Museum.)

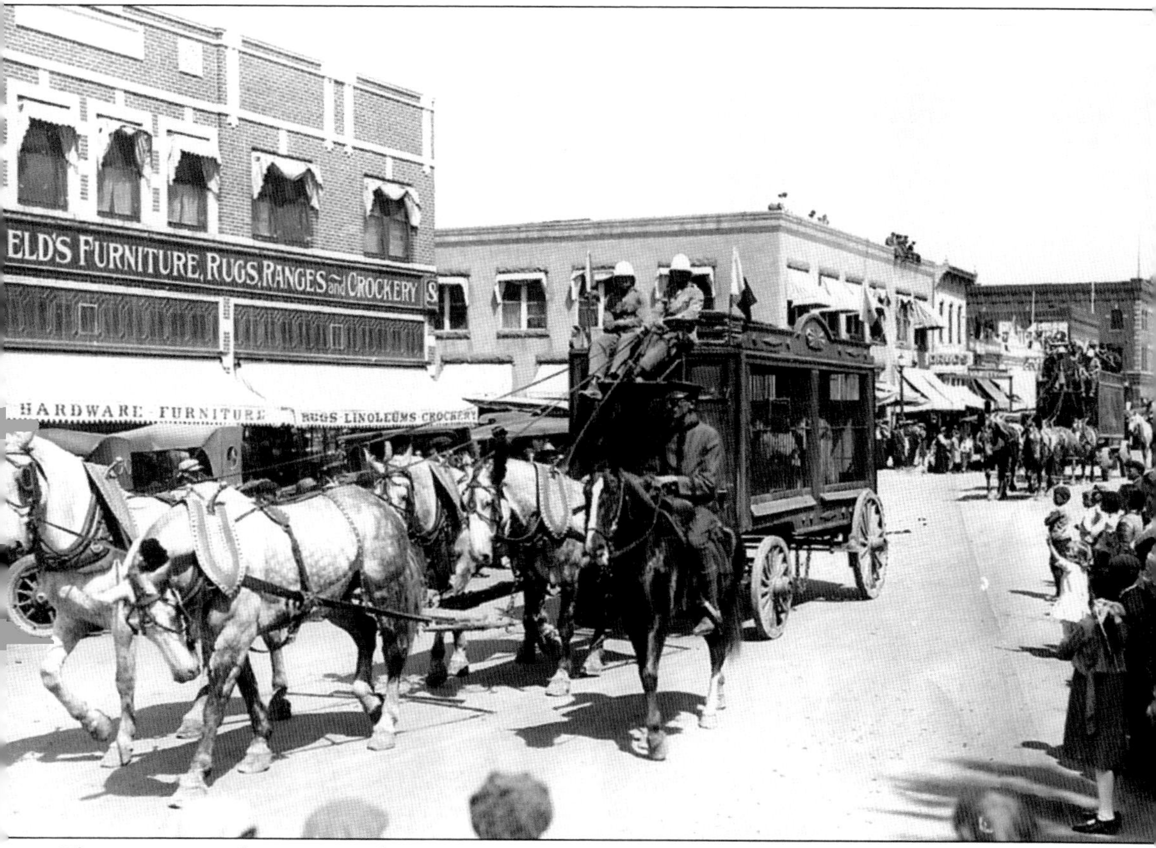

This is a picture of a circus parade entering Sterling from the railroad yard. The horse-drawn wagon is between Second and Third Streets on Main Street. (Courtesy Overland Trail Museum.)

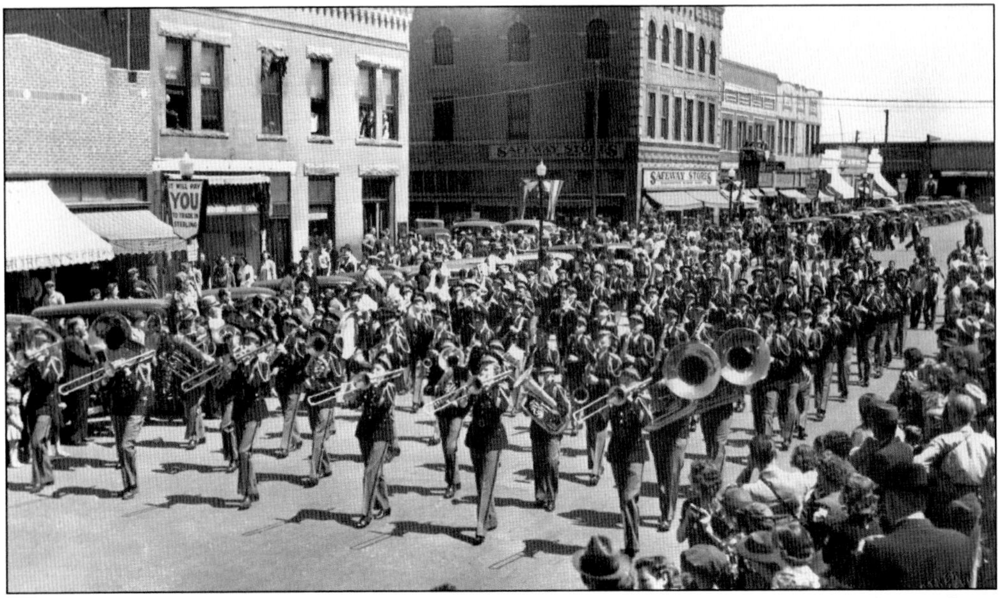

This photograph, noted by the Overland Trail Museum as taken in the late 1930s, is of a marching band, possibly part of a parade progressing west on the north side of the 100 and 200 blocks of Main Street. Many people and cars line the streets. (Courtesy Overland Trail Museum.)

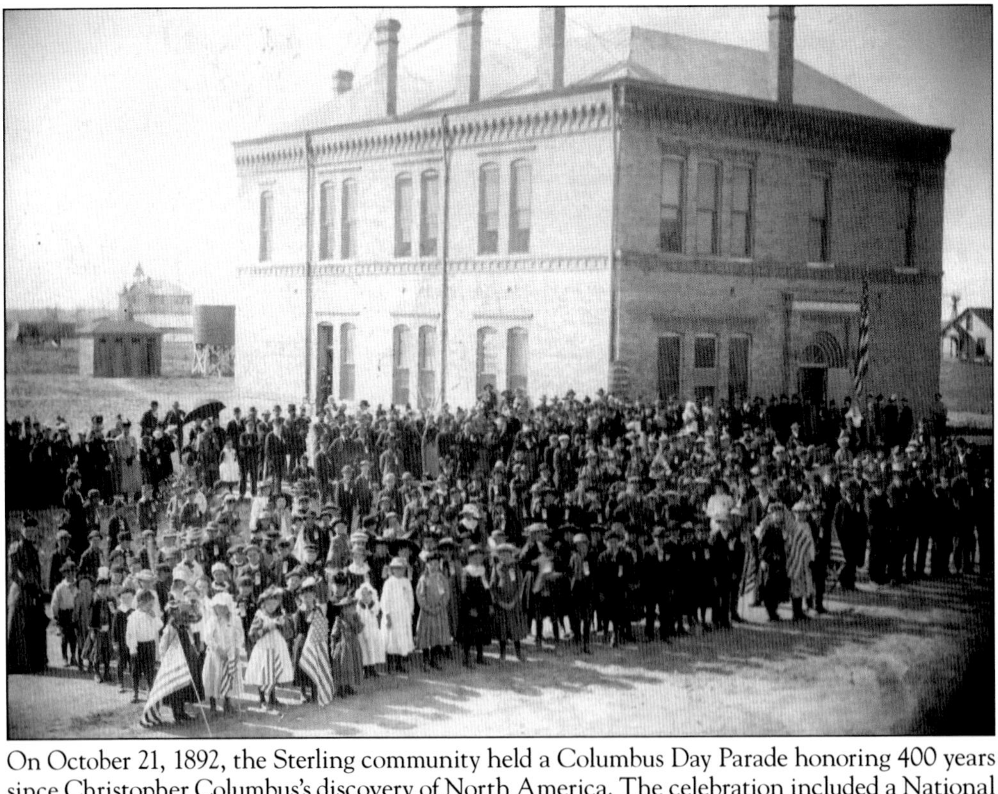

On October 21, 1892, the Sterling community held a Columbus Day Parade honoring 400 years since Christopher Columbus's discovery of North America. The celebration included a National Public School Celebration official badge issued to schoolchildren. In the background of the pictured courthouse is the Hamblin School. (Courtesy Overland Trail Museum.)

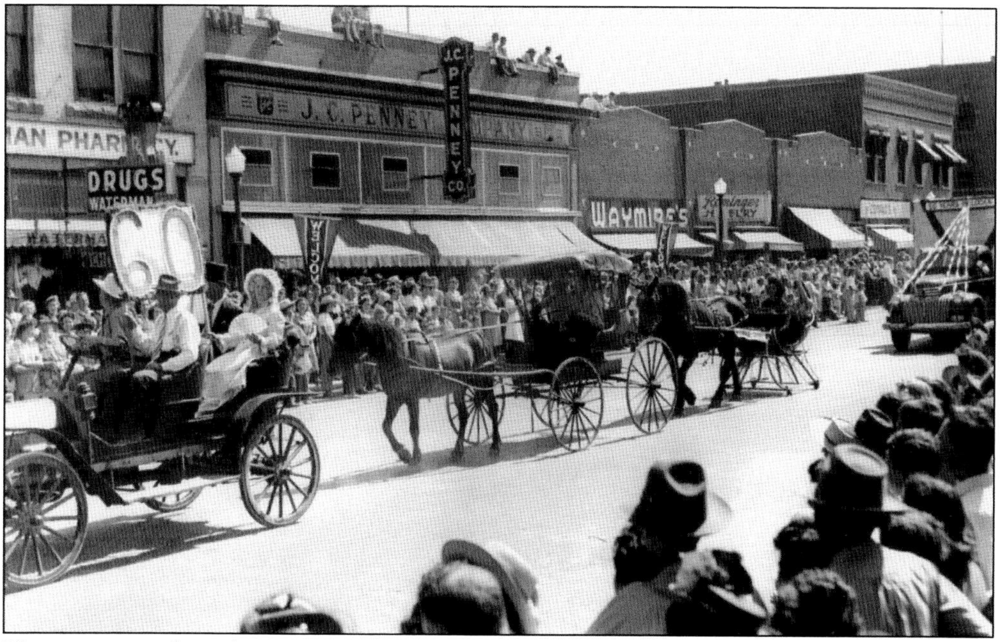

This is a picture from the 1944 Logan County Fair parade. The picture was taken between Second and Third Streets on Main Street. (Courtesy Overland Trail Museum.)

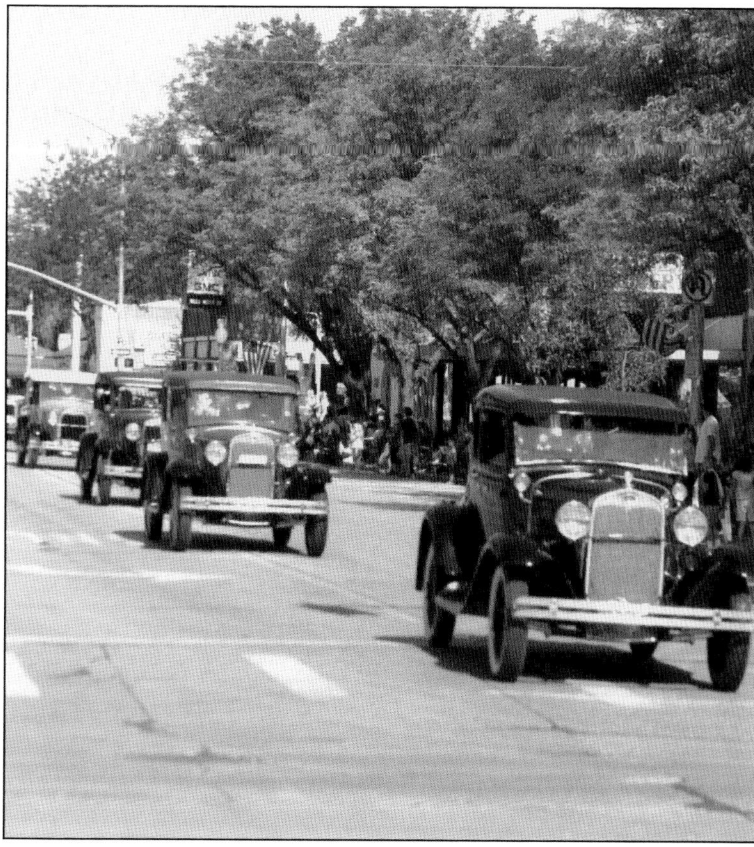

Old meets new in this photograph of a recent Logan County Fair parade, with cars from yesteryear traveling east on Main Street in celebration of the annual fair. (Courtesy *Sterling Journal-Advocate*.)

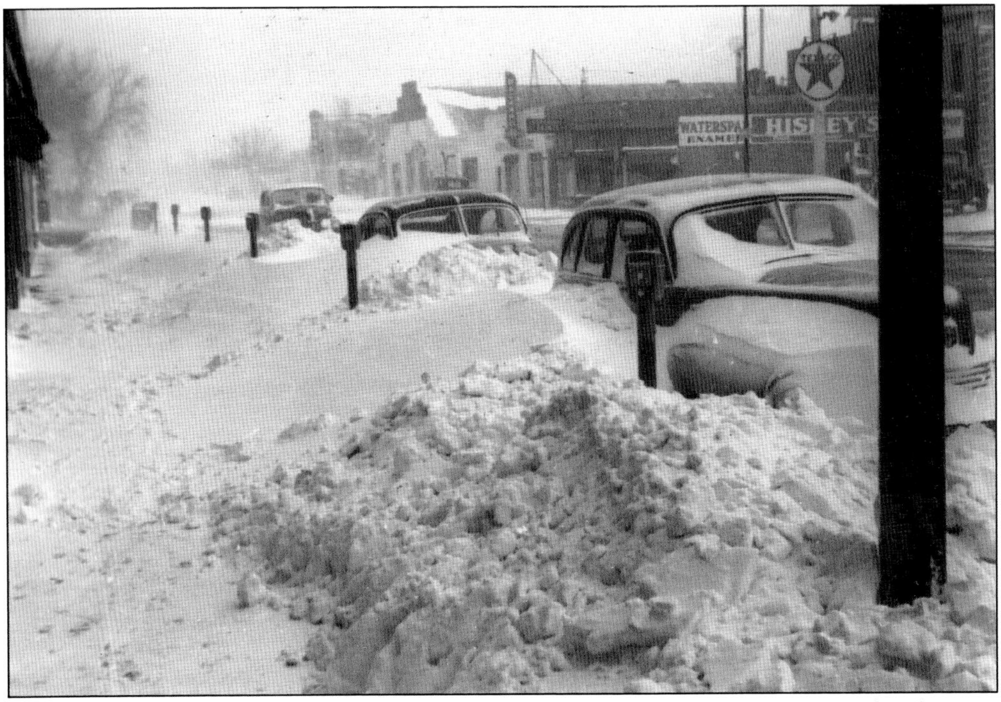

Weathering large snowstorms has long been a part of daily life in Sterling. Pictured is the view from Croft Drug (then on the corner of North Third and Poplar Streets) only hours after the blizzard of 1949 dumped a large amount of snow on Sterling. Parking meters poke out of the piled up snow on the sidewalks. The streets downtown were once dotted with parking meters, but they were removed sometime in the late 1980s or early 1990s. In the background to the right is Hiskey's Glass Shop, which once was located next to the old city hall. (Courtesy Overland Trail Museum.)

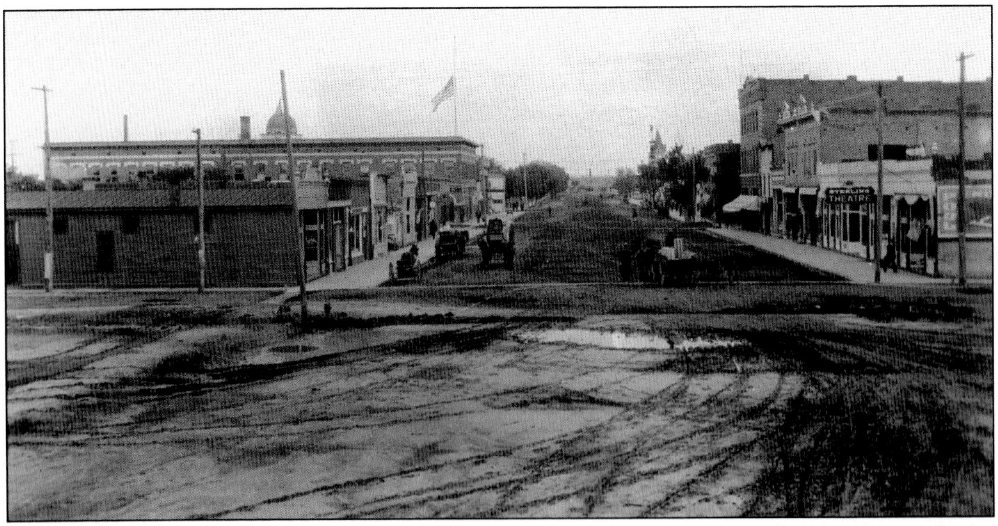

Pictured is Main Street looking west from the Union Pacific depot. A good rainstorm made the unpaved Main Street muddy with tire and wagon wheel ruts. Spring and early summer in Sterling usually brings a great amount of rain, thunderstorms, and lightning—and even tornado warnings are familiar events for most longtime residents. (Courtesy Overland Trail Museum.)

Seven

Clubs and Organizations

Strength in Numbers

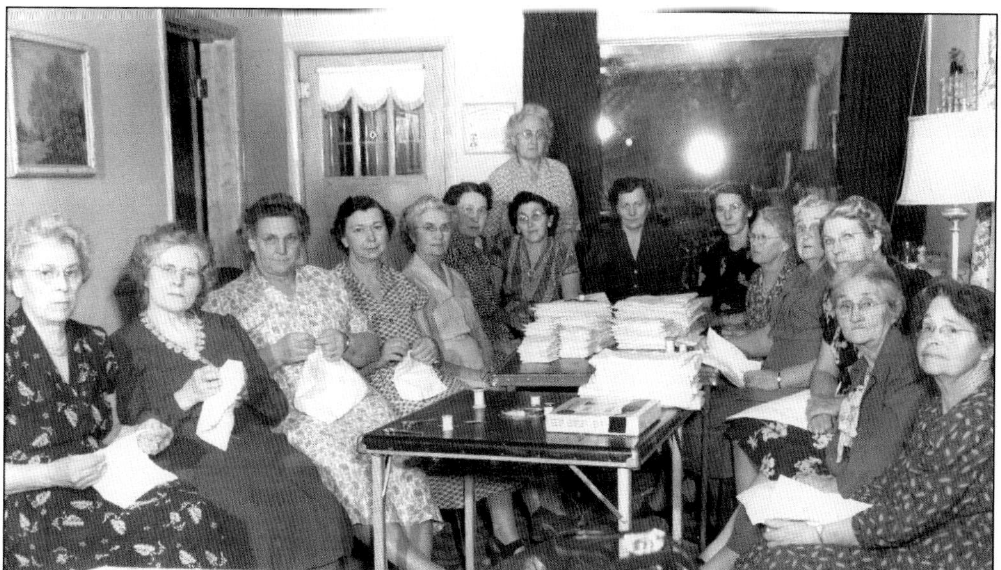

The members of the Sterling Homemakers' Club are sewing cancer dressings. From left to right are Mrs. Guenzi, Mrs. Bartholomew, Mrs. Knudson, Mrs. Rieke, Mrs. Browner, Mrs. Christner, Mrs. Knifton, Mrs. Ils, Mrs. Grubbs, Mrs. Johnson, Mrs. Stuck, Mrs. Dunn, guest Mrs. Coates, Mrs. Coakley, and Mrs. Dickinson. (Courtesy Overland Trail Museum.)

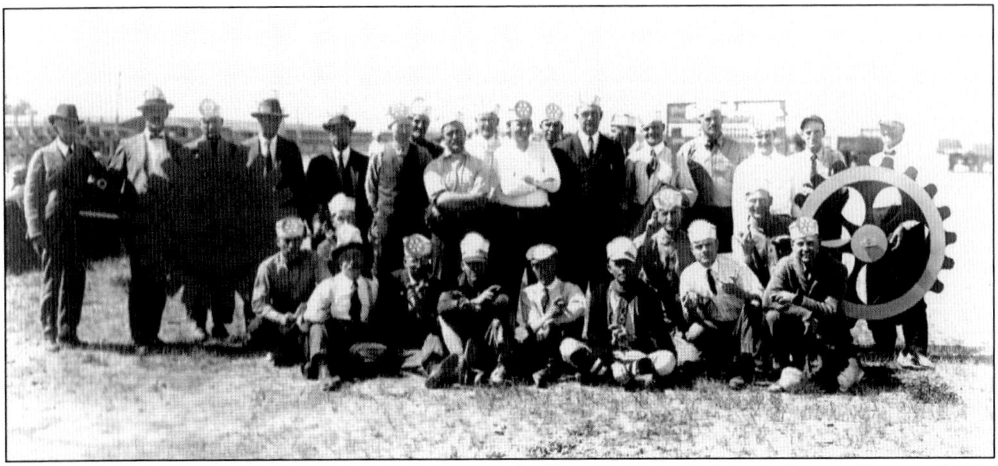

Pictured are the members of the Rotary Club baseball team. From left to right are (first row) Mr. Hogan, P. D. Barney, James H. Jay, Jim Morrison, Art D. Jackson, Charlie Evans, Harry Vail, Mabry King, H. B. Swedlund, B. C. Johnson, and an unidentified man; (second row) Colonel Paschal, W. E. King, Mr. Woodruff, F. H. Blair, Dr. W. E. Kellogg, Carl H. Greenawalt, John Mathis, J. L. Marstellan, Dr. F. E. Palmer, Roy A. Caunley, John A. Strom, Harvey Zink, B. M. Scofield, Charles A. Brink, Jack Robertson, H. L. Titus, and George Schillig, and an unidentified man. (Courtesy Overland Trail Museum.)

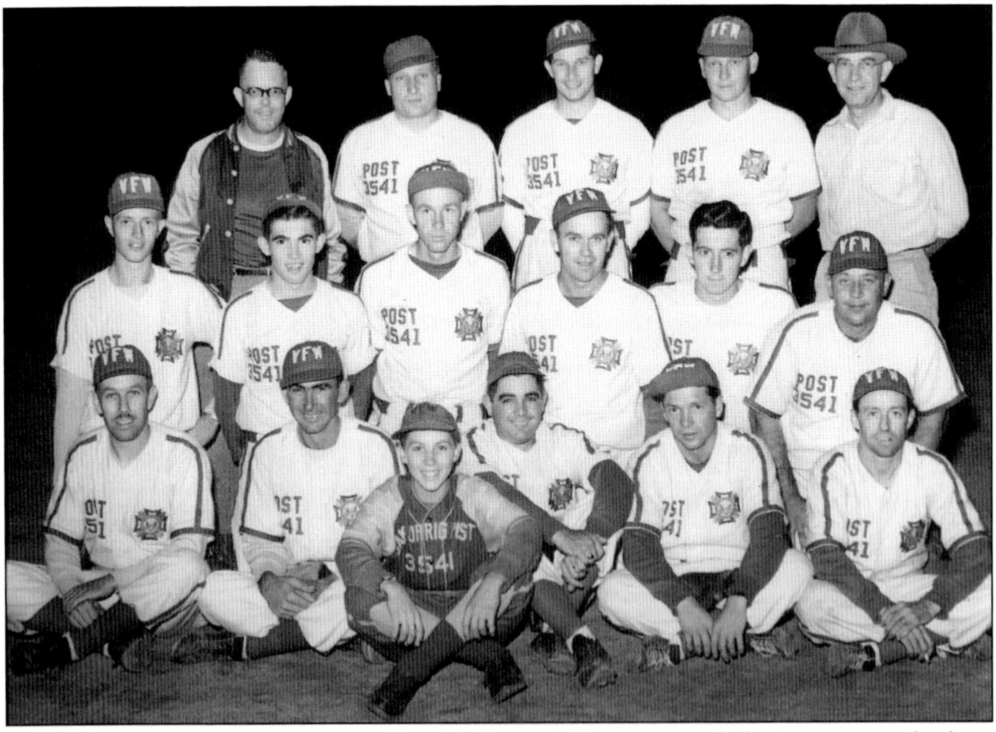

This is a 1953 photograph of the VFW softball team. This team includes many men who later became community leaders, such as Ernie French, who was president of Northeastern Junior College at one time (E. S. French Hall was named after him). Roy Edwards later became a coach at Northeastern Junior College, and John Edwards became a prominent attorney in the community. (Courtesy Overland Trail Museum.)

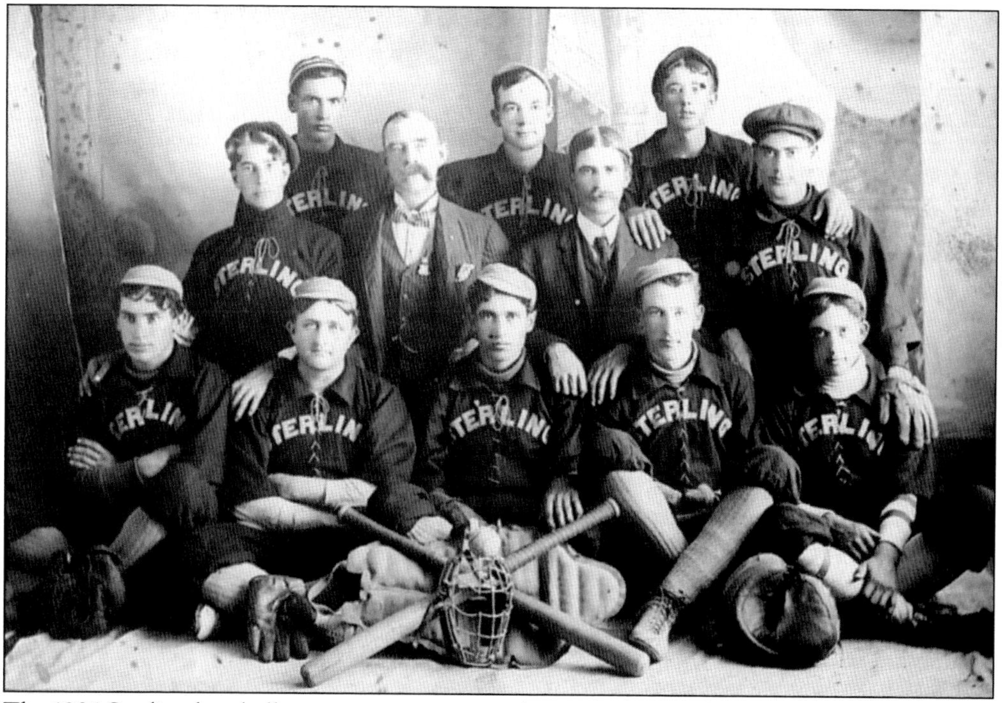

The 1904 Sterling baseball team won every game that season, according to information from the Overland Trail Museum. They are pictured here in a photograph by John C. Johnson. (Courtesy Overland Trail Museum.)

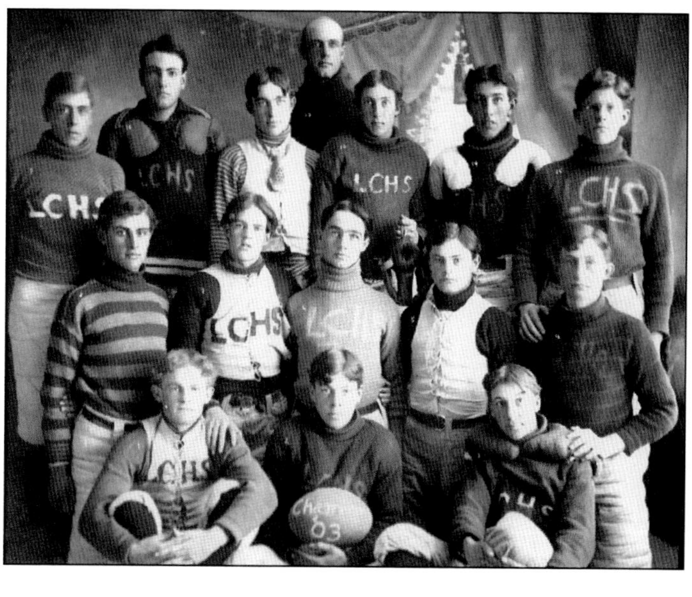

Pictured is the Logan County High School football team with a 1903 championship football. From left to right are (first row) Horace Davis, Louie Campbell, and Earl Ramsey; (second row) Jess Bartholomew, Everett Kelsey, Lon King, Edward Giacomini, and Colonel Goddard; (third row) unidentified, Harr Scott, Otto Chipman, Guy Ramsey, unidentified, and Lawrence Giacomini; (fourth row) coach F. H. Merten. (Courtesy Overland Trail Museum.)

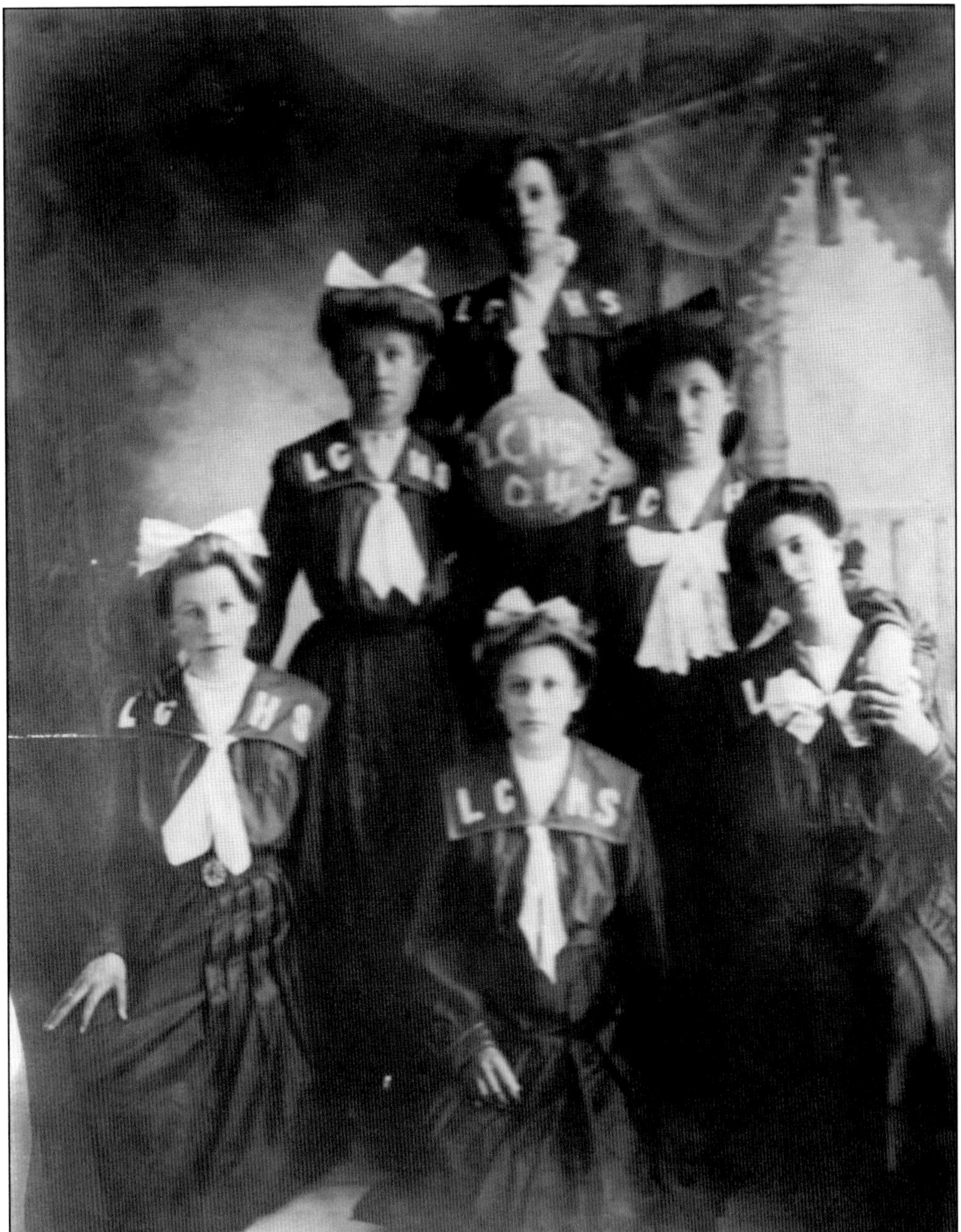

The members of the 1904 Logan County High School girls' basketball team are seen here wearing their uniforms—dresses. Pictured from left to right are (first row) Helen Parr (Sherwin), Belva Robuck (Andrews), and Alemada Sheridan (Chipman); (second row) Margaret Davis (Duffield) and Minnie Johnson (Rauscher); (third row) Werdna Delzell (Ginn). (Courtesy Overland Trail Museum.)

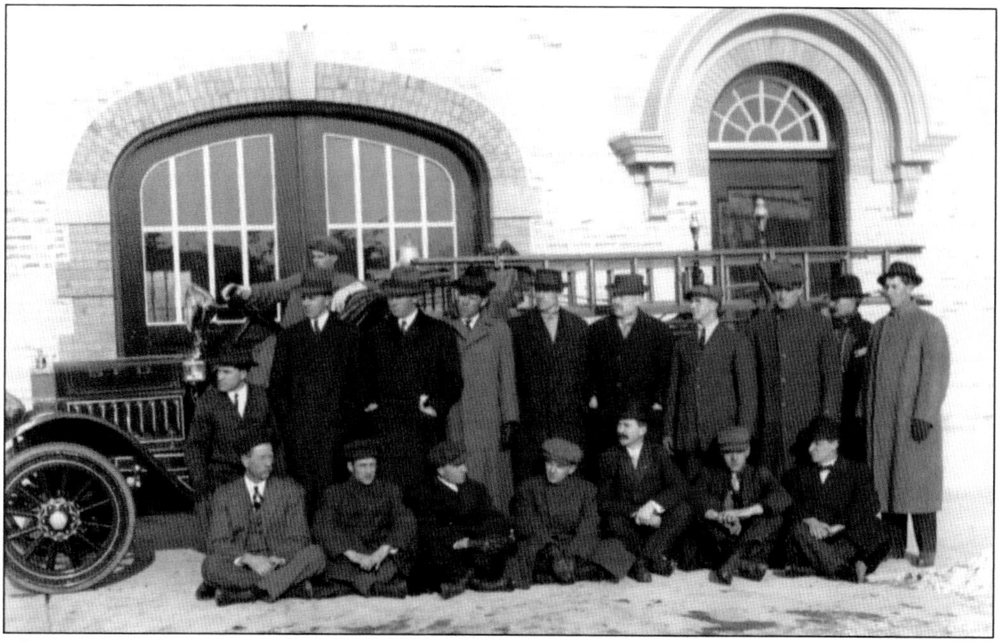

The 1912 Sterling Volunteer Fire Department poses in front of the new city hall with the recently delivered fire truck. From left to right are (first row) J. W. Arnold, Bob Chapmann, O. B. Holman, George Breil, C. R. Bauman, George Holcomb, Frank Mentgen; (second row) O. V. Chipman, N. C. Davis, L. R. Goodwin, J. E. Koenig, Bill Johnson, George Green, J. D. Liebee, unidentified, W. E. Greenman, and unidentified. Driving the truck is Frank Merrill. (Courtesy Overland Trail Museum.)

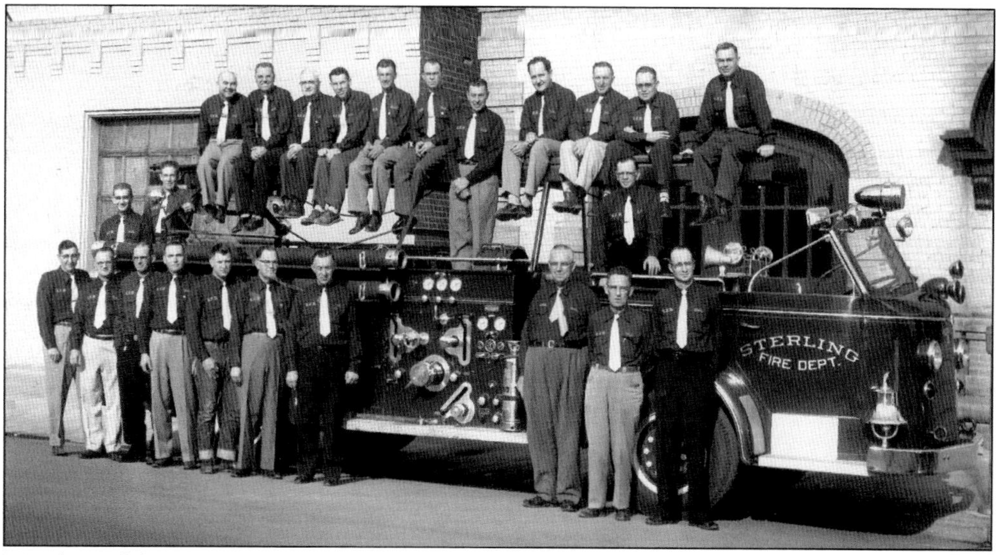

Members of the 1957 Sterling Fire Department are pictured with a 1957 American LaFrance fire truck in front of city hall on Poplar Street. From left to right are (first row) Pete Seeley, Bob Lawrie, Bill Weber, Bob Galbraith, Russ Castor, Jim Walker, Bud Backes, Dean Dowis, Mel Nix, and Stan Heist; (second row) Dick McGill, Larry Hunt, and G. W. Turner; (third row) Woodrow Heist, Bunk Koenig, Don Koenig, Skinny Flater, Bud Graham, Dick Backes, Richard Dowis, Alan Yost, Don Benge, Charles Stafford, and an unidentified man. (Courtesy Overland Trail Museum.)

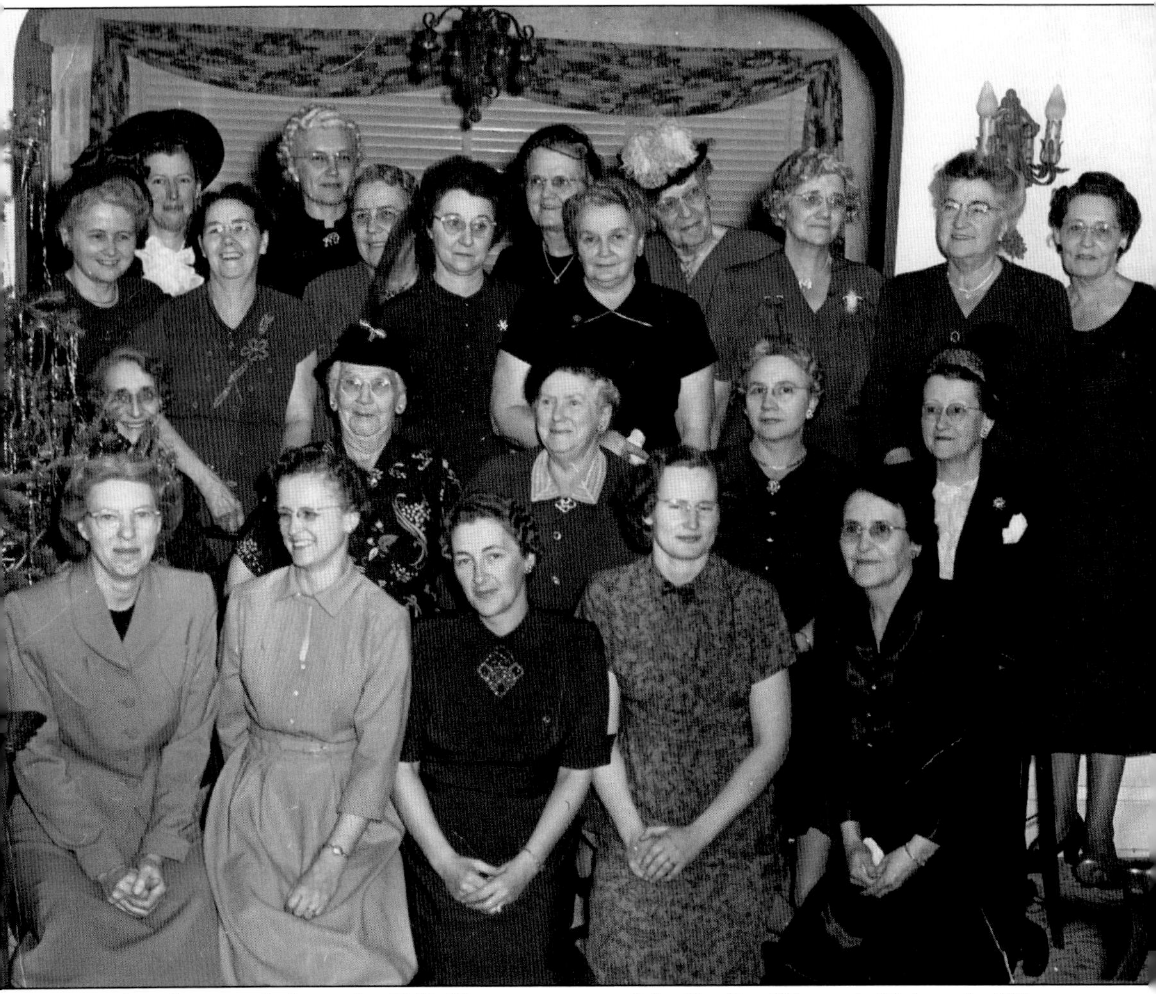

This photograph shows the 1950 Christmas party of the Sterling Women's Club at the Whyman home. Attending the meeting were Mrs. Clinton Astell, Esther Palmer, Mrs. Harley Berry, Ann McDiviets, Mrs. Nathan Thorpe, Mrs. F. R. Anderson, Sarah Arnold, Myrtle Roe, Mrs. Arthur Imig, Mrs. Harry Lingrison, Blanche Potter, Mrs. C. J. Whyman, Mrs. G. B. Andrews, Alice Clark, Mrs. Lloyd Bence, Mrs. Harry Earnhart, Mrs. Clayton Astell, Janet Hurst, Mrs. P. J. Timpleton, Mrs. O. F. Pirrson, Mrs. E. G. Buehler, and Mrs. Arch Monroe. The Whyman residence was a funeral home at 205 Beech Street. It is currently an apartment house. (Courtesy Overland Trail Museum.)

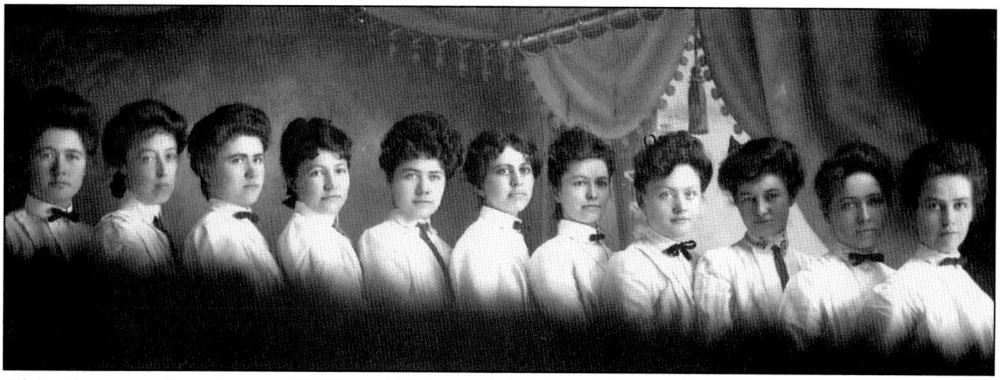

This photograph, taken in 1905 or 1906, is of the members of the Fortnightly Club. Pictured from left to right are Carrie Perkins Naylor, Daisie Usher Morlan, Minnie Yonge, Lottie Landrum Cheairs, Reta King Biles, Viola Davis Curran, Greta Gillett Read, Bertha Gleason Ragatz, Lizie Fennasay Rockwell, Mrs. Texa Moore, and Leta Eldon. (Courtesy Overland Trail Museum.)

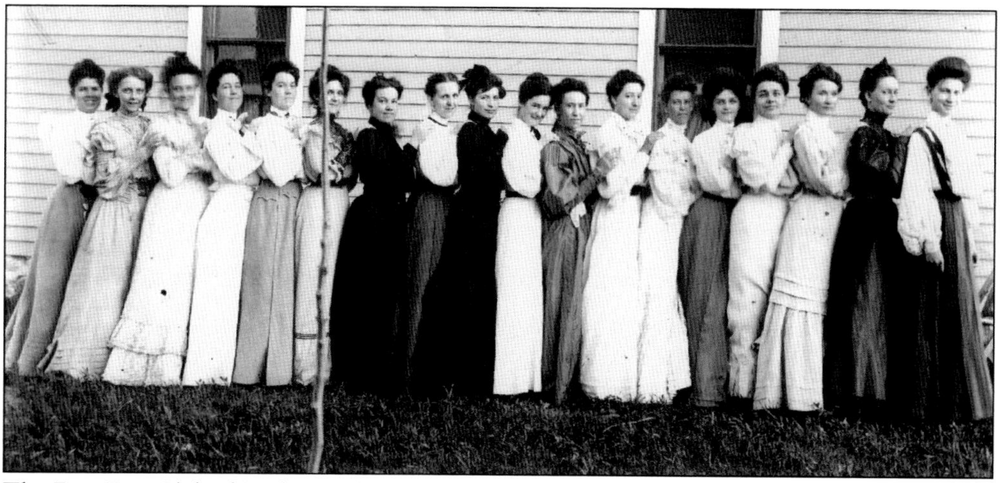

The Zeta Zeta Club of Sterling is shown during its early days. Pictured from left to right are Mrs. A. D. Jackson, a club visitor, Mrs. Werner, Pearl Miller Head, Norma Jackson Young, Mrs. Mabel Forbes, Dora King Fletcher, Louise Day Booth, Lida Morris Watts, Mary Parker, Mrs. Clint Forbes, Elsie Silver Rose, Mrs. W. E. Kellogg, Bernice Smith, a club visitor, Ells (Frank) Watts, Mary Silver Day, and a club visitor. The Zeta Zeta Club was instrumental in raising funds for the old Carnegie Library at the corner of South Fourth and Ash Streets. (Courtesy Overland Trail Museum.)

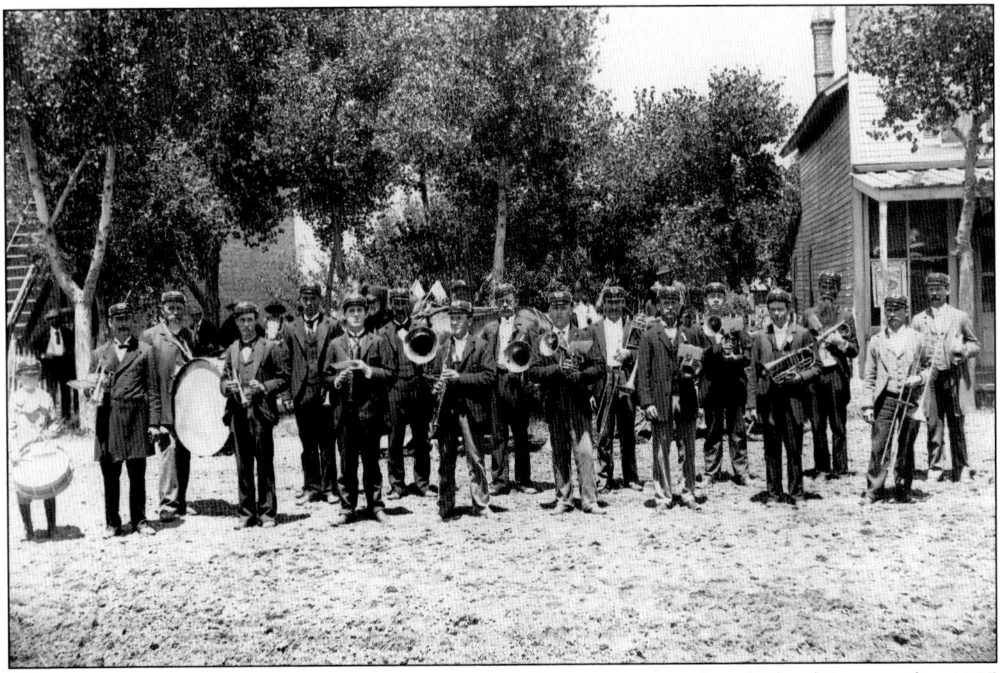

About center of the block, north side of Main Street between Second and Third Streets, this 1885 photograph shows the Sterling Brass Band readying to perform in downtown Sterling. Pictured, from left to right, are Homer Rogers, J. C. Fasher, Joe Haredesky, Sidney Propst Jr., D. C. Smith, Jimmie Boyd, J. C. Scott, V. S. Watts, Jim Wells, Will Bolyd, John Henderson, Art Hudspeth, J. C. Aiken, Eliza Humphreys, H. D. Hinkley, and two unidentified men. (Courtesy Overland Trail Museum.)

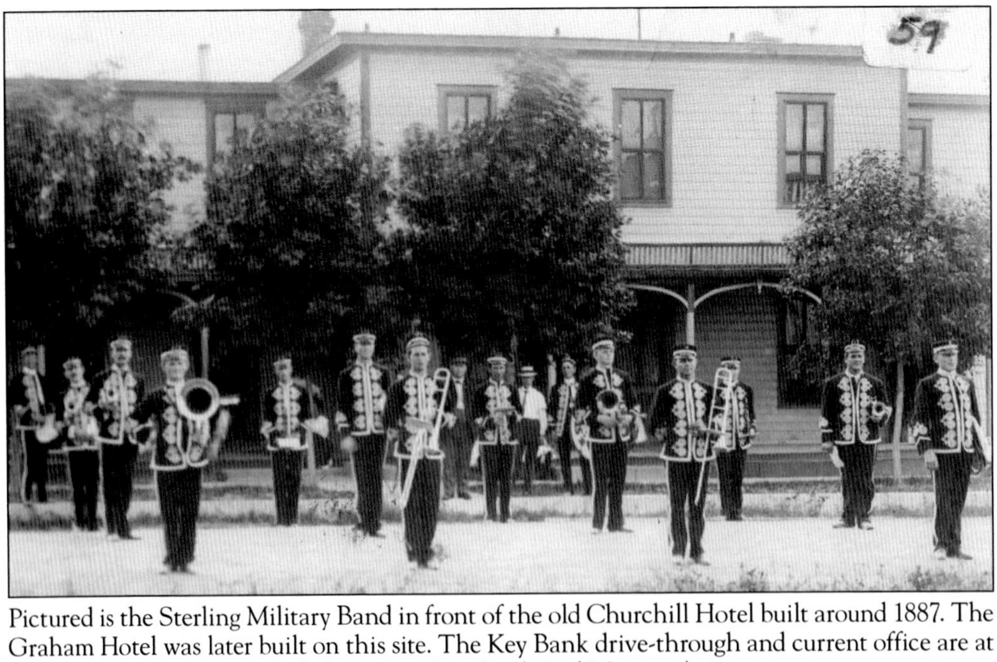

Pictured is the Sterling Military Band in front of the old Churchill Hotel built around 1887. The Graham Hotel was later built on this site. The Key Bank drive-through and current office are at the site of the Graham Hotel. (Courtesy Overland Trail Museum.)

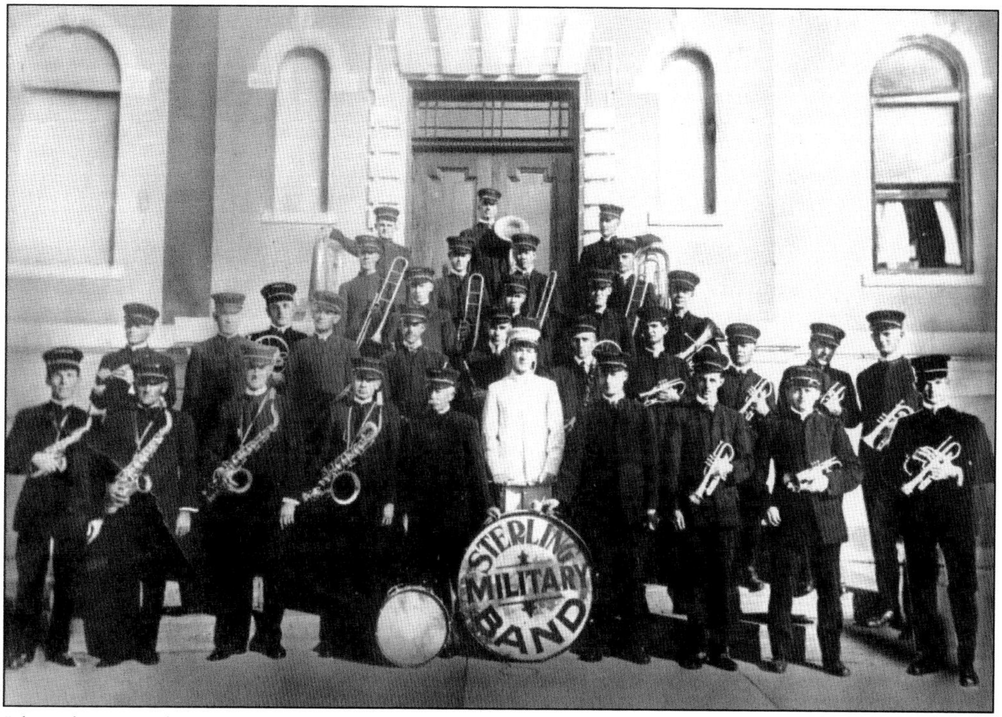

This photograph of the Sterling Military Band was taken in the fall of 1917 or spring of 1918. Pictured at the center is band director C. W. Seymour. (Courtesy Overland Trail Museum.)

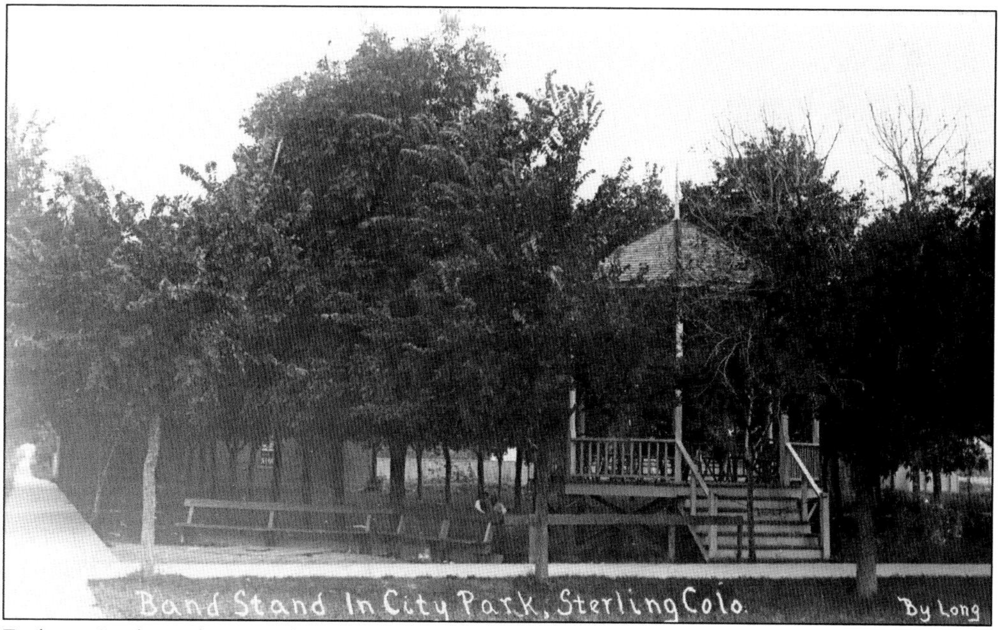

Early in Sterling's history, the area surrounding the Logan County Courthouse was known as City Park. The bandstand, surrounded by trees in this picture, offered afternoon entertainment for city residents. (Courtesy Overland Trail Museum.)

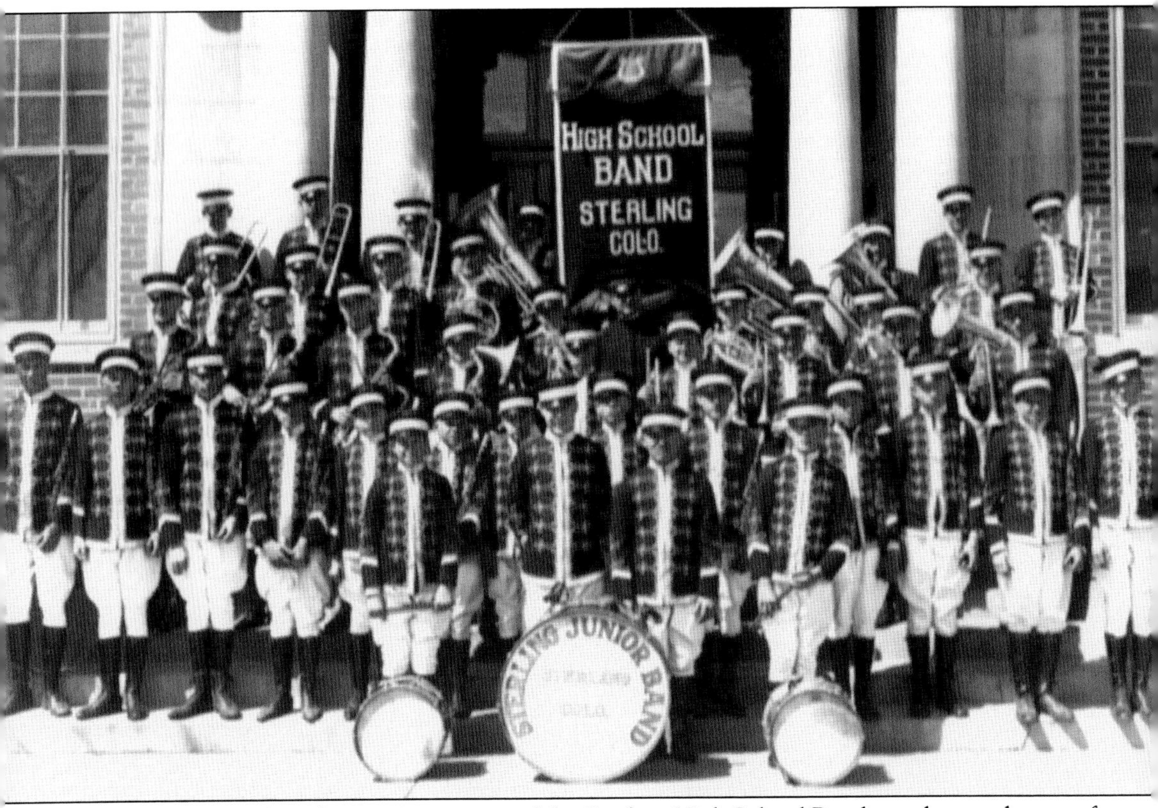

This picture, taken about 1924, consists of the Sterling High School Band members and some of the Sterling Junior High School Band members. The picture came from the Ozro Yenne estate and was given by his sisters, Mildred Reifsneider and Billie Parsons. L. E. "Dick" Smith (wearing a dark uniform under the banner) was known as the flying bandmaster because of his love of airplanes. (Courtesy Overland Trail Museum.)

Eight

Small Town
Big Education Opportunities

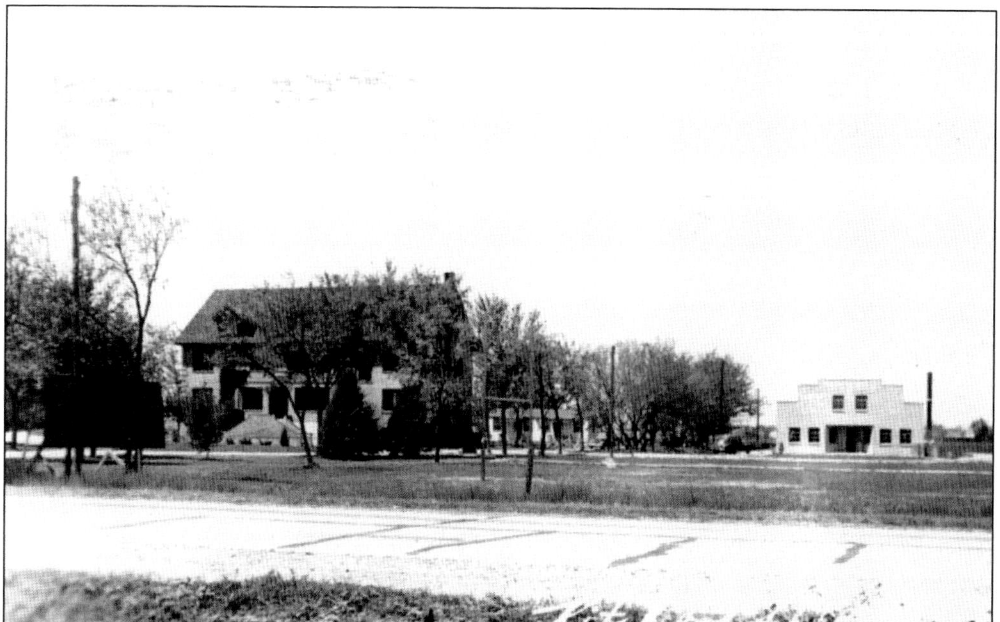

Pictured is the campus of Sterling Junior College (now called Northeastern Junior College) sometime before 1950. The large building on the left is Smith Hall, the campus's original building, which served as a poor farm during the Great Depression. (Courtesy Russell Johnson.)

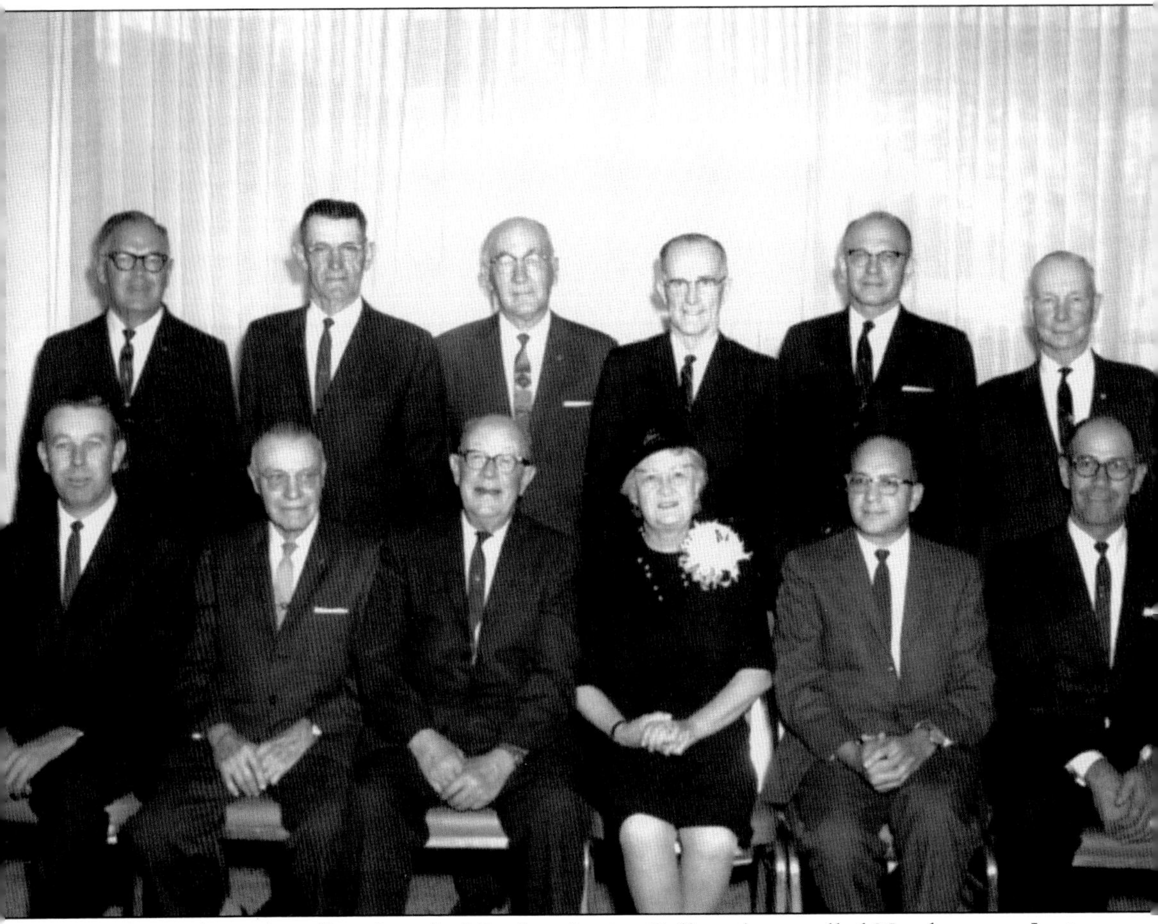

This is the early college board of Sterling Junior College (now called Northeastern Junior College). Pictured from left to right are (first row) college president Ervin S. French (1948–1979), E. C. "Sammy" Williams (1956–1958), Dr. James H. "Doc" Jackson (1941–1976), Ormilda Dowis (1942–1967), Dr. C. J. Jankowsky (1963–1975), and Clarence Lebsack (1963–1978); (second row) James Walker (1950–1962), Amory Beede (1947–1963), Reeder Phillips (1941–1943), Harold Whyman (1941–1950), David Hamil (1947–1956), and Bailey Jamison (1941–1957). (Courtesy Northeastern Junior College.)

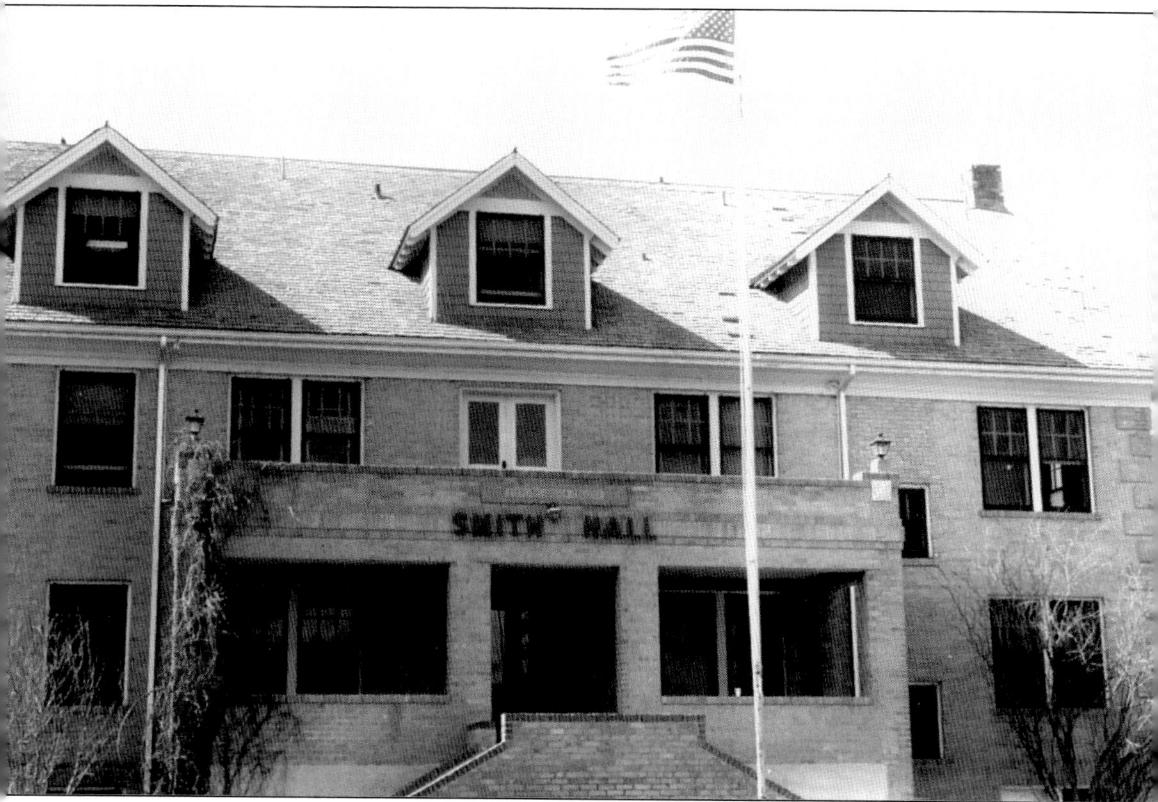

The original building at Northeastern Junior College was Smith Hall. The building and 10 acres were purchased from Logan County in 1944, when the college was named Sterling Junior College. The building was named in honor of Frances Smith in 1956. (Courtesy Northeastern Junior College.)

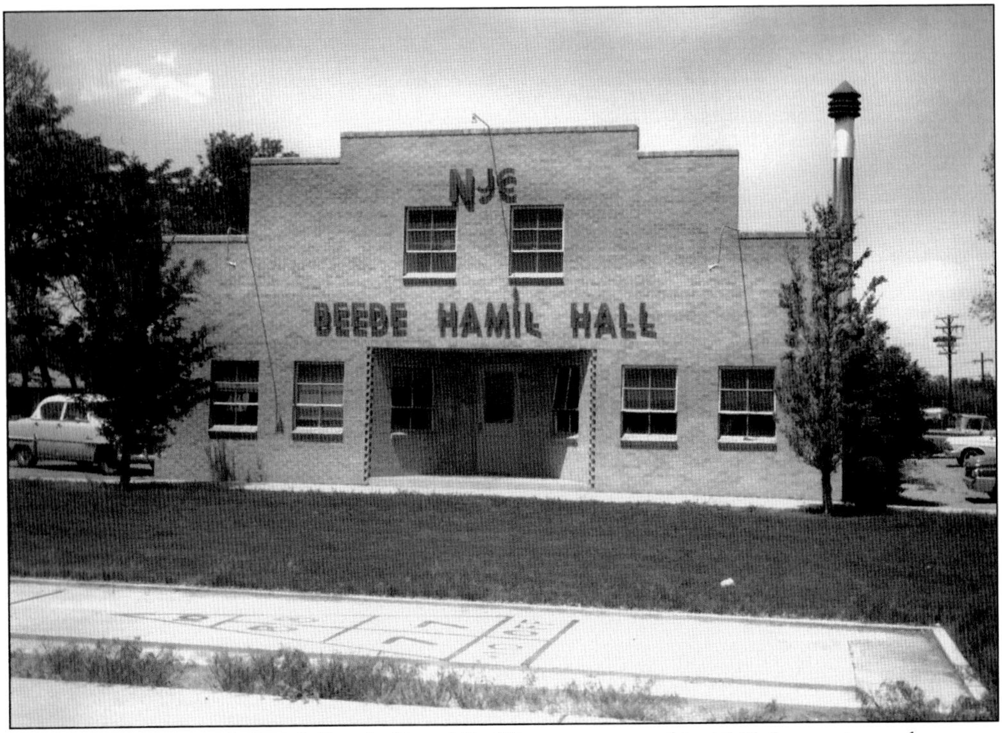

Northeastern Junior College's Beede-Hamil Building was erected in 1965. It remains a classroom building more than 40 years after its construction. (Courtesy Northeastern Junior College.)

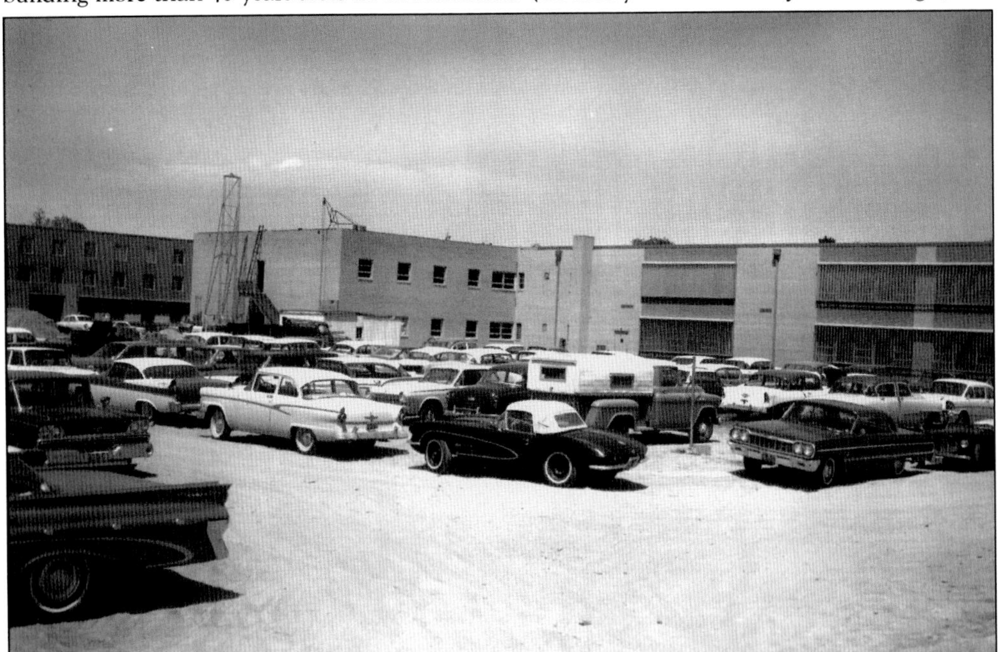

Northeastern Junior College's Phillips-Whyman Hall, a dormitory, was built in 1958. The second floor was added in 1961, and the west wing was added in 1963. (Courtesy Northeastern Junior College.)

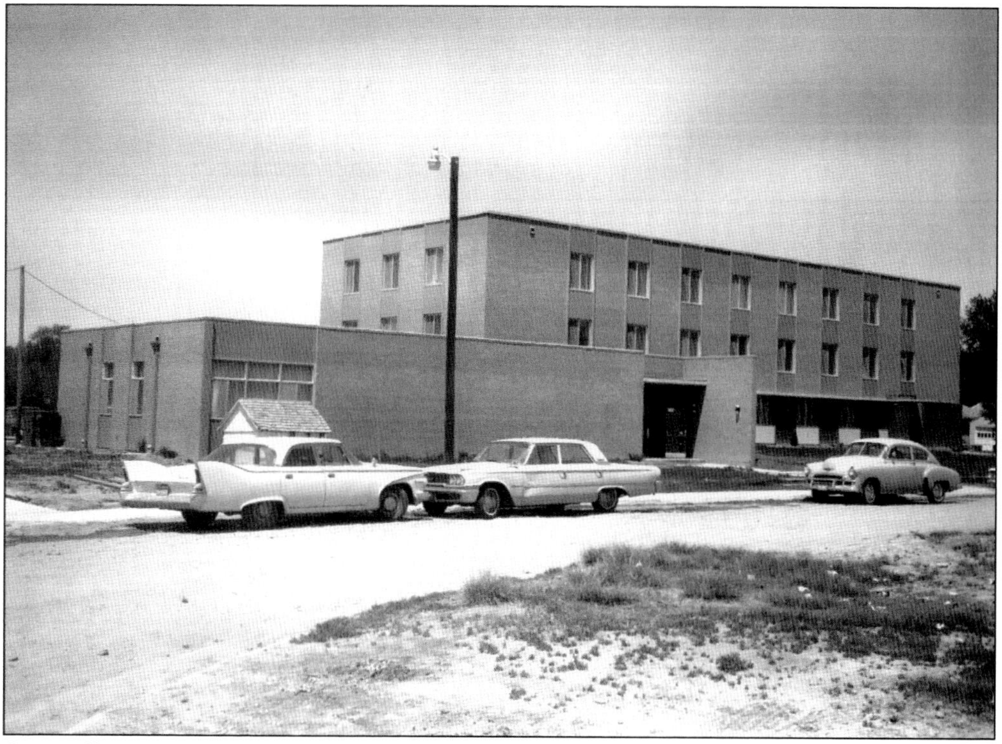

Originally named West Hall, this dormitory was built in 1963 and renamed Poole Hall in 1968. Pictured below are Northeastern Junior College student John Hodgson, college president Ervin French, and Charles and Annie Jo Poole. (Both, courtesy Northeastern Junior College.)

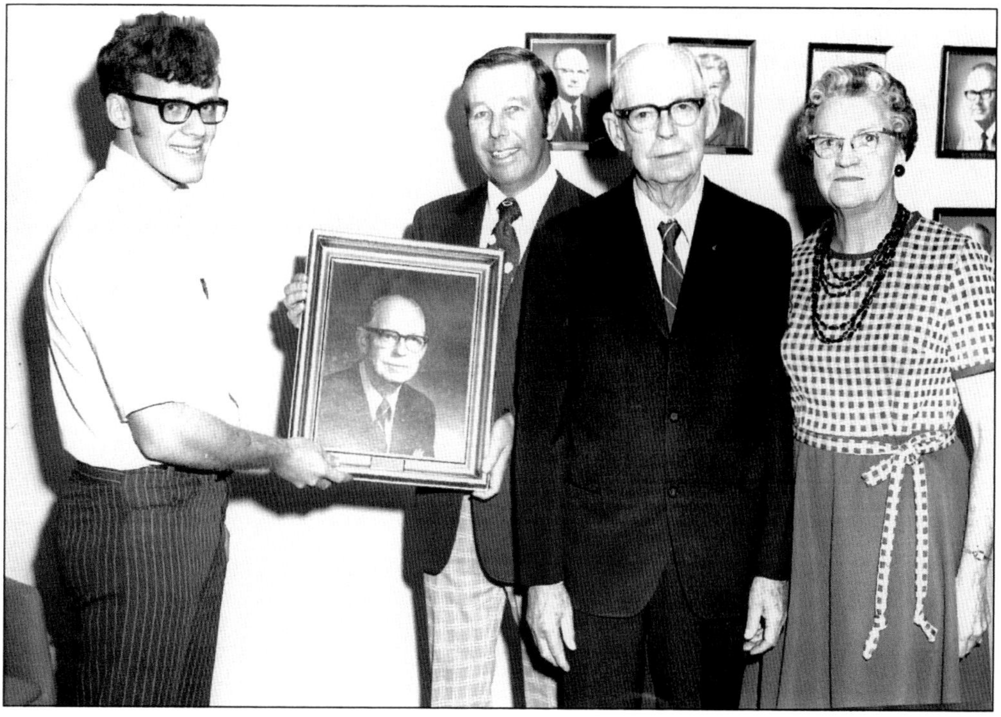

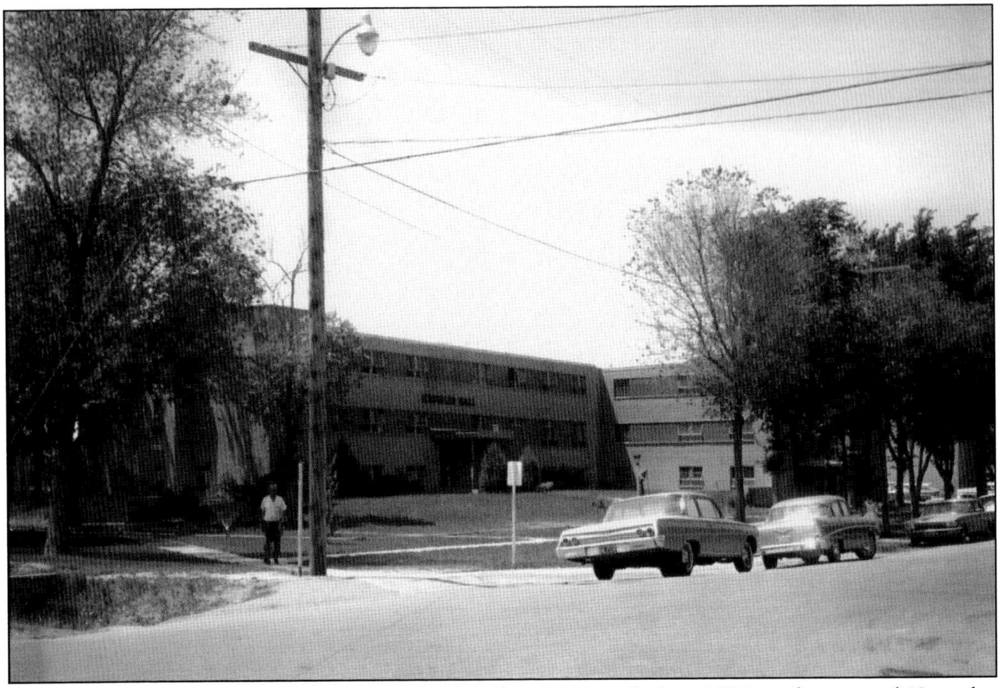

Knowles Hall was built in 1961. It was updated and expanded in 1994 and renamed Knowles Hall-Monahan Library. The building now houses educational offices, classrooms, meeting rooms, and up-to-date library amenities. (Courtesy Northeastern Junior College.)

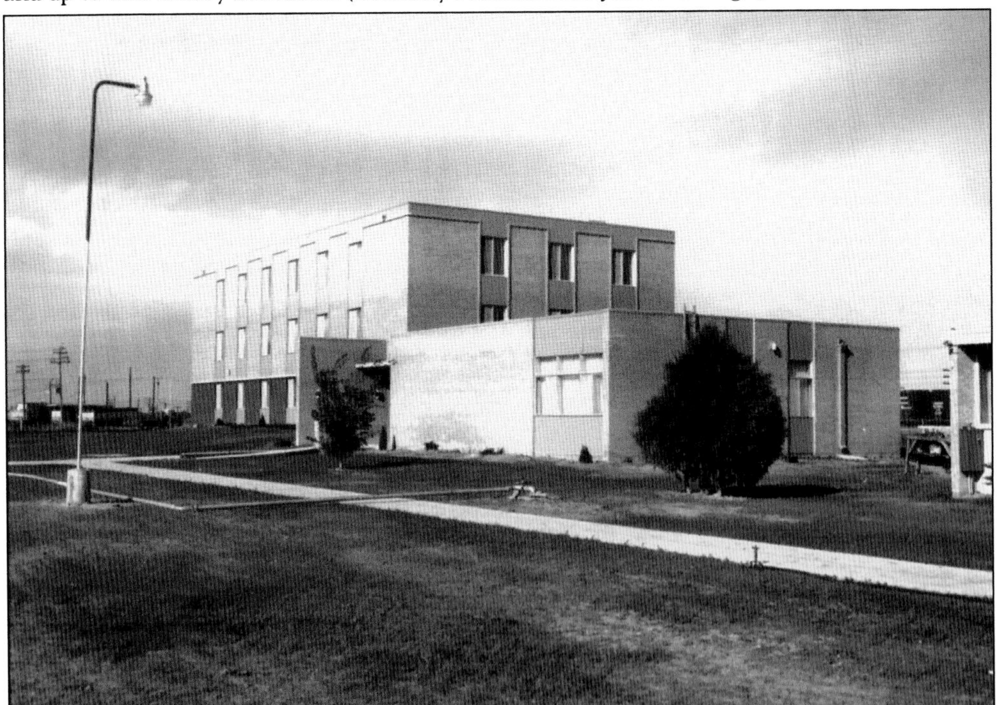

Built in 1963, Herboldsheimer Hall was first called North Hall. (Courtesy Northeastern Junior College.)

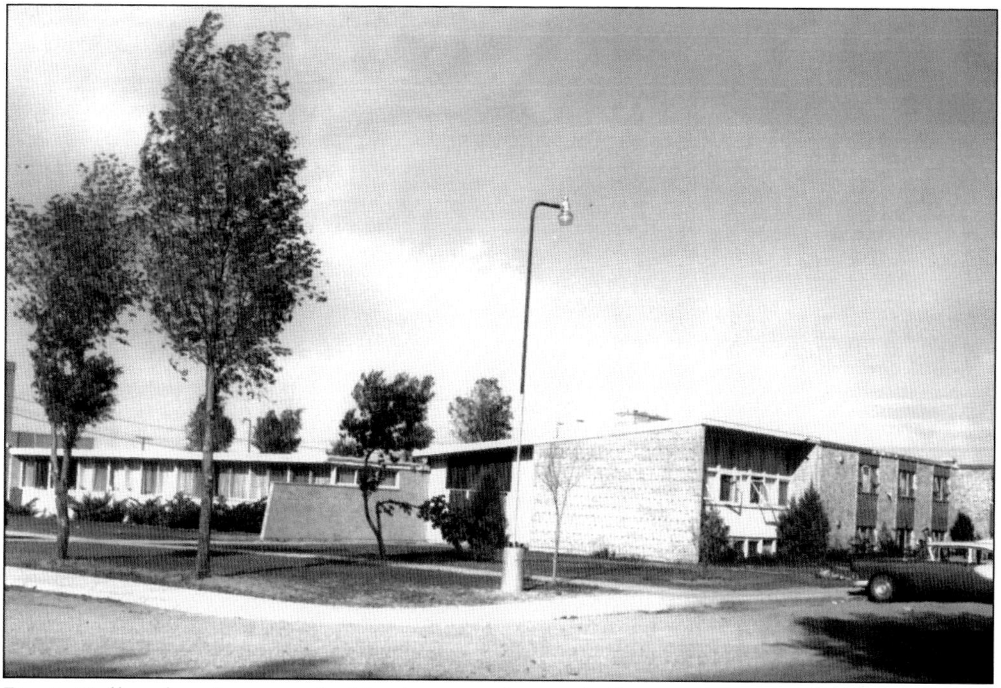

Dowis Hall, a dormitory on the Northeastern Junior College campus, was built in 1953. An addition was later constructed. (Courtesy Northeastern Junior College.)

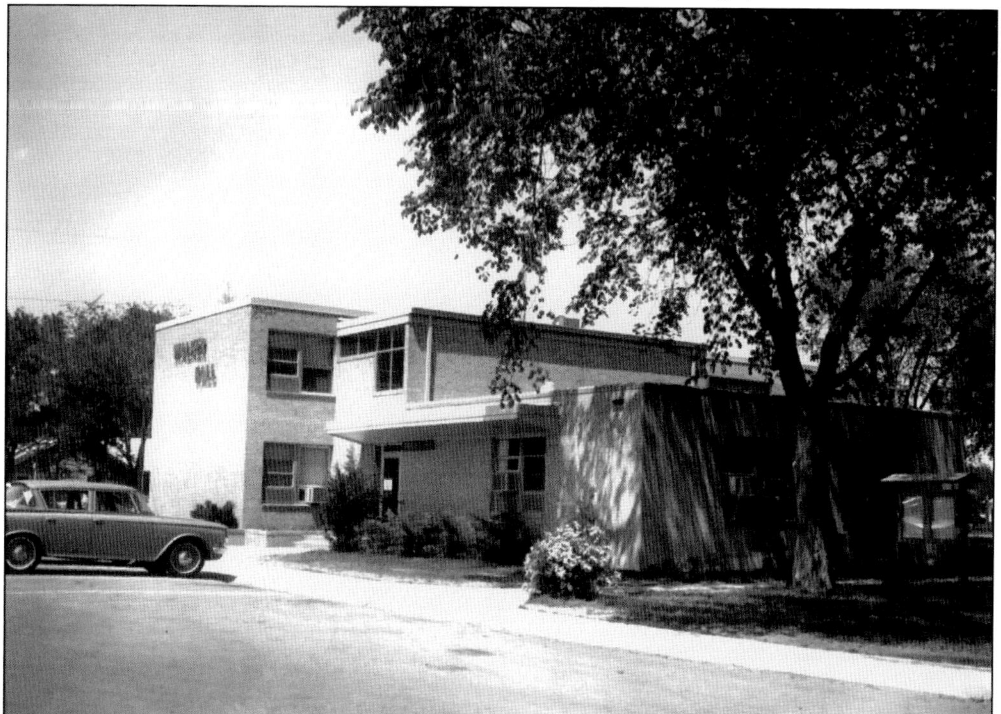

Walker Hall, presently the administration building for the college, was constructed in 1955. An addition was erected in 1971. (Courtesy Northeastern Junior College.)

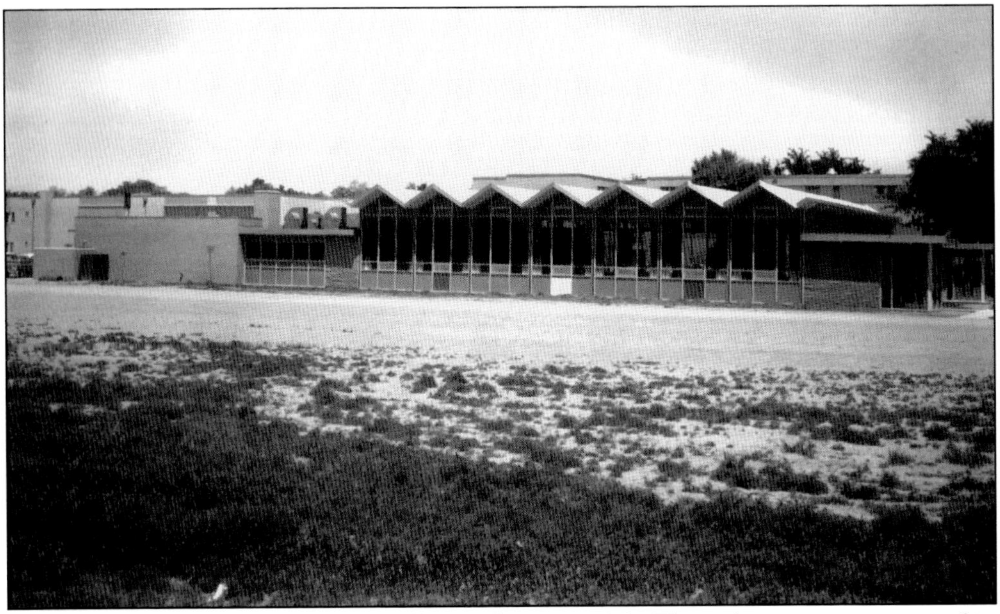

Pictured is the Northeastern Junior College cafeteria in 1968. The cafeteria was constructed in 1962. The Hayes Student Center was added to it in 1968. The photograph was taken from about where the entrance to the Bank of Colorado Event Center now stands. The Bank of Colorado Event Center replaced Jackson Hall, the first gymnasium at the college. (Courtesy Northeastern Junior College.)

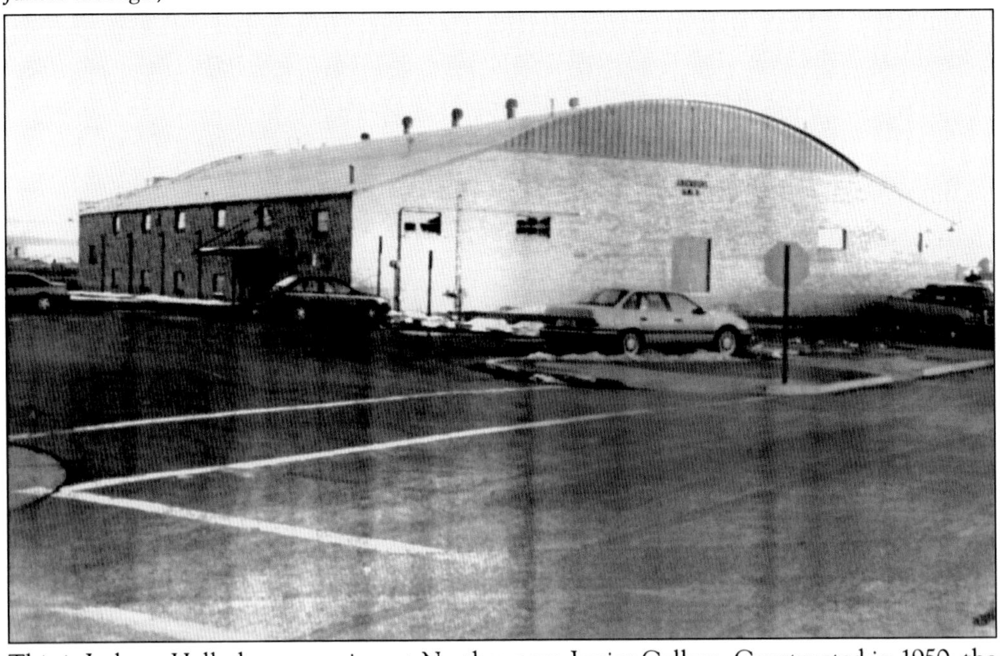

This is Jackson Hall, the gymnasium at Northeastern Junior College. Constructed in 1950, the building was dedicated as Jackson Hall in honor of Dr. James H. "Doc" Jackson on November 11, 1951. The facility remained the focus point for athletic events until the Bank of Colorado Event Center—a 62,000-square-foot, multipurpose arena—was built in the mid- to late 1990s. (Courtesy Northeastern Junior College.)

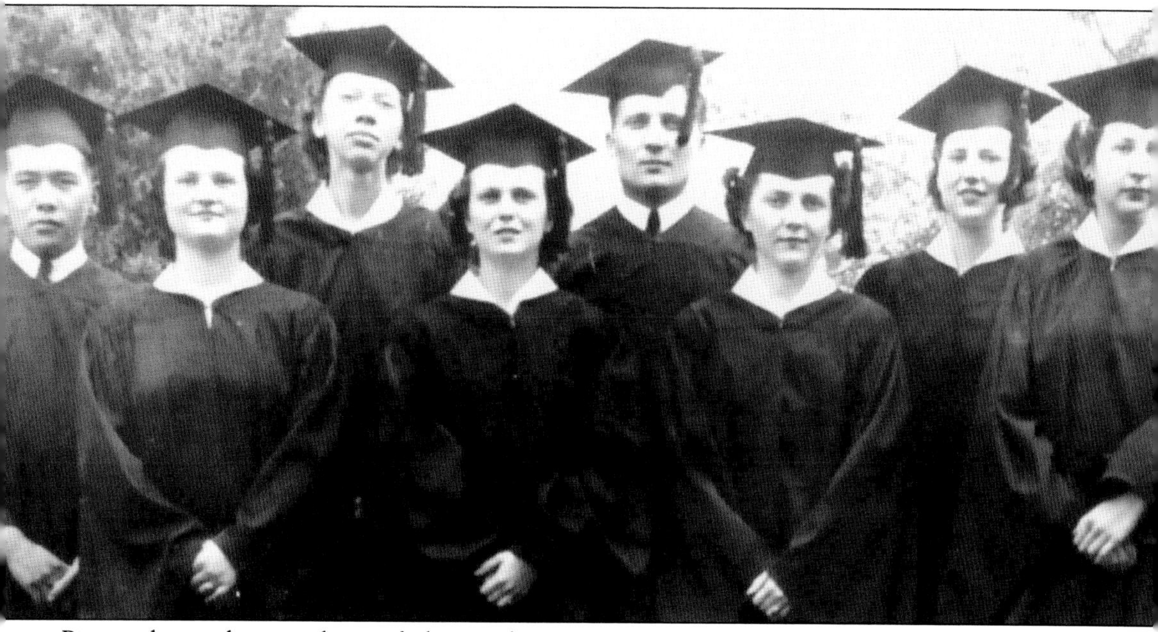

Pictured are the members of the graduating class of 1943. (Courtesy Northeastern Junior College.)

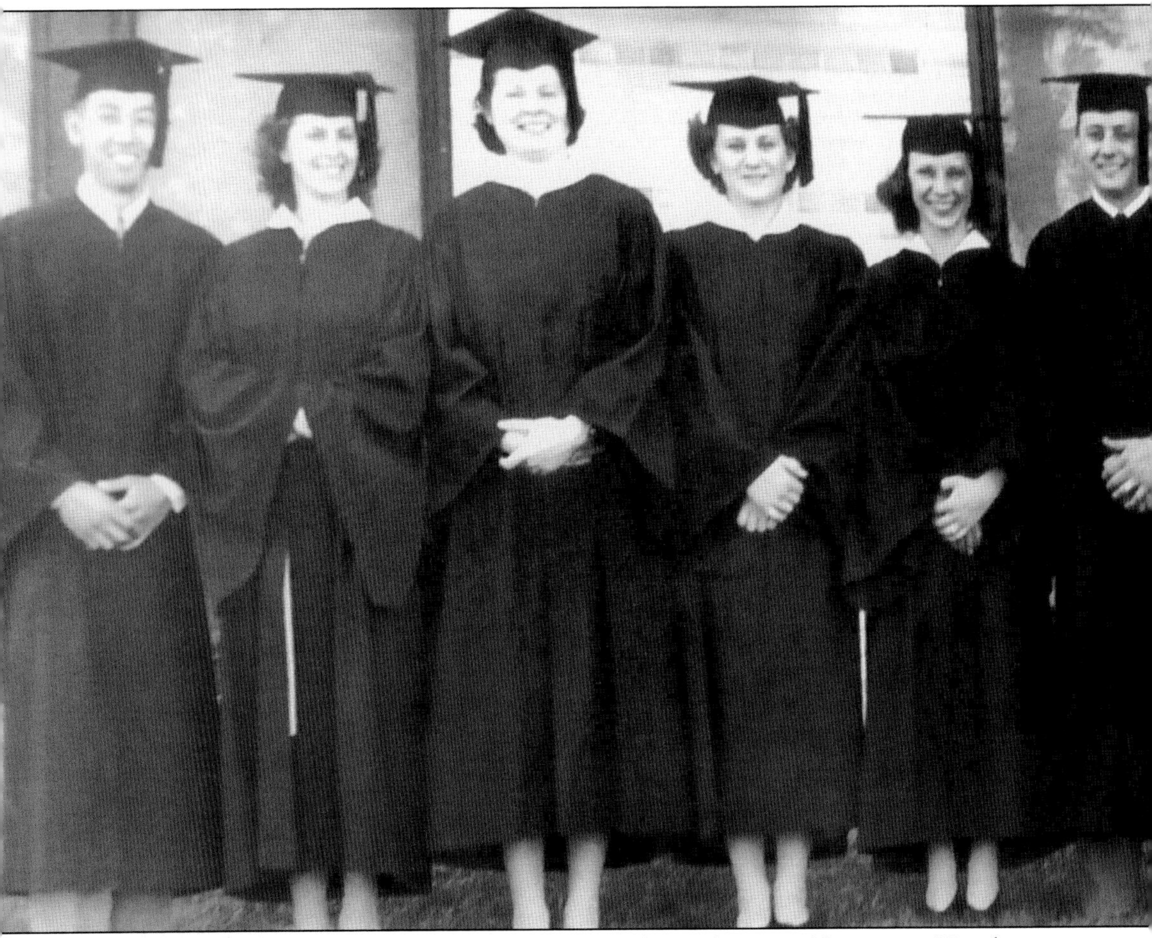

These are the members of the graduating class of 1944. (Courtesy Northeastern Junior College.)

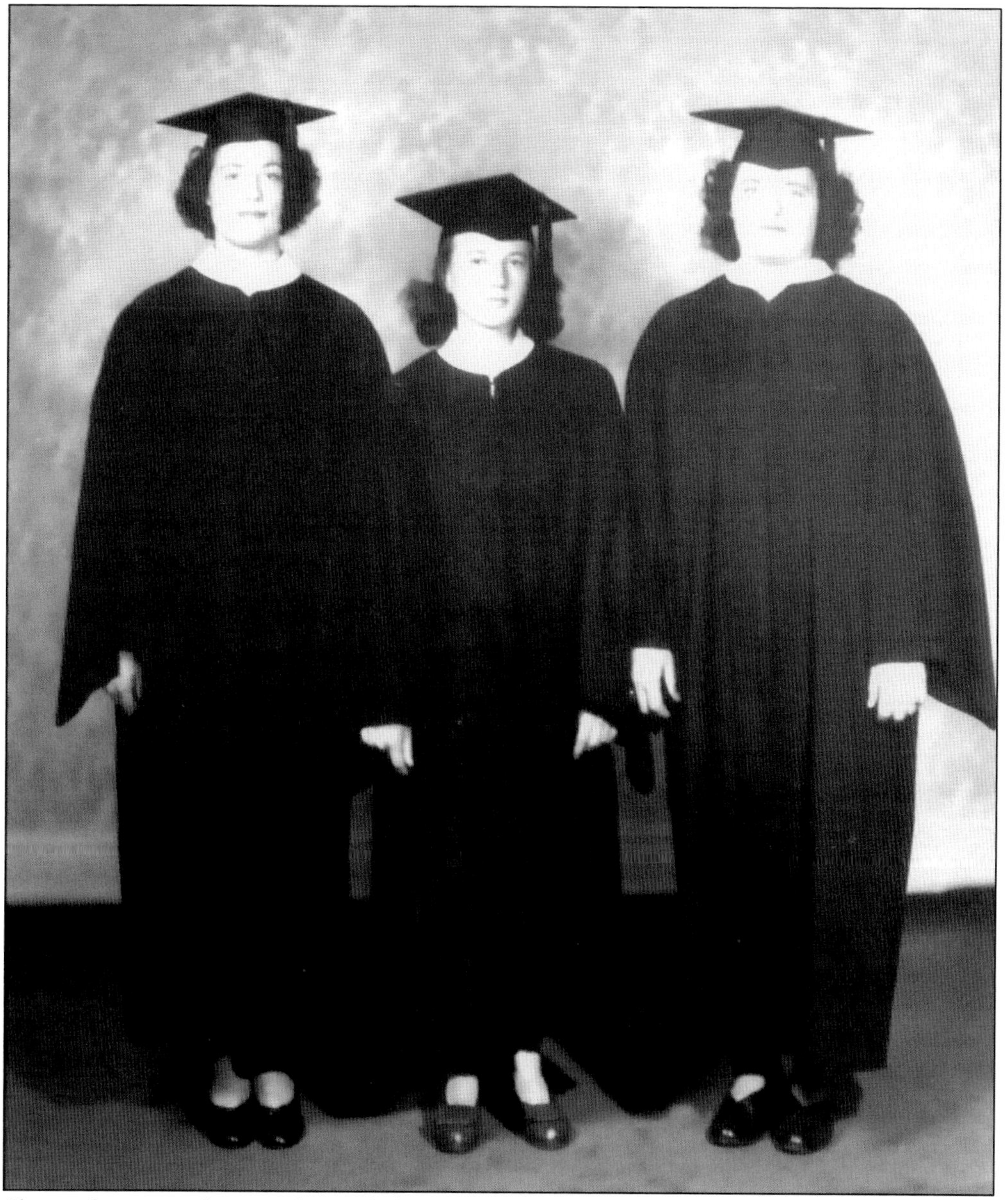

Shown here are the members of the graduating class of 1945. (Courtesy Northeastern Junior College.)

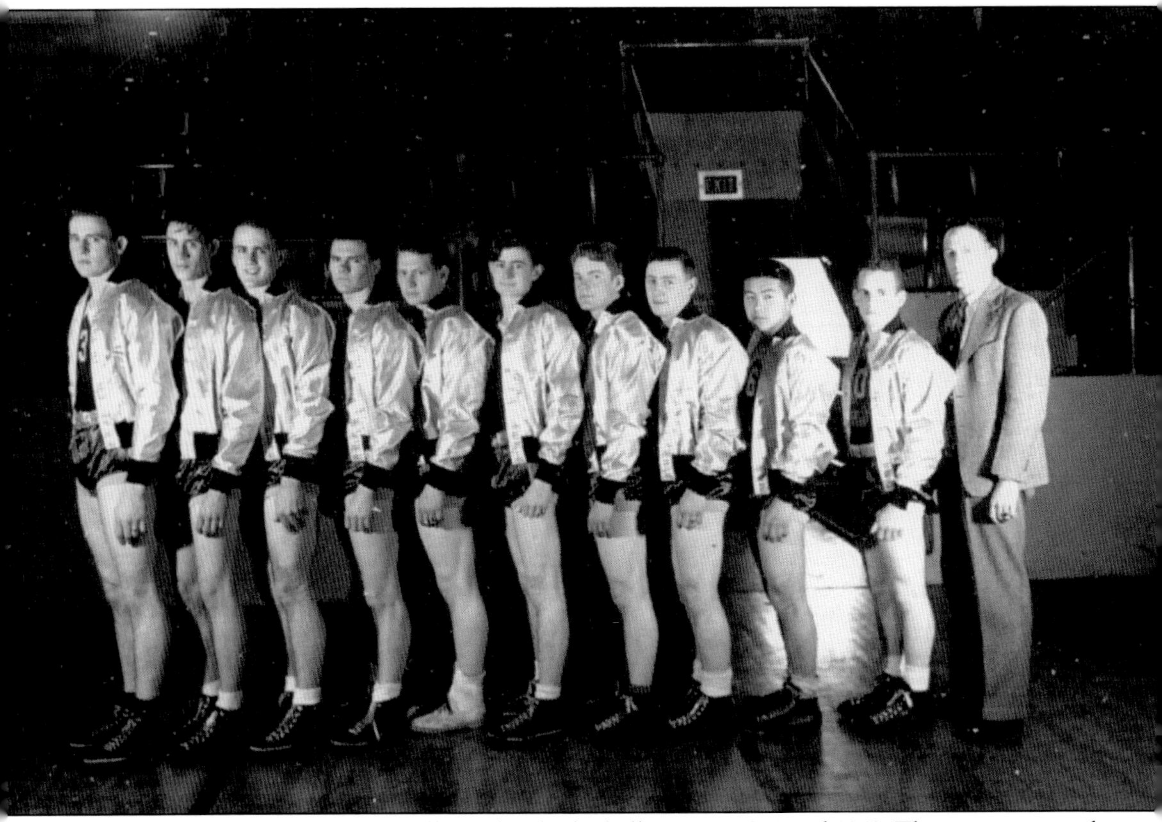

This is Northeastern Junior College's first basketball team in 1941 and 1942. The team consisted of, from left to right, Elmo Hagemeier, Leland Erickson, Eldon Phillips, Keith Baird, Roy Edwards, Harry Warner, Keith Fountain, Neal Gregory, Jimmy Nukaya, Frank Long, and coach Doug Wright. (Courtesy Northeastern Junior College.)

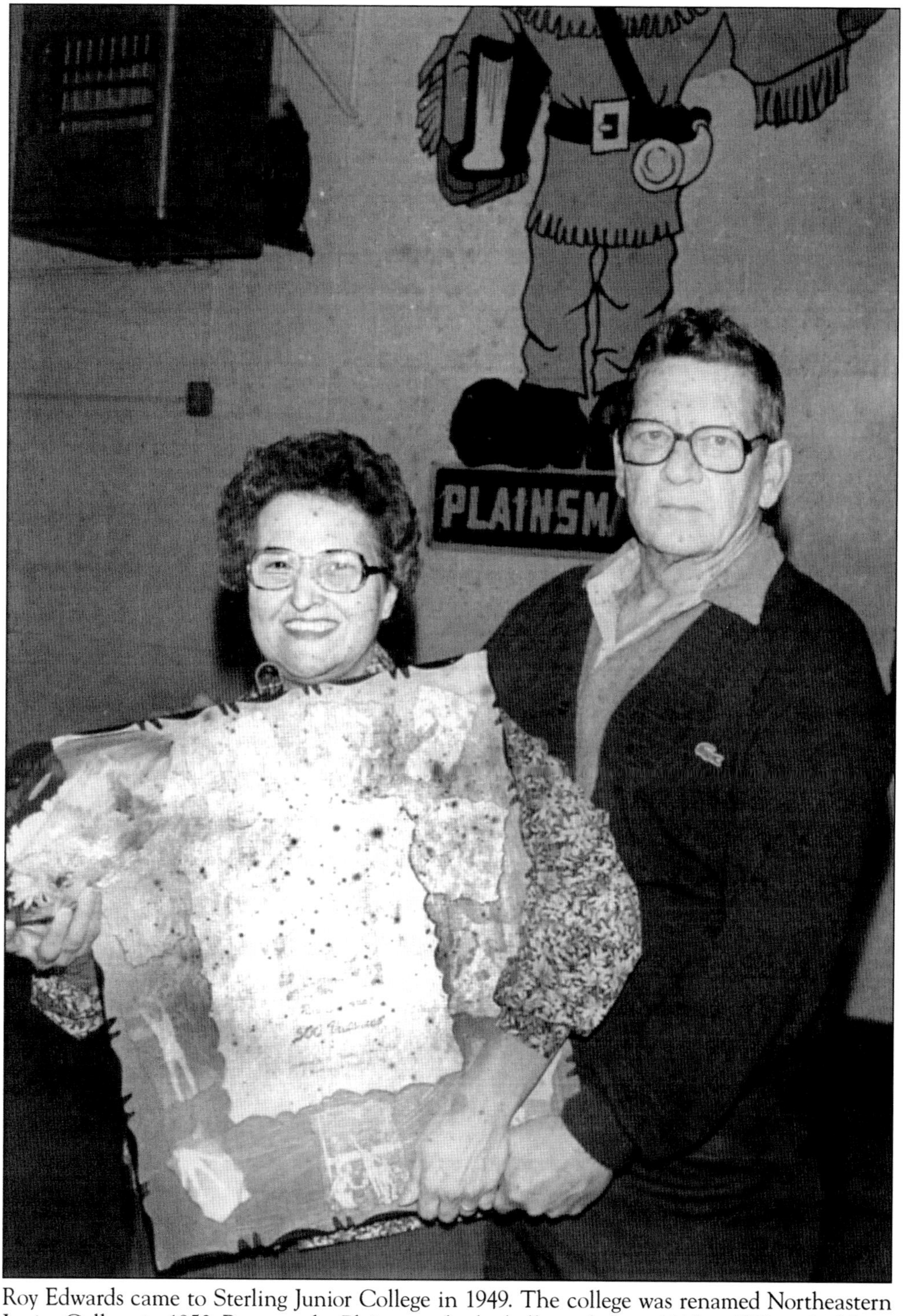

Roy Edwards came to Sterling Junior College in 1949. The college was renamed Northeastern Junior College in 1950. Roy was the Plainsmen basketball coach from 1949 to 1981 and athletic director until 1986. Roy and his wife, Ann, were presented with a plaque at the last home game of the season in 1981. (Courtesy Northeastern Junior College.)

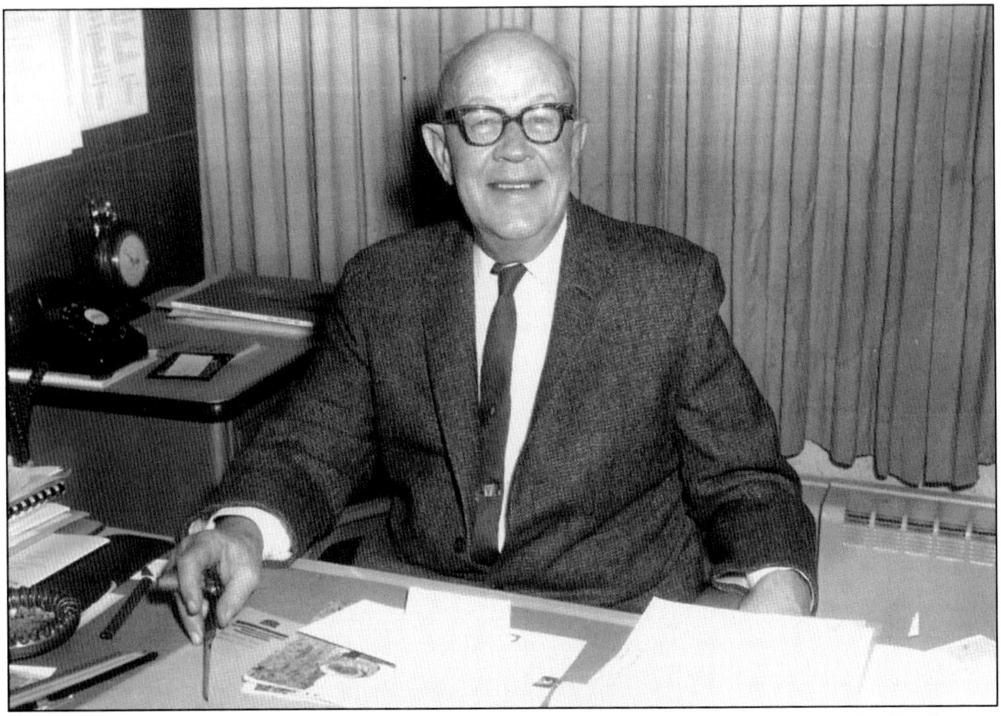

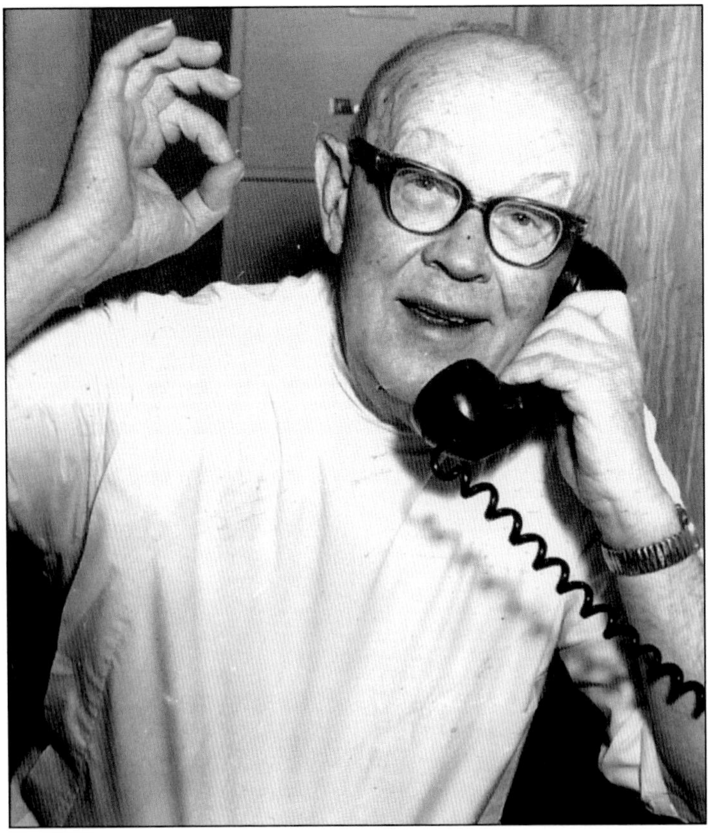

Dr. James H. "Doc" Jackson is pictured at his desk. He was a member of the college board from 1941 to 1976 and was president of the board from 1947 to 1976. (Courtesy Northeastern Junior College.)

Doc Jackson gives the okay sign as he learns by telephone that Northeastern Junior College has received full accreditation by the North Central Association of Colleges and Secondary Schools on April 7, 1964. (Courtesy Northeastern Junior College.)

Ervin S. French was the president of Sterling Junior College from 1948 to 1979. One of the buildings has been named in his honor. (Courtesy Northeastern Junior College.)

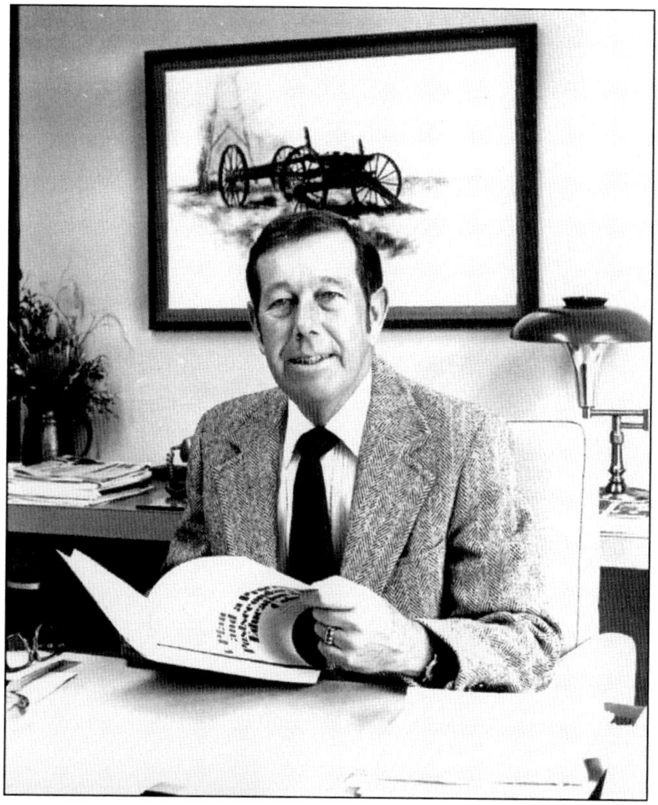

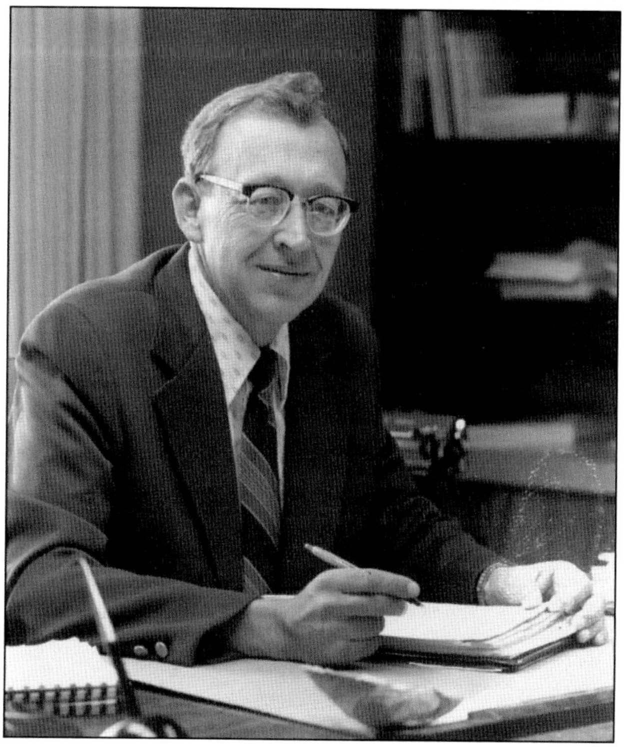

Zane Hayes served the college from 1950 to 1982. He was a business teacher, business manager, dean of faculty, assistant president, and vice president. He was also known as a friend, colleague, and campus leader who believed teaching to be an honorable profession. (Courtesy Northeastern Junior College.)

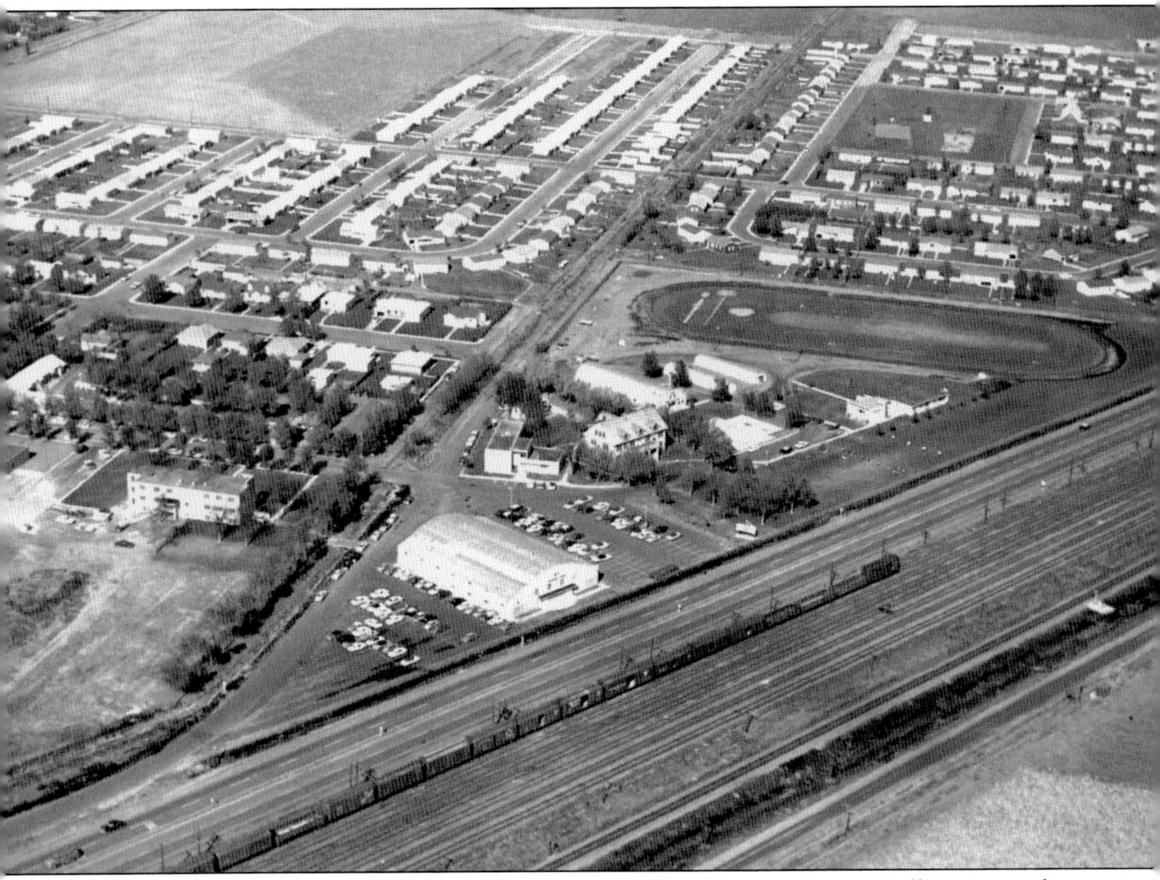

Pictured is an undated aerial view of the campus of Northeastern Junior College in northeast Sterling. The large structure in the foreground is Edwards Hall, the college's gymnasium. The facility was replaced with the Bank of Colorado Event Center, a multipurpose athletic/cultural center. The campus's most recent dormitory, designed for energy efficiency, will be completed in 2011. (Courtesy Overland Trail Museum.)

Nine

Overland Trail Museum
Preserving History

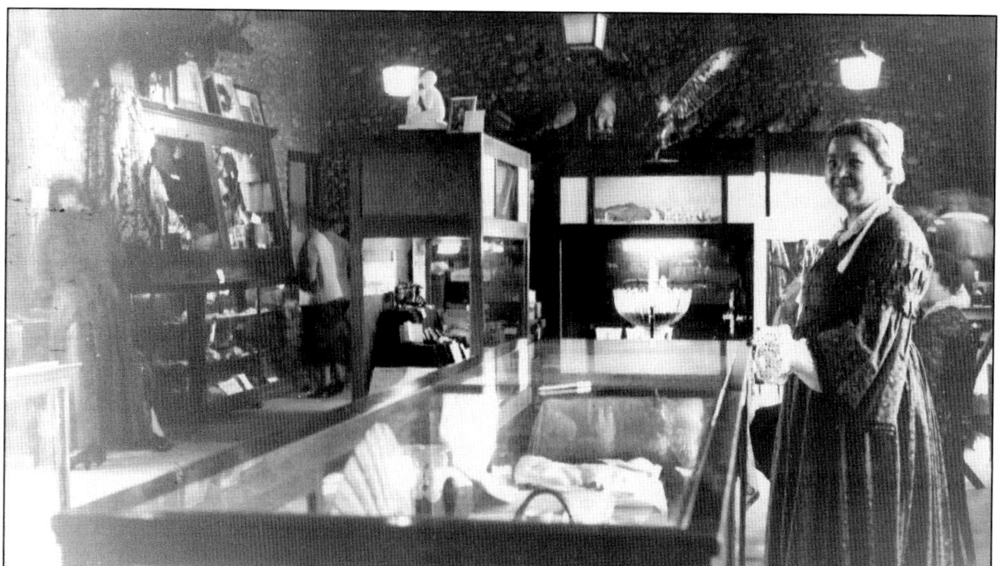

Even early in its history as a cultural center and place of historical record, the Overland Trail Museum hosted events for the public. Pictured is an October 1940 photograph of an Antique and Heirloom Fair at the museum. (Courtesy Overland Trail Museum.)

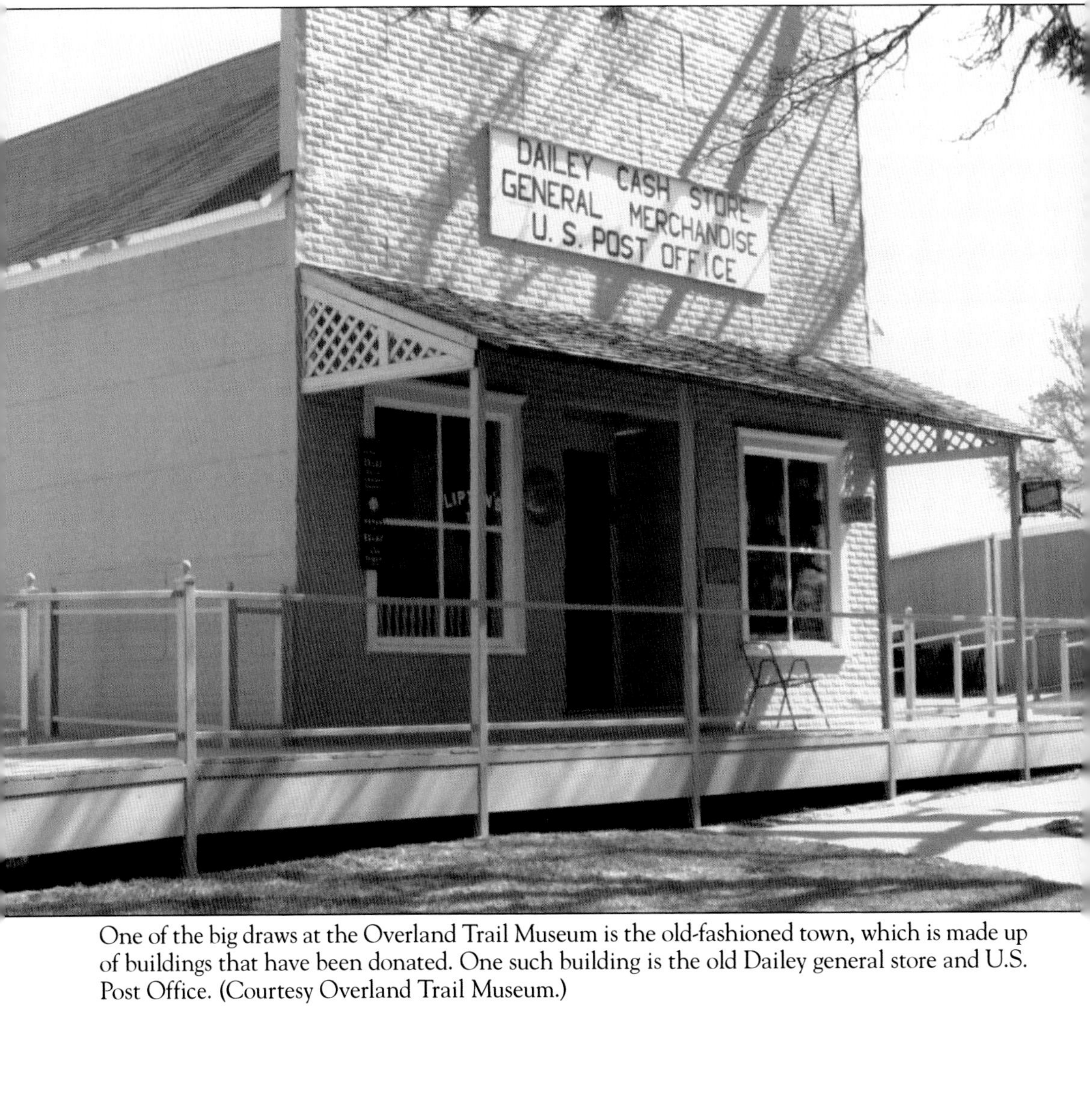

One of the big draws at the Overland Trail Museum is the old-fashioned town, which is made up of buildings that have been donated. One such building is the old Dailey general store and U.S. Post Office. (Courtesy Overland Trail Museum.)

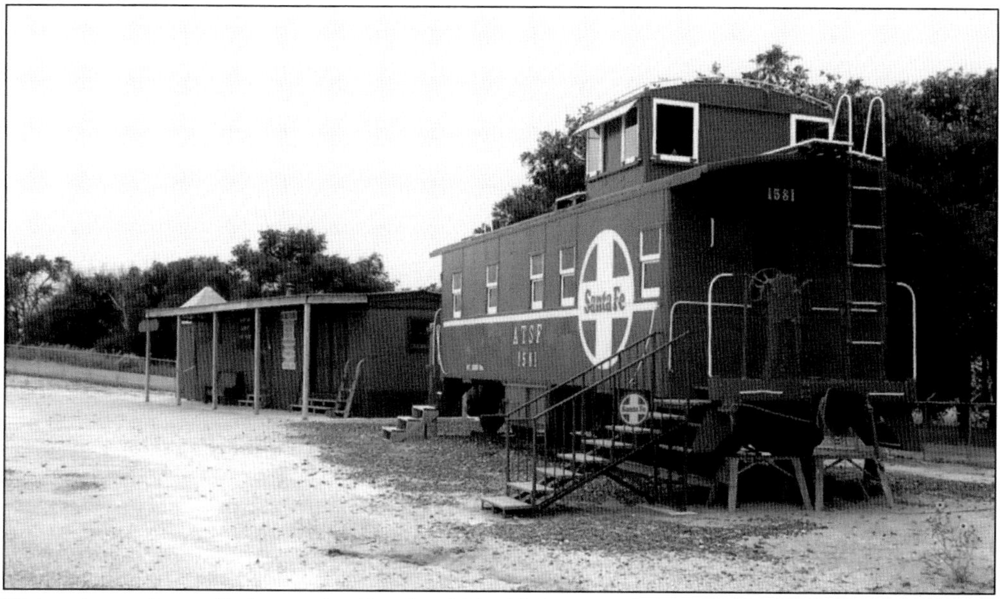

This caboose is on display at the Overland Trail Museum. Cabooses used to be a staple of rail travel and transport, but they are seldom seen at the back of trains nowadays. (Courtesy Overland Trail Museum.)

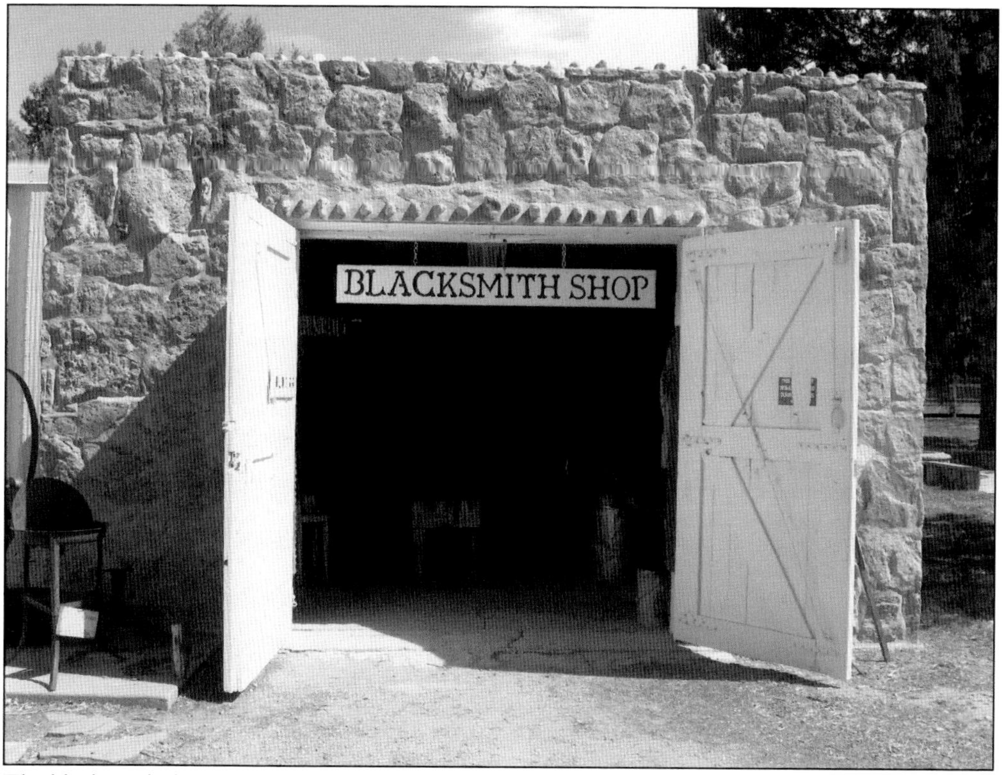

The blacksmith shop is another of the buildings in the Overland Trail Museum's old-fashioned town. During demonstrations, such as at the annual July Fourth Heritage Festival, real blacksmithing can be done in the shop. (Courtesy Overland Trail Museum.)

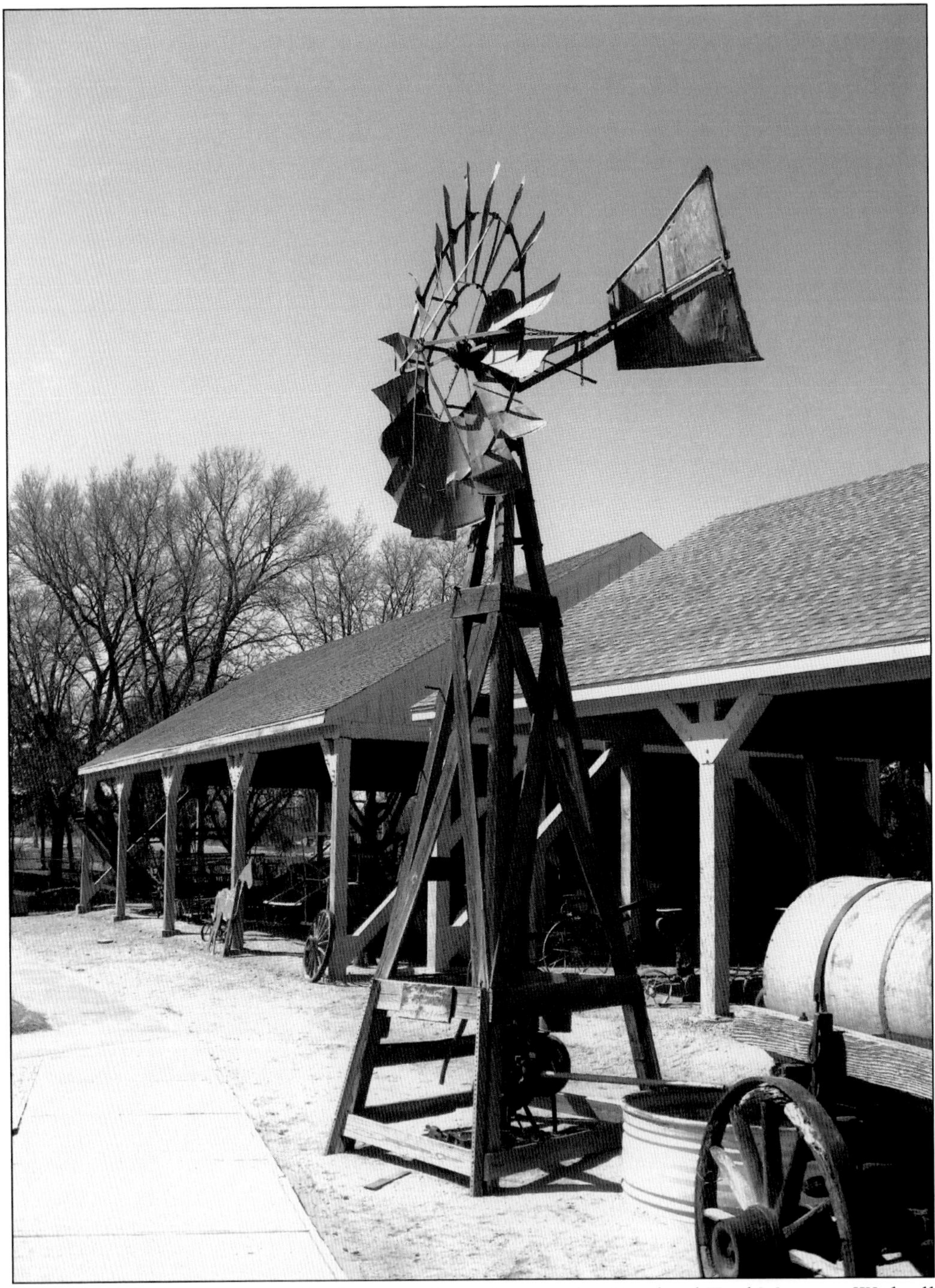

A working, old-fashioned windmill is one of the sights at the Overland Trail Museum. With all the present-day focus on renewable energy and wind farms, it can be easy to forget that pioneers routinely harnessed wind power from windmills, such as the one pictured, as part of everyday life. (Courtesy Overland Trail Museum.)

Ten

Nowadays in Sterling
Different but the Same

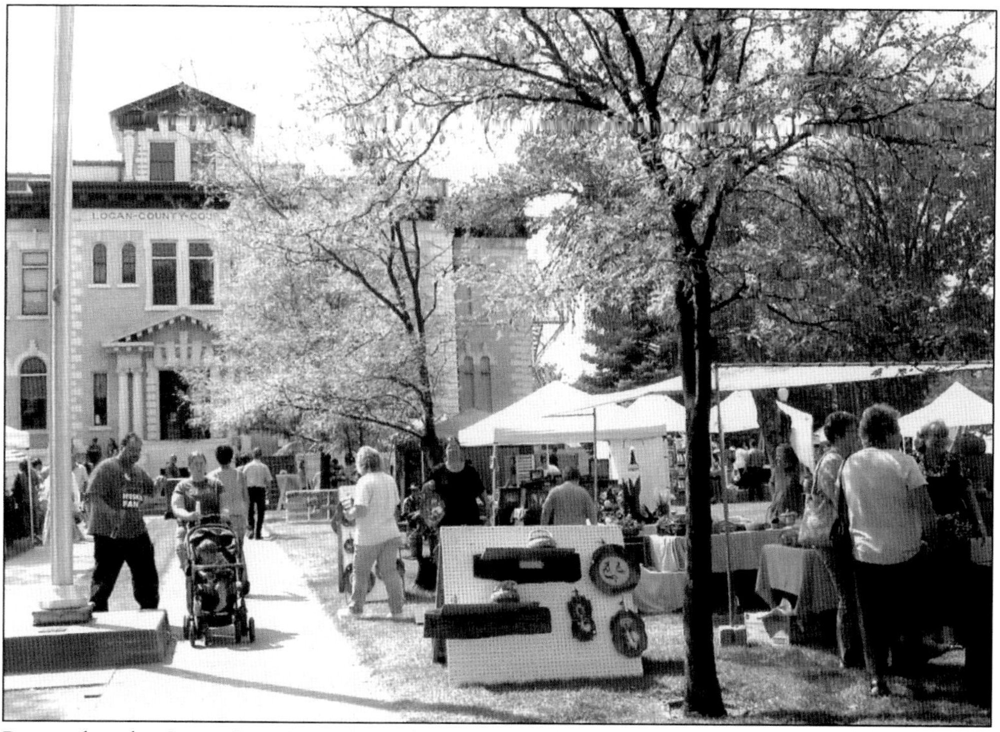

Pictured is the Sugar Beet Days festival in 2007. The annual September event features a wide variety of vendors and groups that sell crafts, food, ideas, and more at booths in the Courthouse Square of downtown Sterling. (Photograph by Forrest Hershberger.)

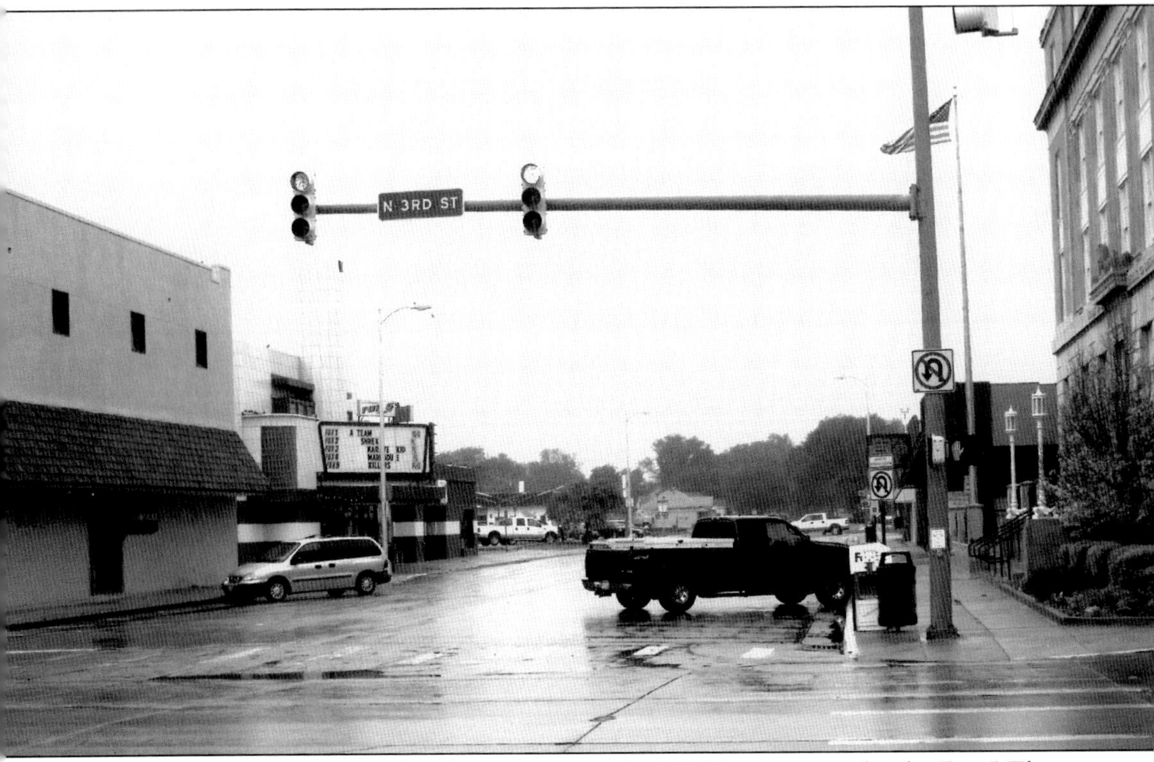

Pictured is the 300 block of Poplar Street around 2007. The marquee for the Fox 5 Theatre can be seen on the left, and the U.S. Post Office can be seen on the right. (Photograph by Forrest Hershberger.)

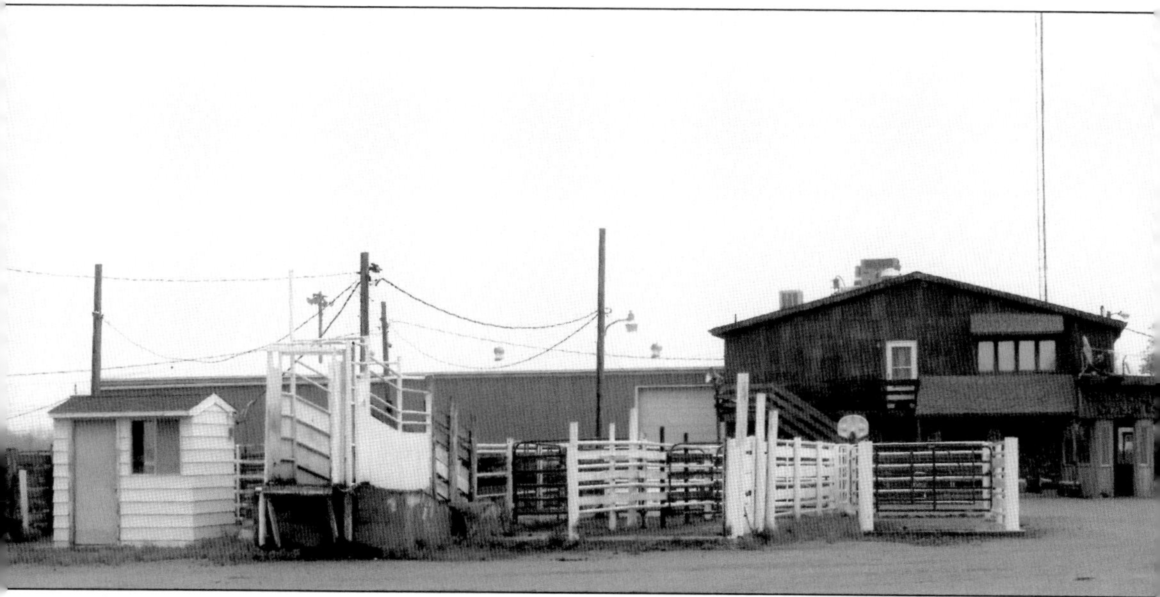

Sterling Livestock Commission Company, located at 20197 Riverside Drive, is a longtime local business that reflects the city's agrarian and ranching history. (Photograph by Forrest Hershberger.)

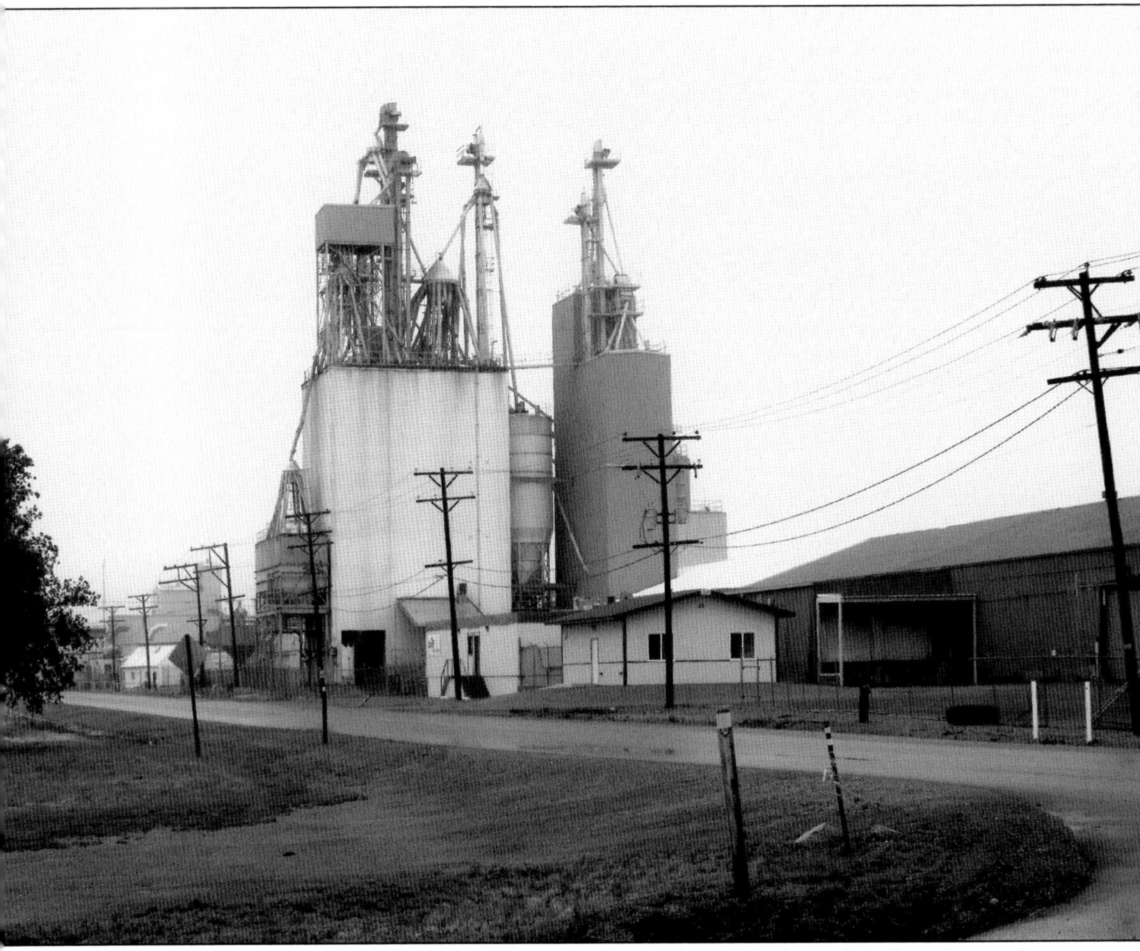

Trinidad Benham Bean and Elevator Company, located next to the railroad tracks on the east side of town, was a major employer in 2010. (Photograph by Forrest Hershberger.)

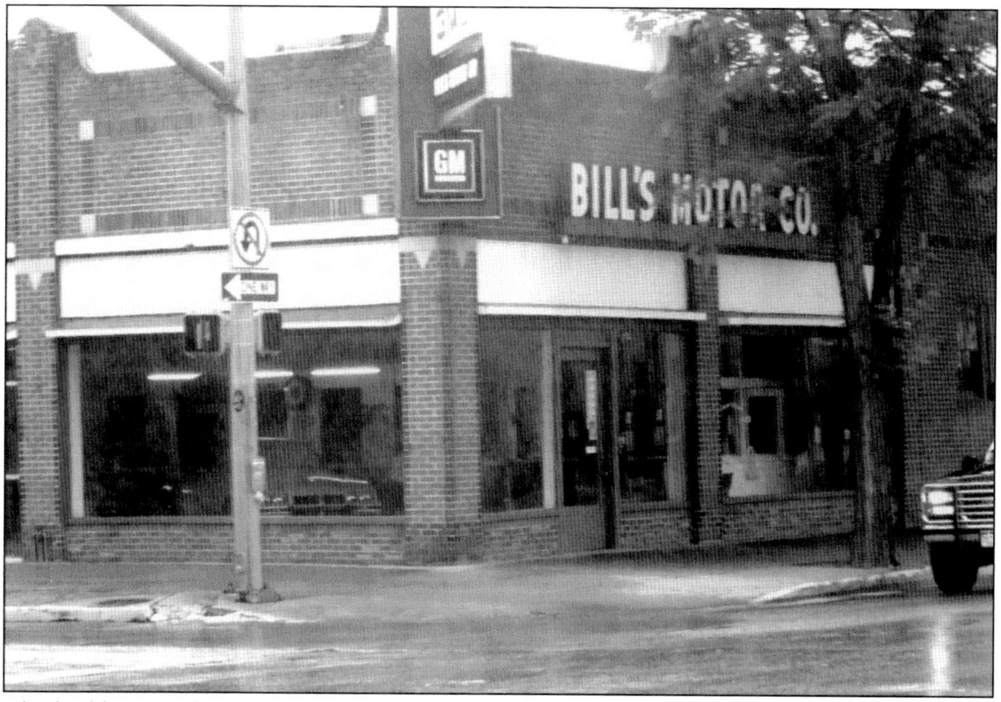

The building on the corner of Main and Fourth Streets, which houses Bill's Motor Company, was constructed in 1926. It was originally erected for McClain Chevrolet. Bill Pospicil moved to the building in 1929. His son, Bill Jay Pospicil, is the owner as of 2006. (Photograph by Forrest Hershberger.)

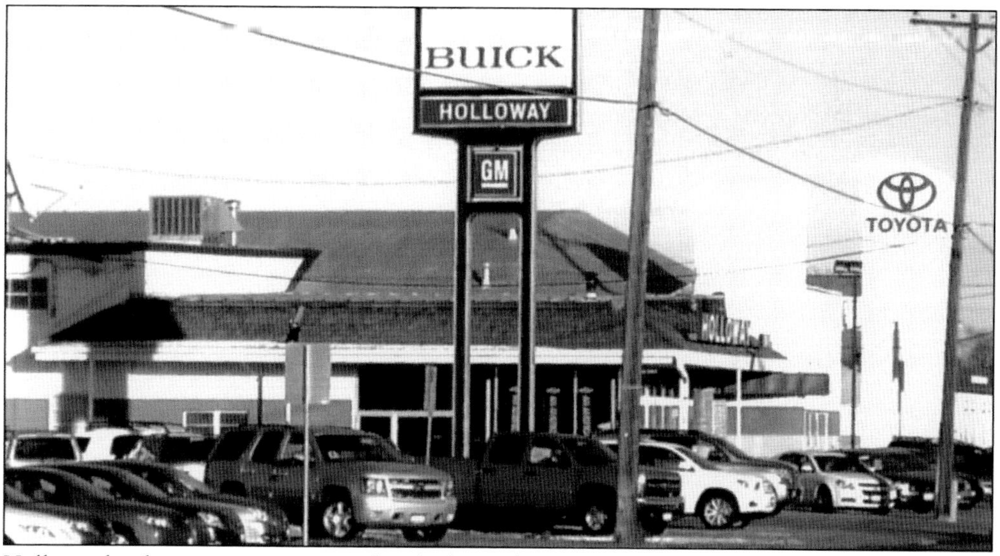

Holloway has been a name associated with the car business in Sterling for more than 50 years. The Holloway car dealership was located at 1200 West Main Street from 1952 until 2008. The Holloway family sold the dealership, which included Toyota and General Motors lines, to Ehrlich Toyota of Greeley. Ehrlich moved the Toyota line to Fort Morgan and sold the General Motors line to Sterling competitor Korf Continental. The Korf dealership remains a General Motors dealer in Sterling. (Photograph by Forrest Hershberger.)

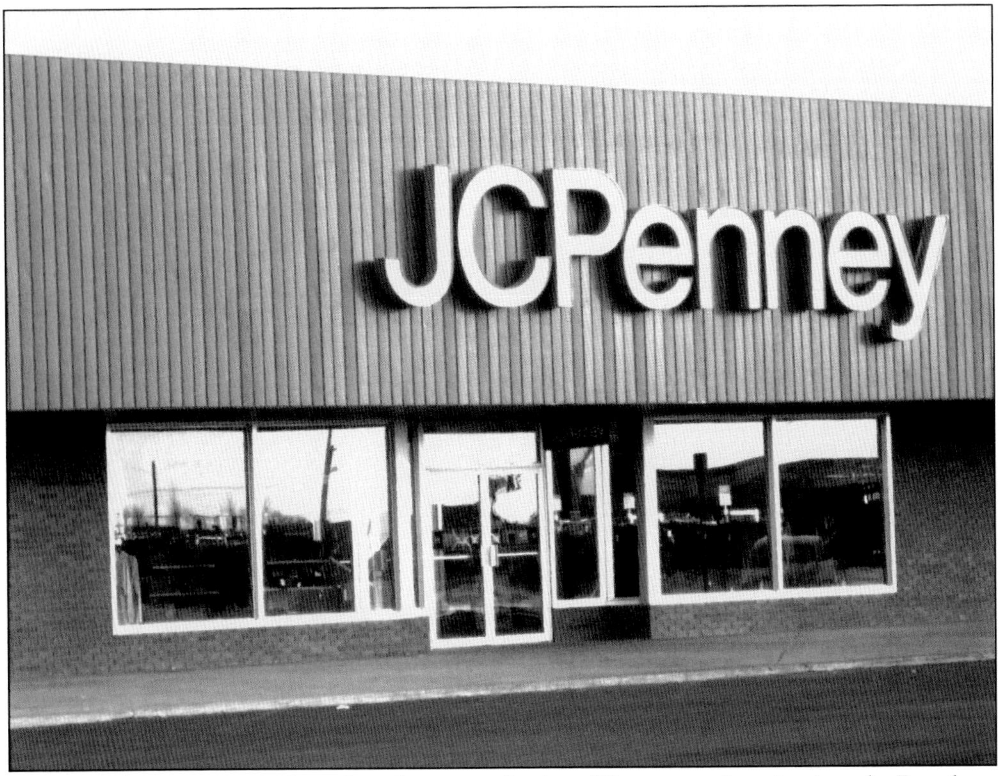

JCPenney department store has a long history in Sterling. The current location is at the Broadway Plaza shopping center. (Courtesy *Sterling Journal-Advocate.*)

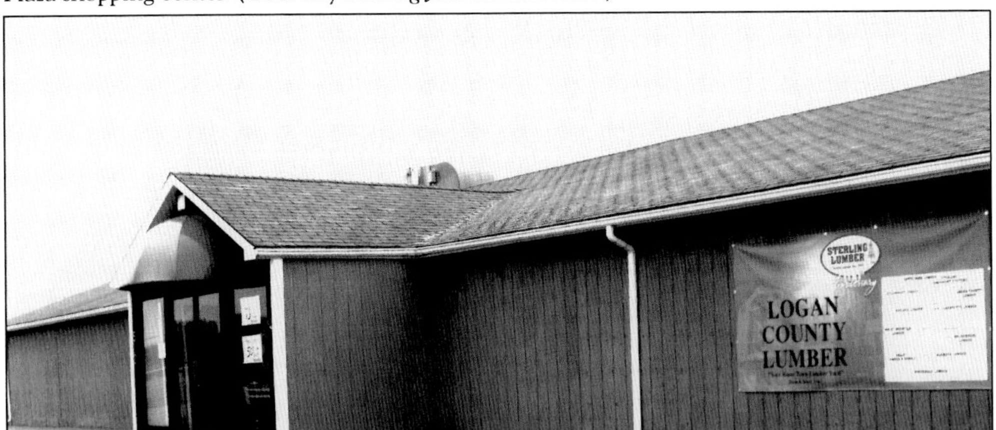

The area of Sterling along South Tenth and Eleventh Avenues has seen a surge of development in recent years. Logan County Lumber Company, located at 502 South Eleventh Avenue, is one such business found in that neighborhood, and it has been there a long time. (Photograph by Forrest Hershberger.)

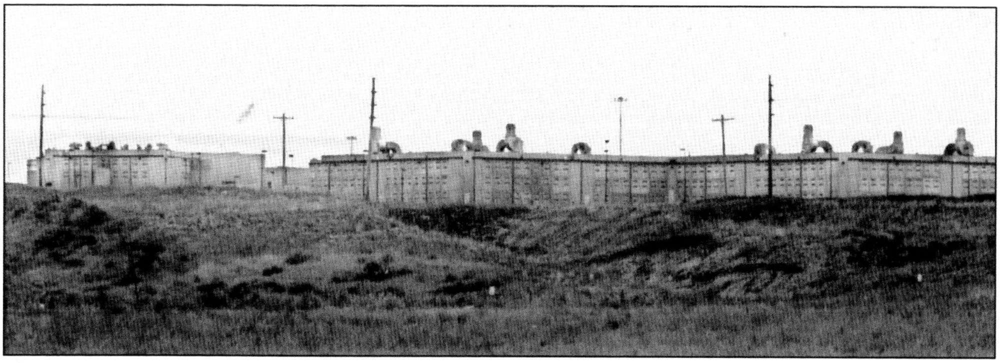

Shown here is Sterling Correctional Facility, which opened in June 1999. The 850,000-square-foot, level 5 facility sits on a 765-acre site. It is one of Logan County's largest employers, with approximately 800 workers. Inmates at Sterling Correctional Facility are able to participate in a number of educational, rehabilitative, and religious programs during their incarceration. (Courtesy *Sterling Journal-Advocate.*)

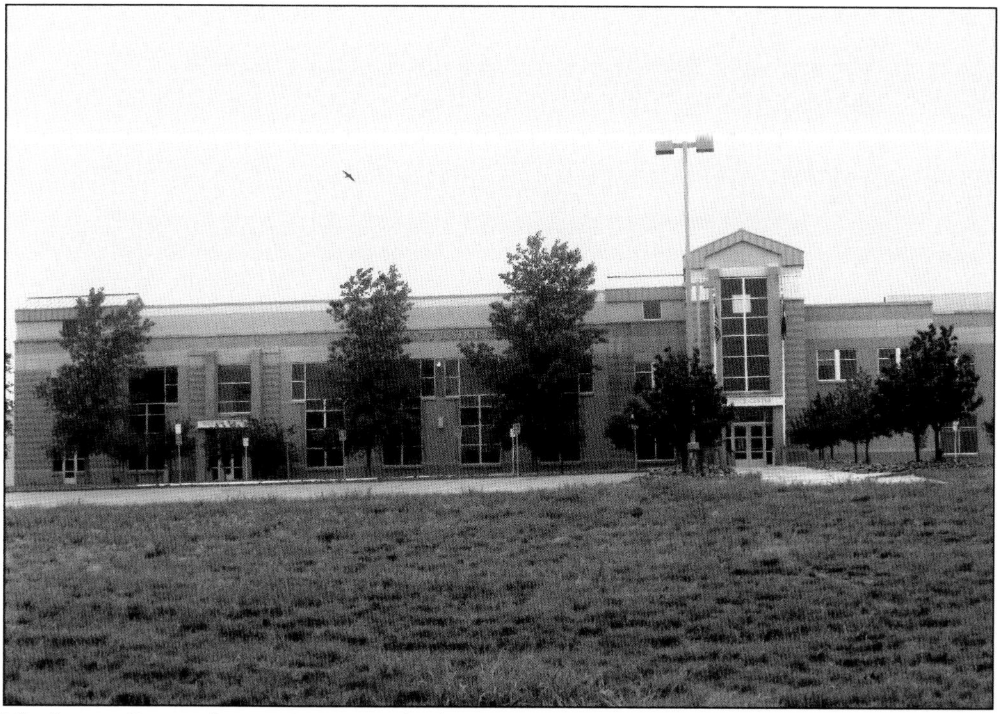

The Logan County Justice Center was built in 2003 and opened in August of that year. The new justice center serves as a replacement for the old Logan County Courthouse and jail and features more office space for the sheriff's office, the commissioners, and the county and district courts. (Courtesy *Sterling Journal-Advocate.*)

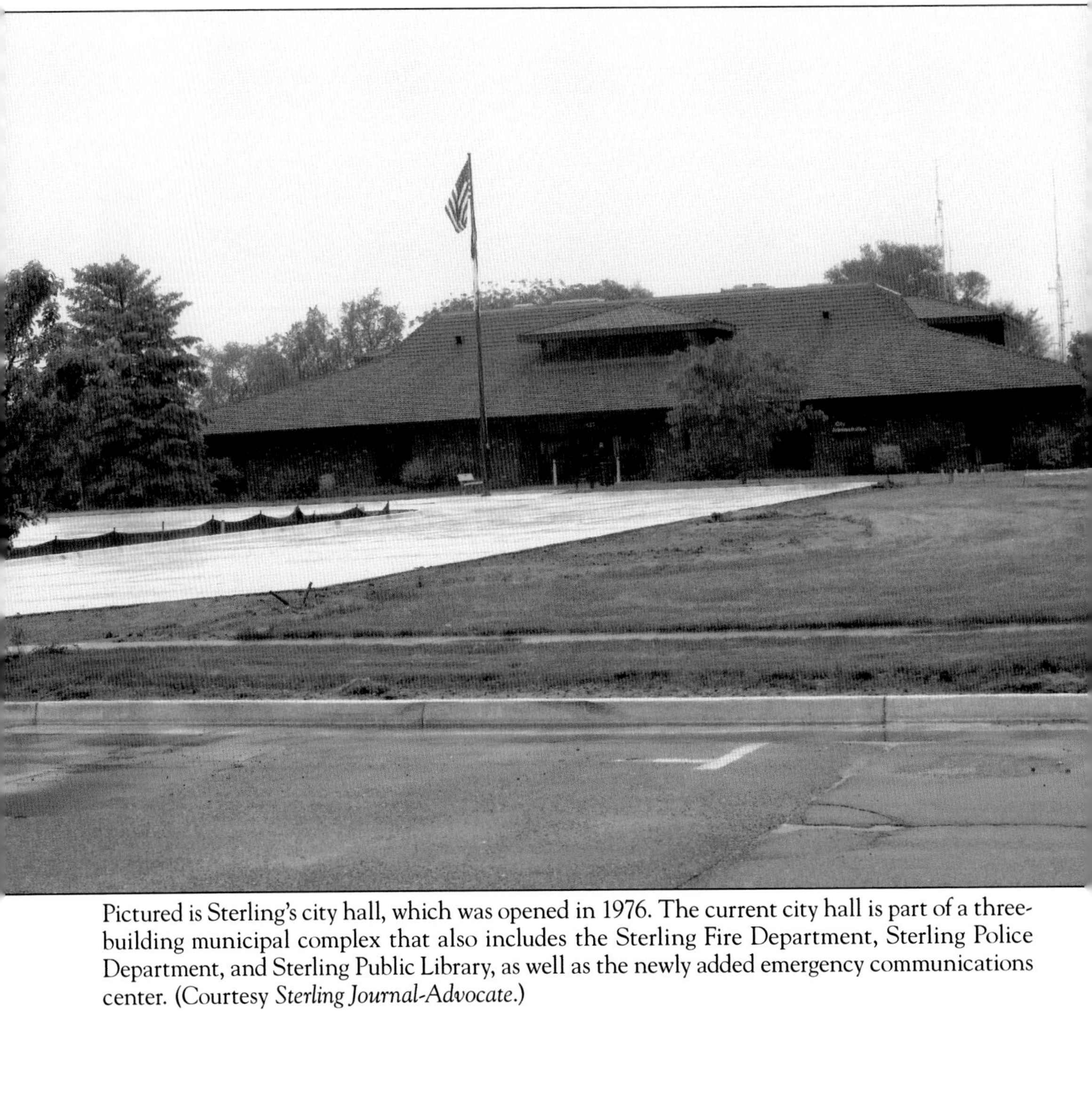

Pictured is Sterling's city hall, which was opened in 1976. The current city hall is part of a three-building municipal complex that also includes the Sterling Fire Department, Sterling Police Department, and Sterling Public Library, as well as the newly added emergency communications center. (Courtesy *Sterling Journal-Advocate*.)

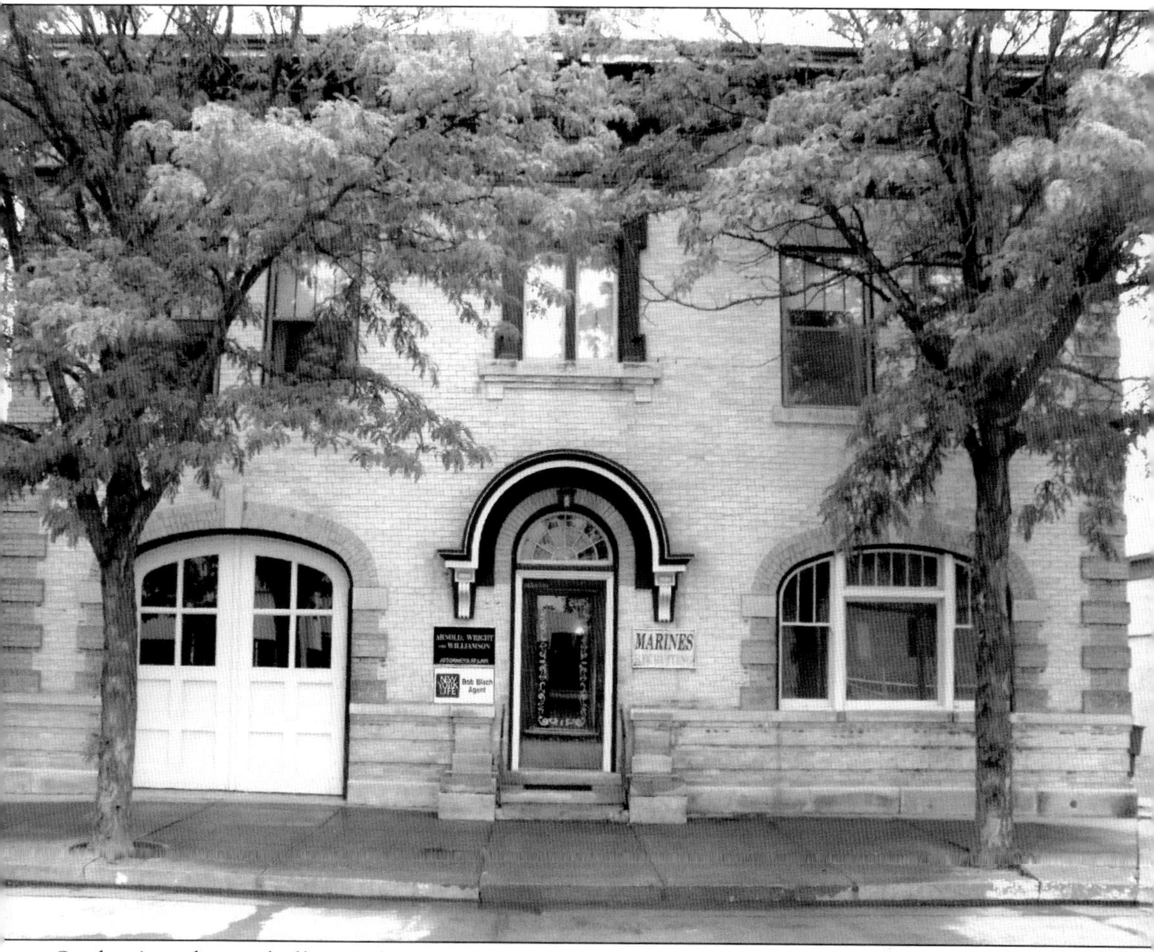

Sterling's early city hall served various functions served from one location. The city hall on Poplar Street housed the marshal's office, the jail, the fire department, and offices. Today it is home to an attorney's office and is a working example of Sterling history. (Courtesy Overland Trail Museum.)

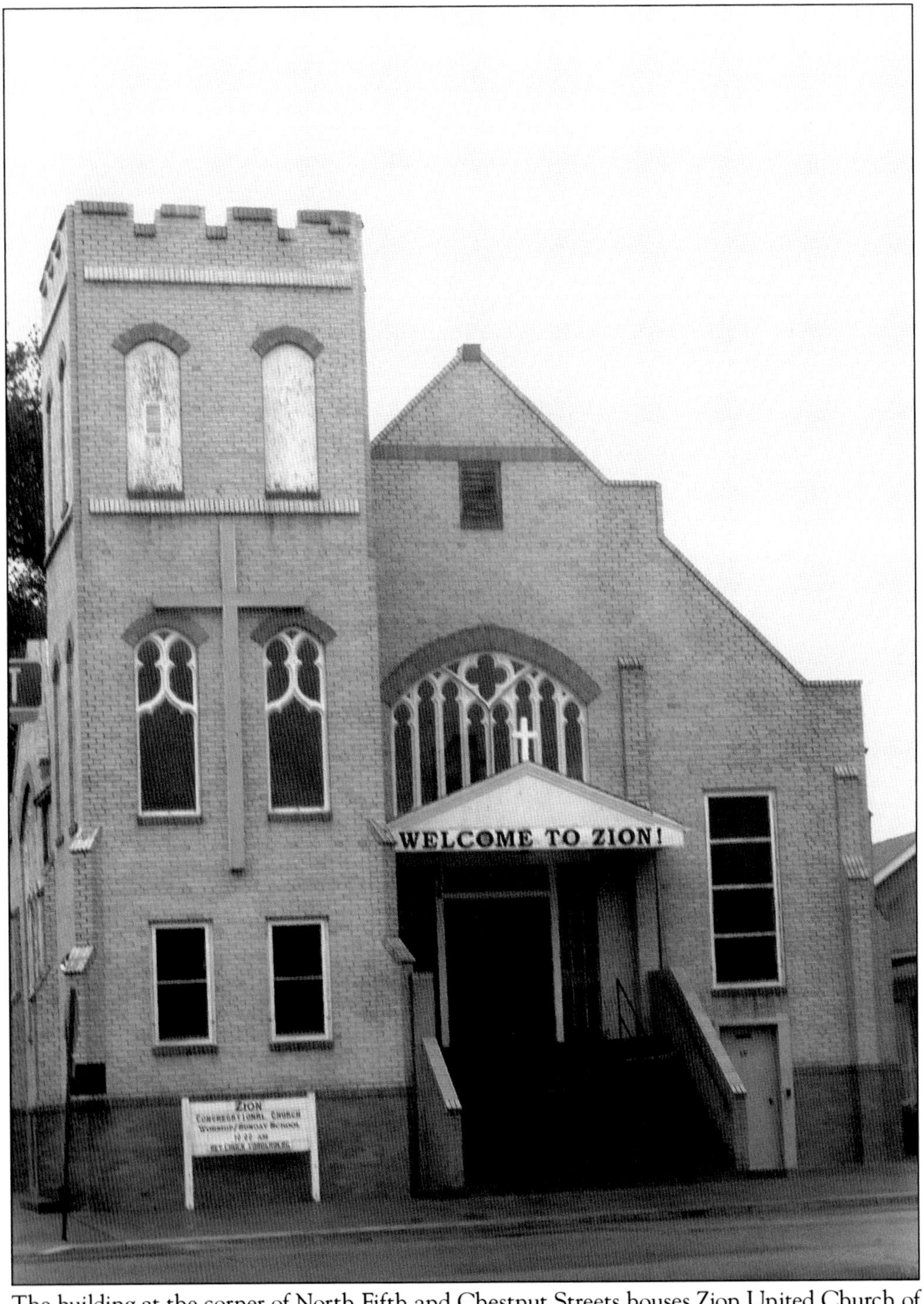

The building at the corner of North Fifth and Chestnut Streets houses Zion United Church of Christ. Organized in 1911, the church was originally known as the German Congregational Zion Church of Christ. After later merging with the Christian Congregational and Evangelical and Reformed Churches, it changed the formal name of the church. (Courtesy *Sterling Journal-Advocate*.)

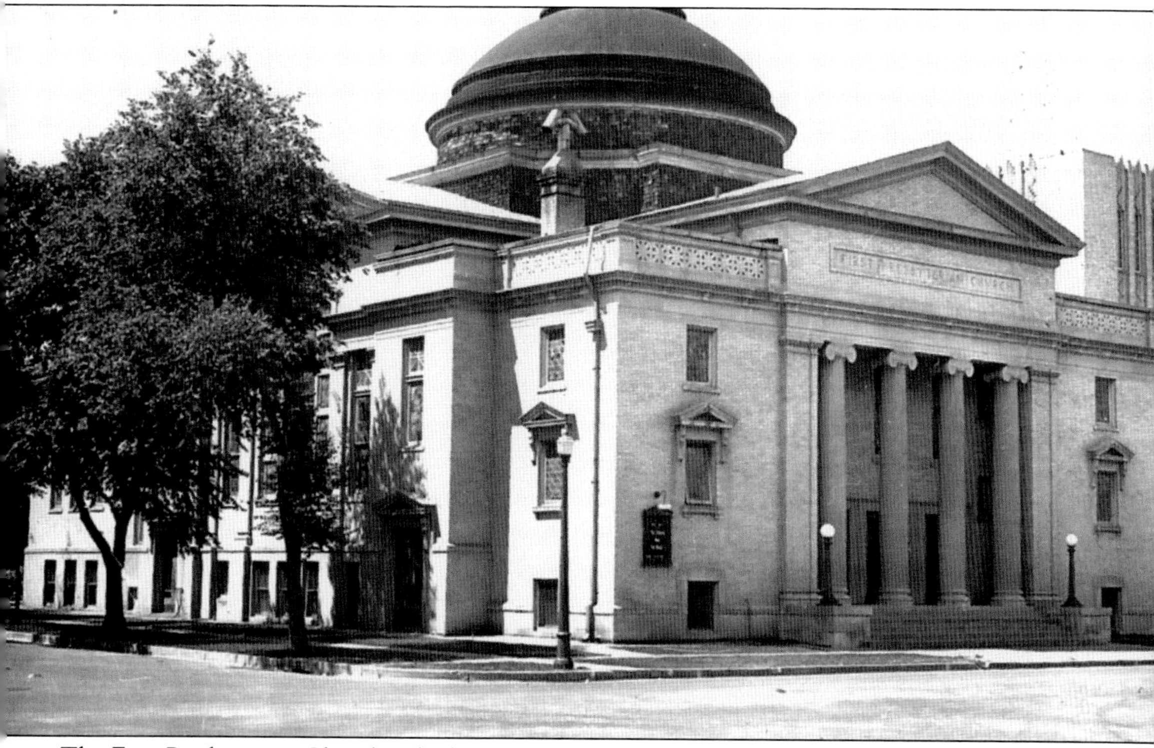

The First Presbyterian Church, which was built in 1918 and has had a place on the National Register of Historic Places since 1982, sits at 130 S. Fourth Street. Members of the First Presbyterian Church can boast that they were first to build their own church in the city and belong to the second oldest congregation in the community. The nearly century-old church has been undergoing renovations in recent years, including preservation and restoration of the dome and stained glass. (Courtesy *Sterling Journal-Advocate.*)

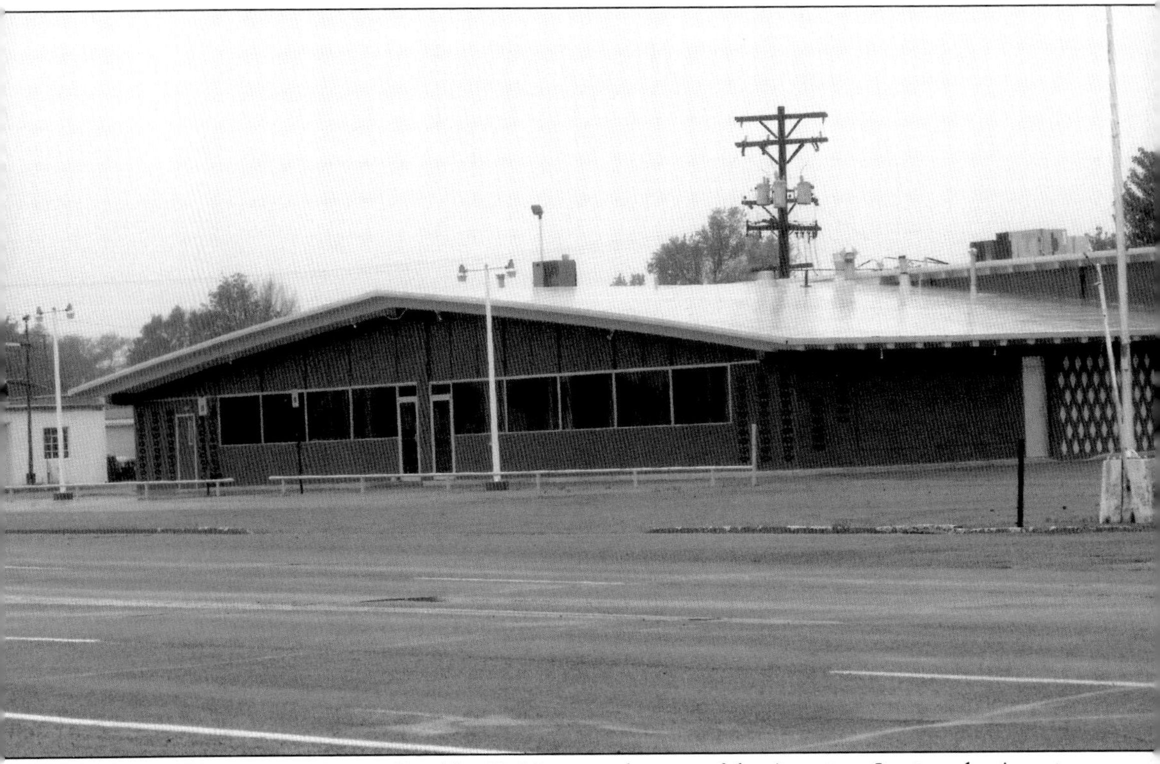

Pictured is American Legion Post No. 20. Home to chapters of the American Legion, the American Legion Auxiliary, and the Sons of the American Legion, the post is a popular hangout for veterans and fans of bingo, which is hosted there weekly as a fund-raiser. The building is also available to rent for parties, wedding receptions, and other events. (Courtesy *Sterling Journal-Advocate*.)

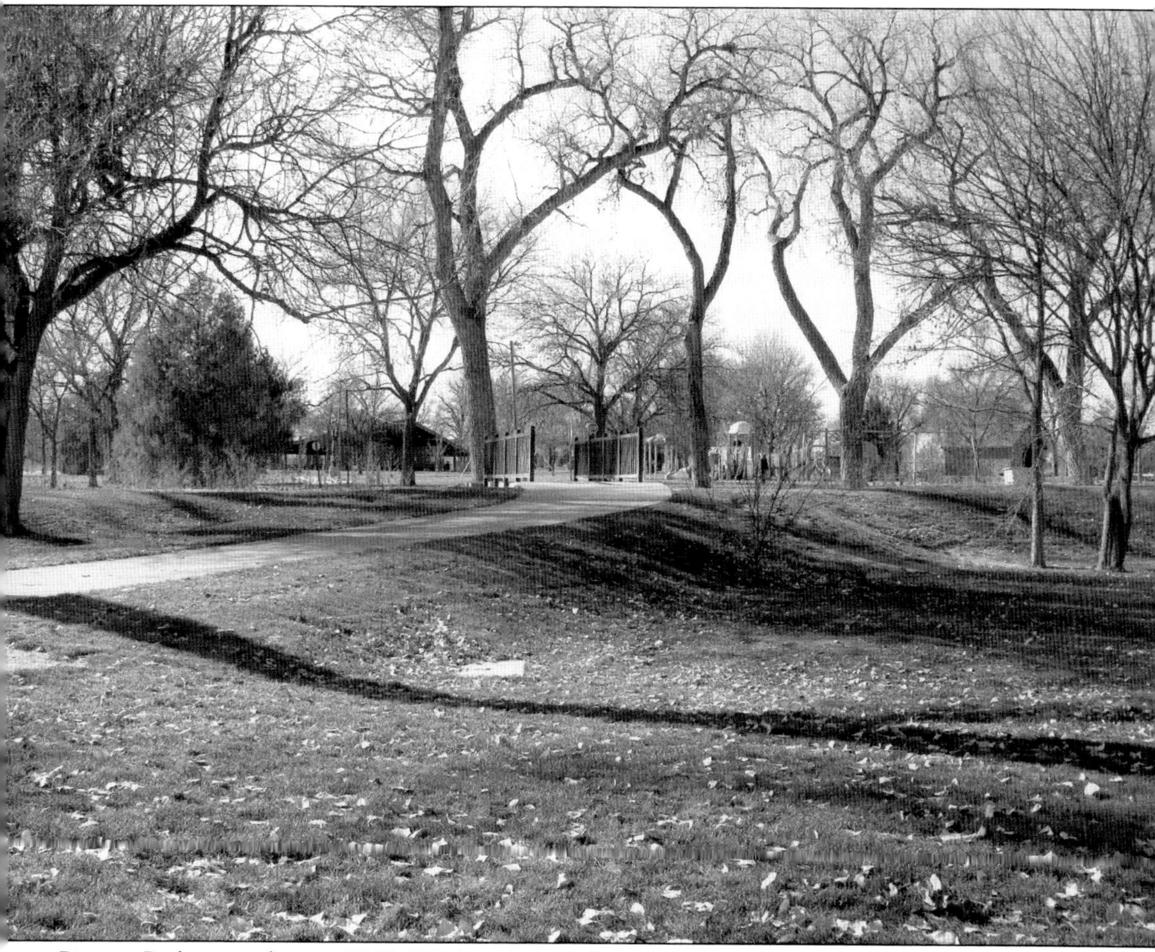

Pioneer Park is seen here in 2009. While only one of many in the Sterling area, the large park on the west side of town is a popular locale for picnicking; playing tennis, volleyball, soccer, or disc golf; hiking through the nearby wooded area; and watching Fourth of July fireworks. (Courtesy *Sterling Journal-Advocate*.)

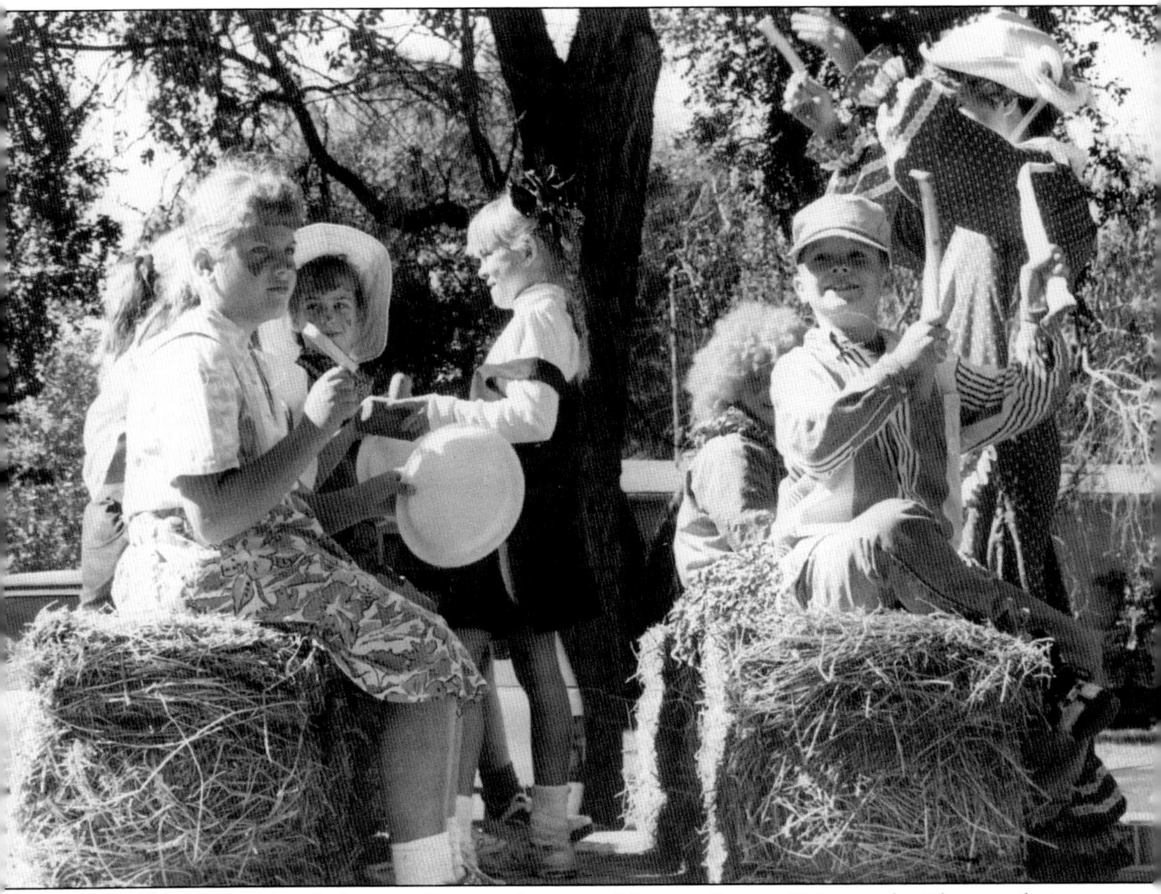

Children sit on hay bales on a float in the annual Logan County Fair parade. The parade is an annual tradition that draw spectators from around the city and county to watch floats travel through downtown Sterling. (Courtesy *Sterling Journal-Advocate*.)

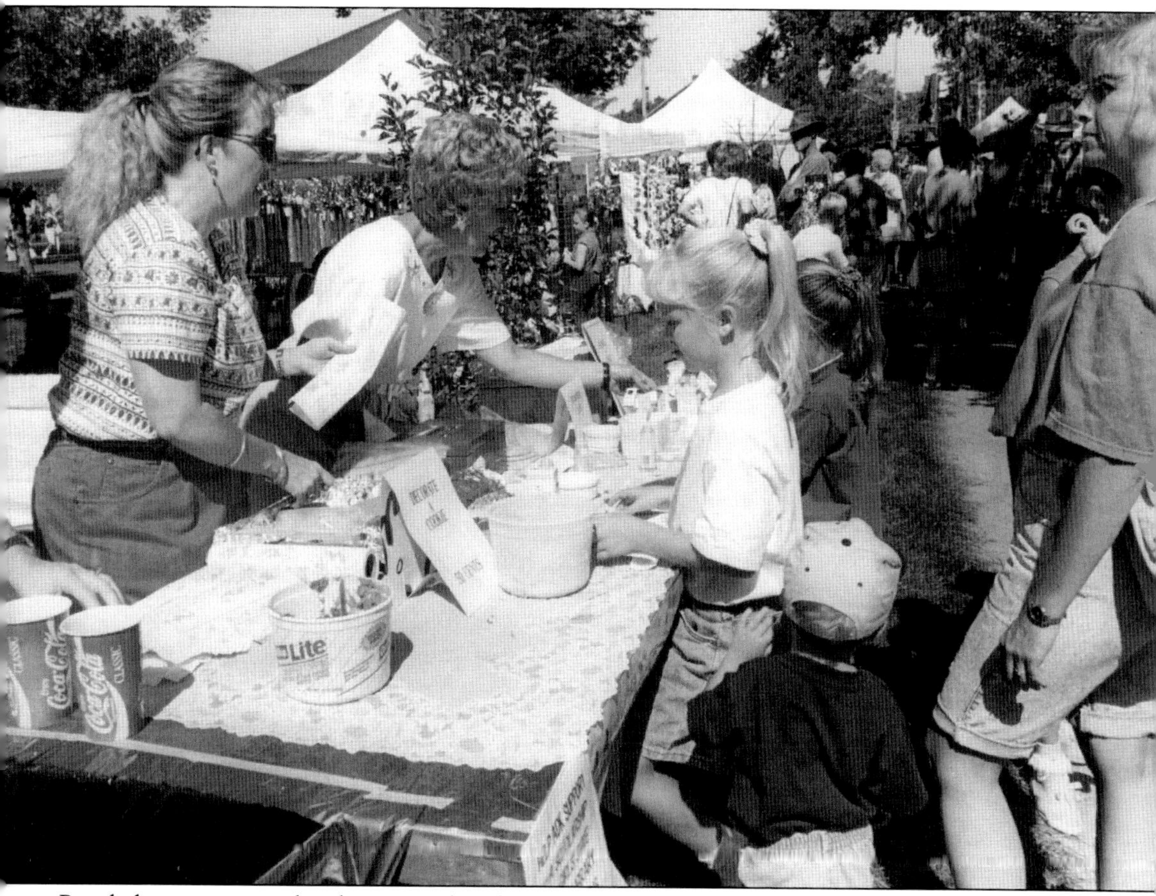

People line up at a cookie decorating booth at Sugar Beet Days in 1995. The annual September festival features a wide variety of vendors and groups selling crafts, food, ideas, and more the Courthouse Square of downtown Sterling. (Courtesy Overland Trail Museum.)